Will you follow me?

Exploring the Gospel of Mark
Leith Fisher

with foreword by Professor John Barclay
Professor of New Testament and Christian Origins,
University of Glasgow

Scottish
Christian PRESS

First published in Great Britain
In 2003 by Scottish Christian Press
21 Young Street
Edinburgh EH2 4HU

Copyright © 2003 Rev M Leith Fisher

Printed in 2003. Reprinted in 2004

ISBN   978 1 90432 503 1

Cover design by Iain Campbell

Cover layout and page layout by Heather Macpherson

Contents

foreword:
Following the Gospel of Mark...

The Gospel of Mark was for a long time in Christian history regarded as an ungifted sibling among the gospels: a legitimate member of the evangelical family, but lacking what made the others rich and famous - their birth narratives, their full gallery of parables and their striking accounts of the resurrection. Since most of the stories in Mark are also to be found in Matthew, one could even ask whether this sibling had much to contribute to the theological conversation of the church.

At last, however, Mark's day has come, and the runt is gaining his proper respect. For a century and more, most scholars have agreed that Mark's gospel was the first to be written, and is thus historically the closest to Jesus and to the first formative generation of Christianity. In the last few decades, literary critics have rediscovered the power in Mark's terse and simple style, in the intricate structuring of his narrative and his ambiguously open 'closure' at Mark 16:8. Most importantly, Mark has come to be appreciated as a theologian with his own distinctive voice, whose rough and sometimes shocking tones are a sign not of literary ineptitude but of a challenging vision of discipleship.

Leith Fisher is fully aware of these newer trends in the interpretation of Mark and has skillfully deployed them in a fresh reading of the gospel of great importance for the church today. Enriched by his long experience in the Church of Scotland, especially in an urban (and West of Scotland) environment, Leith works attentively through the Gospel of Mark to make the text vibrate in the context of our contemporary challenges. His lead questions haunt the reader: 'Who is Jesus Christ for us today and what does it mean to follow him?' As he points out, Mark invites us on a journey of faith, in the company of committed but flawed disciples, who are as ordinary in their strengths and failings as any Christian today. What is more, the Jesus they follow cuts through contemporary assumptions of status and power: Mark's Jesus is a radical figure, turning settled expectations upside down, courting controversy, choosing powerlessness and suffering the consequences. Following Ched Myers and others, this act of listening to Mark is particularly well attuned to the political resonance of his gospel, and places the unconventional Jesus in frontal challenge to our world of global injustice, social polarization and war. Refusing the path of violence, self-glorification or exclusivity, Jesus in Mark invites the disciples to a life of risk, paradox and radical self-giving.

Although it draws effectively on a wide range of reading, this is not a book for the intellect alone. Leading us into the text, and exploring its dynamic potential, Leith directs us out again into the world of ordinary, everyday, experience, the only place where discipleship can be real. Poems, prayers and meditations invite us to personal reflection, while suggested exercises for group discussion at the end of many segments make this book ideal for Bible study groups intent on serious study of Mark. This is rich fare, which I was privileged to hear in an earlier form at Wellington Church and am delighted now warmly to commend to the church at large. It takes us deep into Mark's gospel and, like Mark, invites us to face our greatest challenge with down-to-earth realism and hopeful courage: the challenge to follow Jesus today.

Professor John Barclay
University of Glasgow

Mark's gospel
- An outline

CHAPTER 1: The beginning of the gospel of Jesus Christ... John the Baptist... Baptism... 'You are my son, my beloved'... Temptation... into Galilee... 'the right time has come, turn your lives round'... the call of Peter, Andrew, James and John... 'Follow me'... Exorcism in the Capernaum synagogue... healing Peter's mother-in-law... and many others... time apart... preaching through Galilee... healing a leper.

CHAPTER 2: Healing the paralytic man... 'Your sins are forgiven'... conflict with the Scribes... the call of Levi... table fellowship with publicans and sinners... the question of the Pharisees... 'new wine in old bottles'... the question about the Sabbath.

CHAPTER 3: The man with the withered hand... teaching and healing the crowd... choosing the Twelve... bad mouthed by the opposition... 'he's the devil'... the new community... 'Here are my mother and my brothers'.

CHAPTER 4: Time for reflection... the parable of the Sower... don't hide the light... parables of growing seed, mustard seed,... the calming of the storm... 'How little faith you have!'

CHAPTER 5: Across the lake out of home ground... the man whose name was Legion... the healing of Jairus' daughter and of the woman with the chronic bleeding.

CHAPTER 6: Rejected at Nazareth... sending out the Twelve... the death of John the Baptist... the feeding of the 5000... walking on water... back across the lake... healing at Gennesaret.

CHAPTER 7: Tradition... what makes unclean?... the Syro-Phoenician woman... the deaf and dumb man's healing... Ephphatha.

CHAPTER 8: Feeding the 4000... seeking a miracle (Pharisees)... beware of the leaven of Herod and the Pharisees... healing a blind man... Crux 1... Caesarea Philippi... Jesus and Peter... Who am I?... You are the Christ... The Son of Man must suffer... Get behind me Satan... Take up your cross... Follow!

CHAPTER 9: Crux 2... The Transfiguration... 'This is my own dear son, Listen!'... healing the boy with the evil spirit... Jesus again speaks of his death... who is the greatest? (1 ... the first and the last... the child in the midst... who is not against us is for us... any one who causes any of these little ones to stumble.

Introduction

Mark's gospel has a fair claim to be numbered among the top ten most influential books ever written. Consider its impact on human history and western civilisation. It has fascinated me ever since student days, helped on by *Mark at Work*, by John Vincent and John Davies. Then around ten years ago I read *Binding the Strong Man, A Political Reading of Mark's Story of Jesus*, by Ched Myers, the American peace organiser and activist, lecturer and preacher. Ched Myers opened my eyes and my thinking to new possibilities of understanding and interpreting this gospel, aided by a wide range of recent New Testament studies and approaches.

Myers' study cried out for the attention of a wider audience. So I decided to preach my way through Mark's gospel at Wellington Church in Glasgow over an eighteen-month period, using Myers as guide. I aimed to filter his work and the text of Mark through my own experience of living and working in Scotland over the last thirty years. My profound thanks are due to the evening congregation at Wellington who not only lasted the course but encouraged me in my efforts.

With the guidance of Professor John Barclay of Glasgow University's Divinity Faculty, I have edited this sermon material without, I hope, losing the immediacy of the spoken word. Muriel Pearson, a member of my congregation, has helped greatly in the suggestions for prayer and study at the end of each section. The production of this study would also not have been possible without the enthusiasm and care of Gill Cloke, Janet de Vigne and Kath Davies at the Scottish Christian Press.

The root of the word 'sermon' comes from the Latin *sermo*, 'a conversation'. I am gratefully aware of conversations over the years which have gone into this book's making, particularly with fellow members of the Iona Community. The book is offered in the hope that it may provoke many more 'conversations', particularly since in the Church of Scotland we are encouraged to 'live in dialogue' with one gospel each year. It is also offered with apologies and thanks to my long-suffering wife and family. I am blessed that they share with me the concerns of Mark's gospel for a world of justice and care for the marginalised.

Getting to grips with Mark's witness to Jesus and its significance for us is the heart of this study. Let this brief introduction encourage the reader to engage *immediately* (a favourite word of Mark's) with the gospel text. My prayer is that through Mark's own words the living Jesus may appear to us in our time, inviting faith, announcing the reign of God and calling us to be disciples now.

HOW TO USE THIS BOOK - SOME SUGGESTIONS

Any book has a life of its own in the hands of a reader or group of readers. This book is intended for personal and group reading. It could form the basis for a year's preaching or a series of group studies. Having forty sections, it could also be used on a daily basis through Lent.

Some stimulus for personal reflection is suggested. Keeping a journal of your thoughts as you journey through the gospel will deepen study and reflection. Another aid is to put a question mark against anything which puzzles you; a cross against anything you find difficult or don't agree with; an exclamation mark against anything you find surprising or see in a new light; a tick against anything that makes you want to cry out 'Yes!'

Group work material is offered for around half of the sections. These can be picked-and-mixed. Do them all or pick out a few. If your group decides to use some of the studies, it is worthwhile taking some from the first half of Mark (up to Chapter 8) and some from the second (Chapters 9 to 16).

Mark's gospel is a story in two halves about the good news of Jesus Christ. Before you begin, you might jot down your answers to the question, What do I know about Jesus which excites, scares, perplexes, challenges, reassures me? Ask yourself the same question when you come to the gospel's end. Bible references are from the Good News Bible, unless otherwise attributed.

One last word before you start. In any book, first words matter. They introduce many of a book's moods and themes. The first section, 'Gospel Genesis', is therefore particularly worth close reading and study. Now you can start 'immediately'.

Leith Fisher
2002

chapter 1

Gospel Genesis

MARK 1:1-8

The Preaching of John the Baptist

(Matt 3:1-12; Lk 3:1-18; Jn 1:19-28)

This is the Good News about Jesus Christ, the Son of God. It began as the prophet Isaiah had written:

God said, 'I will send my messenger ahead of you to clear the way for you'.

Someone is shouting in the desert, 'Get the road ready for the Lord; make a straight path for him to travel!'

So John appeared in the desert, baptising and preaching. 'Turn away from your sins and be baptised,' he told the people, 'and God will forgive your sins'. Many people from the province of Judea and the city of Jerusalem went out to hear John. They confessed their sins, and he baptised them in the River Jordan.

John wore clothes made of camel's hair, with a leather belt round his waist, and his food was locusts and wild honey. He announced to the people, 'The man who will come after me is much greater than I am. I am not good enough even to bend down and untie his sandals. I baptise you with water, but he will baptise you with the Holy Spirit'.

'WILL YOU COME AND FOLLOW ME?'

Let one radical questioner and disciple introduce us to another. In his letter of 30 April 1944 from a Berlin prison, Dietrich Bonhoeffer, thinker and martyr, comments, '... the thing that keeps coming back to me is, what is Christianity, and indeed, what is Christ for us today?' Bonhoeffer was not the first nor will he be the last to be bothered by those questions, though few will be as creative and committed as he was in dealing with their disturbance.

Very early in the story of the Christian church, the writer of the Gospel of Mark was concerned with just such radical questions. He sought to answer them, not only for himself, but for the community of faith to which he belonged. Scholars debate where that community was - possibly a mixed community of Jewish and Gentile Christians living in or near Galilee towards the final quarter of the first century, some time after CE70. That was his immediate audience, but Mark's gospel is an invitation for Christians of any time and place to wrestle with those questions. This gospel has been called 'the gospel of radical discipleship' with good reason. In one sense, the challenge which Mark throws out could be reduced to two deceptively simple questions, 'Who is Jesus Christ?' and 'What does it mean to follow him?' These questions walk with us from beginning to end of Mark's gospel.

What follows in these pages is an exploration of the rough, exhilarating, liberating road which Mark outlines as the way of Jesus and the way of Christian discipleship. It's quite a road - at its very beginning we should be clear that this is a road which never ends, since Mark presents Jesus and his way as a continuing journey. The journey is not only his but ours. This is living history, our history. The answers to the two fundamental questions are not merely about 'head' knowledge, they are in the shaping of our lives; in the responses we make to the call of the one Mark entitles 'the Son of Man'. With a proper respect for inclusive language we will call him simply 'the Human One'. 'The Son of Man'/'The Human One' is not simply the main title which Mark gives to Jesus, the very name makes clear from the outset that Jesus has come to clarify the meaning and purpose of our humanity.

'THE BEGINNING'

The gospel starts, 'The beginning of the gospel of Jesus Christ' - 'beginning'... 'gospel'... 'Jesus'... 'Christ'. Each of these first words has an echo and a history. 'Beginning' evokes the primal - the story of creation. Remember the Bible's description of all beginning, 'In the beginning God' ... 'In the beginning God created ... the heavens and the earth.' (RSV) Here is the first signal. This story is about something as real and basic as the creation itself. It tells of the possibilities of a new creation; it invites us to consider the possibility that the God who took the initiative at the start of all things is about to take the initiative again. 'There is another first time despite the fatigue of world history.' (Via 1985 p.45) The air is heavy with meaning and possibility.

'Gospel'

The next word is 'gospel'. Surely that's simple enough? We know 'gospel' as the word used for the telling of Jesus' life-story in the Bible - the authoritative, canonical story. Indeed it is. Few words have become more completely Christianised. 'Gospel truth' has entered our language as a description of what is thoroughly trustworthy. Throughout his book, Mark suggests the authoritative handing down of what is genuine. The transmission of 'gospel' goes like this,

> Jesus receives the gospel from God,
> Mark receives the gospel from Jesus,
> we, the readers, receive the gospel from Mark.

Mark wants to stress that the story he tells is authentic. He was writing at a time when eye-witnesses to Jesus' life and ministry were dying out and it may well have been that the stories about Jesus circulating in the early Christian communities as oral tradition were liable to misrepresentation and distortion. Mark's claim is that he offers pure 'gospel', going back to the source, Jesus himself. 'Gospel' literally means 'good news' - the nature of the good news will be unfolded in the telling of the tale itself.

Before the word 'gospel' became associated with the story of Jesus Christ, it was most often used in relation to the Roman Emperor. Rome's power and imperial claims form the political and cultural context of the story, and we should bear in mind the reality of Roman power and influence as we read Mark's story of Jesus. 'Gospel' was the word used to announce the Imperial Roman Army's victories; it meant 'News of Victory'. It was also used whenever a new emperor came to power. Roman propaganda talked of the emperor as 'the Divine Man'. By claiming that he was part of the company of the gods, Rome sought to legitimate the emperor's exercise of power. To anyone brought up on the traditions of the Old Testament, any such claim was idolatrous. Throughout Mark's gospel we are witnesses to the contest developing between 'the Divine Man' and 'the Human One'. 'Mark is taking dead aim at Caesar and his legitimating myths.' (Myers 1988 page 124) Here is early intimation of a conflict which rumbles through the gospel, the battle between the carpenter's son from Nazareth and mighty Caesar. The odds might have seemed long on Caesar, but the gospel has a shock or two in store.

One bonus of ministering in different places is the acquisition of distinguished predecessors! In Glasgow's East End, I used to sit on the chair of Thomas Chalmers, father of the Disruption of the Church of Scotland in 1843 and one of the first leaders to recognise how rapid urbanisation would challenge the church's effectiveness. The Disruption - over the right of congregations to appoint their own ministers - was in part about keeping civil powers in their place. However, Chalmers pales before Andrew Melville, sixteenth-century Principal of Glasgow University and minister of the parish of Govan, where I was ordained. Melville, one of the second generation of leaders of the Scottish Reformation was author of the Second Book of Discipline. He took issue with his king, James VI, concerning the spiritual independence of the Scottish Kirk. It was Melville who reminded his king that, '... in Scotland there are twa kings and twa kingdoms. There is Christ Jesus the King and his kingdom the Kirk, whose subject King James the Sixth is, and of whose kingdom not a King he is, nor a Lord, but a member' (Burleigh 1960 pp204,5).

The 'good news' challenges the authority of all earthly rulers. Mark makes plain at the outset the validity of such a challenge, not only within the sphere of the church, but everywhere. We can look forward to Mark's unfolding of a clash of powers, a confrontation between the claims of Caesar and the claims of Christ. And we clearly see that battle continuing in our world now.

'JESUS'

'The beginning ... of the gospel ... of Jesus'. In the four gospels the name 'Jesus' occurs almost six hundred times and the composite name 'Jesus Christ' only four. While we think of the name 'Jesus' as very special, in Jesus' own time and society it was extremely common - it was the Greek form of three Old Testament names, Joshua, Jehoshua and Yeshua. Think of it as equivalent to the Glasgow name for everyman, 'Jimmy', or the universal 'John Smith'. It has suggestions of profound humanity, of Jesus as *everyman, the human being.*

The name Jesus also had a particular meaning among his people. It was a name of honour and significance. Joshua was the inheritor of Moses' task in leading the people of Israel into freedom and promise after their deliverance from Egypt, a task which he fulfilled. The name means, 'God is my help' or 'The one who saves'. 'Jesus' means freedom.

'CHRIST'

'The beginning ... of the gospel ... of Jesus Christ'. In other words, 'the beginning of the good news of Jesus Messiah'. 'Messiah' is not so much a name as a title, meaning 'God's Anointed', or 'Chosen One'. In the time of Jesus his people were once again suffering under occupation, chafing against foreign rule, this time from Rome. Ever since the days of the great King David, the life of the nation had suffered one shock and disaster after another at the hands of outside aggressors. Not surprisingly, the people longed for a return of the great king, or someone of like power. They prayed continually for deliverance and, over the years and generations, the belief grew that a new David, the Messiah, God's anointed, would return to save his people. However, there were many different expectations concerning the coming of the Messiah.

In the 200 years before Christ's birth, more and wilder dreams of the Messiah's coming circulated among the people. These dreams, hopes and longings, born out of a people's sufferings and frustrations, often conflicted with one another. For example, the Pharisees thought the Messiah would not come until the Law of Moses was kept to every last 'jot and tittle', while other people prayed that the Messiah would come like an avenging *deus ex machina*, a great warlord, the first century equivalent of Superman, who would rout their enemies before leading the nation in triumph up Zion's holy hill.

Mark is quite prepared for Jesus' being seen as the answer to his people's longings. At the start of his story he intimates to us, his readers, that Jesus is indeed entitled 'Messiah'. Much of the drama of the gospel itself will centre around the question, 'What does being the Messiah mean?' Very early in Mark's account, Jesus disappoints the Pharisees - by the end he will have failed to live up to the political aspirations of the people. Throughout the gospel, those who discern who he is are told to keep very quiet about it. Although the title 'Messiah' is disclosed to readers at the start, what 'Messiah' means in its fullness is not made plain until the gospel's end. Only on the cross and through the cross will the true nature of Jesus' Messiahship be revealed. 'The Human One' must suffer (8:31, 9:31, 10:33) and only then will we see and know who he is.

We have spent a long time with the first verse of the gospel. The pace will quicken. First words matter; they announce the theme: 'The beginning of the gospel of Jesus Christ'. With this terse announcement Mark invites us to fasten our seat belts for all that is to follow. Note that no comment is here offered on the final words of 1:1, 'the Son of God'. Significant manuscripts omit these words and there will be further comment on them in the course of our gospel reading.

PREPARING THE WAY

The immediate sequel to the gospel announcement is a quotation, 'God said, "I will send my messenger ahead of you to clear a way for you." Someone is shouting in the desert, "Get the road ready for the Lord; make a straight path for him to travel!"' This is a composite quotation from three Old Testament sources. It is significant that at the gospel's start Mark quotes from the sacred scriptures of Jesus' people, lending weight and legitimacy to the startling claim he has already made. Jesus is radically new; he also has roots deep in the traditions of Israel.

Turning to the quotation, the final part comes from Isaiah 40:3, that great chapter of hope which begins 'Comfort, comfort my people'. The first half runs together two other texts from the Greek Septuagint translation of the Old Testament, one from the book of Exodus (23:30) which speaks of God guiding his people on the journey of liberation, the other from Malachi, the last prophet of the Old Testament, 'I will send my messenger to prepare the way for me'(3:1). Together the quotations introduce the image of a journey, a Way. The image of faith as a journey to which Jesus calls us is central to this whole gospel.

There's a particular suggestiveness in Mark's quoting from Malachi. In Jesus' time, the view was widely held that authentic prophecy had ceased in Israel with the last prophets, Haggai, Zechariah and Malachi. Many people believed that the voice of God had gone silent. The reference to Malachi suggests that the voice of God will speak again - that Jesus, in the tradition of the great prophets, will speak for God.

JOHN, THE FORERUNNER

The appearance of John the Baptist offers confirmation. He is a striking figure. He wears the clothes of the great prophet, Elijah, who dared to enter into headlong conflict with the power of the house of King Ahab (1 Kings:17-22). The presence of one who stands dressed in Elijah's clothes speaks also of battle about to be joined.

John announces the coming of one greater than himself, greater than Elijah, one 'whose sandals I am not fit to unfasten'(1:7). The one who comes, for whom John, inheritor of the mantle of Elijah, is not worthy to perform this act of simple, lowly service, must be mighty indeed. As ever in Mark's story, it's not that simple. When Jesus appears on the scene, he seeks from John no act of physical service. Instead, he freely seeks out and submits to John's spiritual gift of baptism. Some strange truths about high and low, about the nature of greatness and service, are about to be revealed.

The Gospel of Mark is full of surprises. Here's the first. Malachi, last of the prophets, has just been introduced. He foretold that God would next appear in the great Temple of Jerusalem, the centre of Israel's life. With that prophecy in our minds, where does John, prophet and baptiser, first appear? He comes from the wilderness and belongs in the wilderness. In the history of the Bible, the wilderness is a complex symbol. Certainly wilderness is the antithesis of the city. The geography of Mark is always significant. Here 'wilderness' is symbolic of the edges, the margins - the opposite of metropolitan Jerusalem, hub of the Jewish universe, or London, the great siren capital of contemporary Britain. To the faithful with their eyes fixed on their religious/political centre, Mark says, 'Look elsewhere, it isn't going to happen there; it will happen where you least expect it'. In terms of power and prestige it will happen 'nowhere'.

Already, four major themes of the gospel have been unveiled - the way of discipleship, the clash of powers, the hidden Messiah, the overturning of long-held beliefs and expectations. The one who comes, the Human One, the new voice of God, comes to turn things upside down, to set at naught the things that are, to bring to life that which is yet to be, to challenge the powers that be and set before us all a new way. 'The right time has come, the Kingdom of God is near, turn yourself round and believe the good news.'(1:15)

STUDY

BY YOURSELF
A prayer for beginning our journey through Mark
God of life, speak to us through the lively words of this gospel. Open the doors of our ears, hearts and minds to the truths you will reveal to us through Jesus, Messiah. *Amen*

- What have you found unsettling and what have you found illuminating in the gospel introduction?

FOR GROUP WORK
- Does 'Gospel Genesis' extend/upset/confirm what you know about Jesus?

chapter 2

'God is Near!'
The First Great Sign

MARK 1:9-15

The Baptism and Temptation of Jesus

(Matt 3:13-4:11; Lk 3:21-22; 4:1-13)

Not long afterwards, Jesus came from Nazareth in the province of Galilee and was baptised by John in the Jordan. As soon as Jesus came up out of the water, he saw heaven opening and the Spirit coming down on him like a dove. And a voice came from heaven, 'You are my own dear Son. I am pleased with you'.

At once, the Spirit made him go into the desert, where he stayed forty days, being tempted by Satan. Wild animals were there also, but angels came and helped him.

After John had been put in prison, Jesus went to Galilee and preached the Good News from God. 'The right time has come,' he said, 'and the Kingdom of God is near! Turn away from your sins and believe the Good News!'

WHERE DO YOU COME FROM? A QUESTION OF ADDRESS

Every good fairground has its roller-coaster, summoning the brave or the foolhardy to the stomach-heaving ups and downs of the ride. The start of Mark is like this, sometimes you're up, sometimes you're down - in bewilderingly quick succession. This is the 'good news', was the initial announcement. News happens 'now', although it also happens in the old familiar world. 'News' is always touched with the unexpected.

The roller-coaster is heaving in this short passage. We begin on a high note with the words of John the Baptist ringing in our ears,

> The man who will come after me is much greater than I am. I am not good enough even to bend down and untie his sandals. I baptise you with water, but he will baptise you with the Holy Spirit. (1:7-8)

The scene is now set for the arrival of the great one. What comes next? 'Not long afterwards Jesus came from Nazareth in the province of Galilee.' (1:9) Remember the significance of geography throughout this gospel. To get on in the world it's a distinct advantage to have the right address. Mark says, 'Here comes the great one, the mighty one, the holy one'. Where did you say he came from? Nazareth. Nazareth - where's that? Two thousand years of telling the story of Jesus of Nazareth have dulled for us the sense of shock which John's hearers would have felt. One commentator puts it thus, 'Nazareth was Nowheresville'. Galilee was worse than nowhere, it was notorious. To the sophisticated inhabitants in and around metropolitan Jerusalem, Galilee was a poor northern province surrounded by suspect Gentiles and despised Samaritans. It was almost bandit territory; regarded much as the Edinburgh establishment viewed the Scottish Highlands of the seventeenth and eighteenth centuries (and perhaps as Scotland looks to some from southern England now). What an anti-climax! Jesus has come from quite the wrong place. He turns up for the first time in the gospel simply as one of the crowd and submits to the baptism of John.

THE BAPTISM

As Jesus comes out of the water so the roller-coaster starts again. 'He sees heaven open,' says Mark(1.10). 'Open Heaven' is a code. It would be understood by Mark's first readers as a sign of a particularly direct word from God. In earthly terms, Nazareth may be nowhere and Galilee worse, but when the heavens open for the man from Nazareth in Galilee it is clear that on him God's favour rests. By association, God is saying something to us about disregarded places in our own towns and cities, and in the shanty towns, the *favelas*, the Third World villages and the refugee camps of today. God is saying, 'Look there, not just for those deserving of the rich world's charity, look there, and listen for evidences of my living word'.

When and where we least expect it, 'the heavens open' and the Spirit descends, both in Mark's story and in the history of faith. Already we have noted the gospel's reference to Malachi, the last of the canonical prophets, after whose time the people believed the heavens were closed and God was silent. Here at the gospel's start the heavens are open again and the Spirit comes to make a living communion between the Father and the Son and, through the Son, with all God's people. The question remains - in what sense are the heavens open for us today? Where do we see the Spirit coming to the contemporary body of Christ, and the word being spoken as a new and living word? One of the deepest divisions within the Church, a divide which follows no party lines, is between those who believe the heavens are closed again and there's no new truth to be revealed or discovered (it's all there already), and those who assert that now is a time when heaven is open, the Spirit is moving and new words are being spoken as new visions of God's purpose unfold. Let the words of George MacLeod, founder of the Iona Community and prophet of our time, words which he repeated like a litany, ring in our ears, 'God is NOW'.

'My Son, the Beloved'

The heavens open, the Spirit comes, the word is, 'You are my own dear Son. I am pleased with you'. (1:11) This sentence from the heavens is again a quotation from the old and familiar word, from two different Old Testament books. 'You are my Son, the beloved,' comes from Psalm 2, a royal coronation psalm which was used as the King of Israel was enthroned.

> You are my son; today I have become your father. Ask, and I will give you all the nations; the whole earth will be yours... Now listen to this warning, you kings; learn this lesson, you rulers of the world... (Ps 2:7,8,10)

By Jesus's time, this psalm featured in the expectations of the coming of the Messiah, the one who would come with power. The quotation points to the kingly role of Jesus, who announces and inaugurates the coming of the kingdom of God.

The second half of the quotation, however, introduces a tension which is central to the meaning of the whole gospel. The reference here is to Isaiah 42:1. 'Here is my servant, whom I strengthen - the one I have chosen, with whom I am pleased.' Mark is reminding readers of the four servant songs of Isaiah which picture the one who is called to bring redemption not through the exercise of power, but through vicarious suffering. Here, early in Mark's gospel, the cross appears at the centre of the Messianic mission. The one, chosen and beloved of the Father, anointed with the Spirit and with power, will come to reign on a cross.

The baptism raises two further questions. Who saw the heavens open and who heard the voice? This scene is not quite as simple as it looks. Jesus certainly saw and heard; Mark makes it plain that Jesus' baptism was for him a moment of calling and confirmation for the ministry ahead, a time of assurance and empowerment. There is no suggestion that anyone else present saw the vision or heard the voice, certainly among his contemporaries. Yet we, the readers, have seen and heard. We now know a secret about Jesus which, as the story unfolds, it becomes clear those around him have not grasped. Mark gives the reader extra information so that from the beginning, concerning the Human One, we may know who he is and where he is going.

The next question asks - why was Jesus baptised? Why did he submit to baptism by John? He didn't need to, he is the holy, chosen one. Here are two lines of thinking which I find helpful. 'For us baptised, with us baptised'. In the first place, Jesus' baptism can be seen as an act of solidarity with we humans in our frail, finite, fallen condition, an act which sets the tone for the whole of his ministry with and among us. It is also an act which is a forerunner of that greater baptism on the hill of Calvary. Secondly, baptism is always linked with repentance, a notion we have spiritualised almost to death. Biblically, repentance is an act of the turning of our whole selves to face in a new direction, as in the story of Levi, the tax collector (1:14). It involves the death of the old way. Jesus' baptism announces the new way. In and through his baptism and union with his Father, Jesus is baptised into freedom. As one commentator says, 'he has become wholly unobliged' (Waetjen 1989 p.69). The new creation begins with a renunciation of the old order. Jesus stands for the new as he enters into the way of radical discipleship associated with the community around John the Baptist.

TESTING TIMES

Immediately after his baptism, Jesus departs into the wilderness. Down we go again. The beginning is not yet. Before the public ministry comes the private testing. Before the public witness where the word is spoken and lived out, comes the prayer and the preparation, the time of profound struggle. Some years ago our church was visited by Dom Mauro Morelli, serving as an Auxiliary Bishop in Sao Paulo, a brave and gracious man of humour and faith, deeply involved in the struggle of the church for justice in Brazil. He said that all those in South America involved in that crucial struggle, seeking to be with and for the poor, had to be steeped in prayer, and not so much petitionary prayer, the prayer of asking, of words, but contemplative prayer, the prayer of silence, of waiting on the word and letting the reality of God envelop us. Is that not what Jesus does when he goes out into the wilderness, divesting himself of all the props and distractions with which we clutter up our lives, to stand before God alone?

Jesus goes not only to stand before God, but to wrestle with Satan. In the forty days the wrestling is intense, but it does not end with the days of temptation. *Binding the Strong Man* is both the title of an exciting book on the Gospel of Mark, to which I am much indebted (Myers 1988), and also a very good description of Jesus' battle with Satan. Struggling with the forces of evil, battling with the powers of darkness are key themes which develop throughout the gospel. The battle is joined here with a vengeance. It is a struggle with a long way to run before the finish.

We need to pay attention to the site of the battle. It takes place in the wilderness, the place of emptiness, nothingness. Is there any place more opposite to our world of personal stereos, incessant radio, twenty-four-hour television and continuous Internet, where we can spend a lifetime being distracted and yet formed by other people's images, other people's noise? In the wilderness we stand alone with the elemental life of nature, with the voices which rise from the turbulent depths of our inner selves, face to face with God and this world's Strong Man. For Jesus, the wilderness is a place of testing, strengthening, purifying. After forty days, symbolic of Israel's forty years' testing, he is ready to go on.

A FUNNY TIME TO START

What next? 'After John had been arrested, Jesus came into Galilee proclaiming the gospel of God.' (1.14) After *what*? One of the attitudes most deeply rooted in the middle class view of the world is a profound suspicion of anyone who has been in prison. It is not after graduating with a brilliant PhD, nor having completed a glittering Assistantship in some plum parish, that Jesus begins his public ministry; it's out of the wilderness, after his forerunner the Baptist has been flung in gaol. 'People don't go to prison for nothing', 'There's no smoke without fire', so we say. However, we also know that some of those who have been incarcerated are among our world's most profound witnesses: Niemoller, Wiesel, Bonhoeffer, Solzenitsyn, Mandela, Luther King, and many more. In a strange way, some speak of imprisonment as the experience of the transforming wilderness; for the people of Israel it was a forty years' transformation, in Jesus' life it is compressed into forty days; for all it was an exercise in discovering the truth that sets free.

THE RIGHT TIME

Jesus returns from the desert. Now comes the climax. Here is what Jesus has come to declare, 'The right time has come, and the Kingdom of God is near! Turn away from your sins and believe the Good News'. (1:14,15) The time is right, although the place is wrong again - the announcement is dis-located out in the sticks of Galilee. The time is right and now, the kingdom is at hand, the King is near. That's the Good News. Here is what is vital, different. Remember, in the time of Jesus many people felt that the Kingdom of God was anything but near. There were some groups, such as the community of Qumran, who believed that the return of God was imminent. There were also many who believed the prophets were silenced, the heavens closed; they felt that in their alien occupation, God had deserted them. The hopelessness and apathy which are so real in our world, were well known to many of Jesus' contemporaries. To them, Jesus' opening words are an announcement of profound liberation.

We live in a time in which the processes of our history and culture over the last two hundred years have seemed to produce in us as a people a consciousness that God is more and more remote from the business of everyday living and thinking. Both in church and society we need to hear the Good News of Jesus' great words of freedom and release, 'God's reign is near, God's presence is among us'. An immense possibility opens up before us - that the kingdom is all about us, if we have eyes to see. Soon we will see that taking the way of Jesus is the way to the opening of our eyes and ears.

'The kingdom is here, the time has come.' The challenge follows. 'Turn away from your sins. Turn your life round, your whole life. Loosen your hold on everything in your character and personality and on everything in the social, political and cultural world in which you live that ties you to the old order, the way of sin and death. Turn your life round and believe. Trust in the gospel.' Trust in the way of Jesus. Repentance is radical, total. The Good News is all about the turning, the radical redirection of our whole lives, focused on the new way Jesus brings, the new being who is Jesus.

Study

By yourself

A prayer: God is near!
'The kingdom is here. The right time has come.'
God, in Jesus we learn you bring sight to the blind. Open our eyes to your present activity in our world now. Help us to see the signs of your kingdom in the midst of our life in the world, and to give you thanks, through Jesus, the giver of sight. *Amen*

• Against the pessimism of his own time, Jesus makes his announcement of God's nearness. There is much pessimism about faith in our world today. Perhaps we look for the wrong things. What evidence of the kingdom can you see in your own life, in the life of your local church, in the life of your community, and in the wider world? Keep your eyes and the eyes of your mind open in the coming week.

Pause

A word about time

It's an odd thing, time. On the one hand, nothing seems quite so linear, measured, symmetrical as the ticking of the clock, with each moment equal in duration. However, that's not at all how we experience time. Sometimes time drags - in the dentist's waiting room perhaps, or waiting for the final whistle while the team barely holds a one-goal lead. Sometimes time flies - when we're late for the train, when we're in the middle of something we greatly enjoy. Time is not simple. I have a friend who on one occasion began a sermon by inviting his congregation to put their watches in their pockets (an idea with real possibility!). 'Right', he said, 'you're now living in God's time'. He was pointing to the danger of living entirely by the regulation of the clock and not taking time to stare, wait, brood, dream, listen, pray. There is a deeper rhythm to time than the sweep of a second hand.

Mark's gospel draws our attention to two different kinds of time. At one level, Mark presents the story of Jesus as a realistic narrative where the time is everyday time and one event follows another. However, there is another dimension. Already we have seen things happen in this story which do not belong to ordinary, everyday time. The long-silent voices of the prophets are beginning to utter again God's word, the closed heavens are opening as a sign of an extraordinary presence and Jesus himself is beginning his ministry by saying, 'The right time has come': that is, God's time. Theologians say that Mark skilfully blends a narrative in which everyday time is often infused with the apocalyptic. If we try to put that important truth into more everyday language, we might say something as follows.

Mark is telling the story of one who is uncommonly ordinary, the unlikely Messiah, the man from nowhere. As the story evolves, we come to see an outsider, who steps outside the Law and the religious Establishment of Israel, who confronts the power of Rome, who journeys outside the safe boundaries of religion, kith and kin, who stretches out his arms to embrace the unclean and the poor. This is one who takes the ultimate step of surrendering the power of his own life and at the end stands deserted, condemned, rejected and frighteningly alone. Yet, by the signs of the other times, the time from heaven, Mark is pointing to the reality that all the way through this story, in this life, through this journey, from its obscure and unexpected origin in Galilee to its awful and shameful end at Golgotha, we are confronted with the ultimate, the last things, the final truth, the living reality of God and human life. The dimension of the eternal shines through the moments of ordinary time. To live through the Gospel of Mark is to go on a journey where our perceptions are widened as the curtains are drawn further and further apart to help us to see the new and revolutionary fullness of what God reveals in Jesus Christ. In him God's time has come, here is the 'Day of the Lord' promised by the prophets, the revealing of God's favour. Here is the long-expected in the guise of the unexpected. We remember the invitation of Jesus himself to his would-be disciples at the beginning of John's gospel, 'Come and see'. (John 1:39)

chapter 3

Fishing for fishers

MARK 1:16-20
Jesus Calls Four Fishermen
(Matt 4:12-22; Lk 5:1-11)

As Jesus walked along the shore of Lake Galilee, he saw two fishermen, Simon and his brother Andrew, catching fish with a net. Jesus said to them, 'Come with me, and I will teach you how to catch people'. At once they left their nets and went with him.

He went a little farther on and saw two other brothers, James and John, the sons of Zebedee. They were in their boat getting their nets ready. As soon as Jesus saw them, he called them; they left their father Zebedee in the boat with the hired men and went with Jesus.

THE CALL TO A NEW VOCATION

Jesus says, 'Come and follow'. Like a scarlet thread these words run through the whole gospel. To whom are these words first addressed? Remember the roller-coaster. We have just come from a high with the portentous words of the announcement, 'The right time has come. The Kingdom of God is upon you. Repent and believe the Good News'. (1:15) In other words, the day of the Lord is near, the presence of the kingdom announced. Crisis, judgement, hope fill the atmosphere. 'Let all mortal flesh keep silence.' We wait for the crowds to gather, for the signs and portents in the sky. Instead we get, 'Jesus was walking by the sea of Galilee when he saw Simon and his brother Andrew at work casting their nets. They were fishermen'. (1.16) We crash back into the world of the everyday. We meet just a few fishermen, working away at the lakeside as they've always worked, four ordinary men at an ordinary trade, not very high, not very low, with no pretensions to greatness of intellect or power, prestige or holiness. Two simple, extraordinary words are spoken. Jesus says, 'Follow me'. (1.17) There follows the action which speaks louder than any words. 'At once, they left their nets and followed him.' This anti-climax doesn't last long.

This scene, described so starkly, is one of the central pictures of the gospel, simple yet powerfully evocative and emotive. It is a scene which may well have been with us from our own childhood, when Jesus had an almost Pied Piper quality, appearing as the great man charming the disciples into following him. One way to read this scene is as a commentary on the passage immediately preceding it. Here is the way to respond to the announcement of the Kingdom. This is what repentance and believing the gospel means. It means to rise up and follow, in the circumstances of our own lives.

TRUE REPENTANCE

'Repentance' and 'conversion' are words with a long history. The Old Testament word for conversion, *shoab*, occurs more than a thousand times. It means to 'turn', 'return', 'bring back', 'restore'. The prophets were continually calling the people of Israel to turn from their sins, idolatries and unjust ways and return to their Lord. The New Testament words for conversion mean to 'turn round', to take a new direction. They have a force which stops you in your tracks: they show you a radically different road. Throughout the Bible, conversion is not about believing something different in your head, or about experiencing some new emotion, it is about the transformation of life in all its aspects. Listen to the words of Jim Wallis, from his book, *The Call to Conversion:*

> In the larger rhythm of turning from and turning to, repentance is the turning away from. Repentance turns us from sin, selfishness, darkness, idols, habits, bondages and demons both public and private. We turn from all that binds and oppresses us and others, from all the violence and evil in which we are so complicit, from all the false worship which has controlled and corrupted us. Ultimately, repentance is turning from the powers of death... they no longer hold us. Conversion leads to faith... faith is turning to belief, hope and trust. Faith opens up our future, by restoring our sight, softening our hearts, bringing light to our darkness. We are converted to compassion, justice and peace as we take our stand as citizens of Christ's new order.
>
> That conversion is always rooted and grounded in history... Biblical conversion is historically specific. People turn to God in the midst of concrete historical events, dilemmas and choices. That turning is always deeply personal, it is never private. It is never an abstract or theoretical concern; conversion is always a practical issue. Any idea of conversion that is removed from the social and political realities of the day is simply not biblical.
> (Wallis, 1981, p 4,5)

'Citizens of Christ's new order', 'historically specific'. In the story of the disciples' call by the lakeside we can see all that. Peter and Andrew leave their nets. They leave their work with all its familiarity. They leave their livelihood - following Jesus has profound economic consequences. James and John leave their work and their father's household. They leave their home with all its familiarity; they leave the ties of family and that crucial network of relationships - following the way of Jesus has the most profound social consequences. Peter and Andrew, James and John stand as paradigms, living examples of the truth of the words of St. Paul, 'When anyone is united to Christ, there is a new world, the old order has gone, the new has already begun'. (2 Cor 5:17, *NEB*)

As the story of the disciples' life with Jesus unfolds, we will see many painful birthpangs on the way to the establishing of the new order - following Jesus is not instant heaven. From the beginning we see that to turn and follow is a turning of our whole lives, the taking of a radical step on the new path to life which is also the path to newness of life.

Jesus says, 'Follow me'. And they rose up and followed him. The story depicts the call to discipleship with stunning simplicity; it is on the way itself that the implications of the call will deepen and unfold. At the turning point of the gospel's centre, after many wanderings and twists and turns, the call will be intensified. Jesus says, 'If anyone will come after me, they must deny themselves, take up their cross and follow me'. (8:34)

The second half of the gospel will unfold the meaning of the way of the cross to a group of very dim and reluctant disciples. Before Jesus' cross itself their following fails completely, and Jesus stands forsaken and alone. Yet that is not the last word. The last word to the failed and stalled disciples comes from the Jesus who is risen, 'Tell them', says the young man at the empty tomb, 'that he is going ahead of them into Galilee'. (16:7) 'Keep on following', is the message from beginning to end. Along the way, the nature of following will be clarified. Here is the first call to rise and walk on.

BEARERS OF THE NEW ORDER

'Follow me and I will make you fishers of men.' (1:17) The piscatorial image has been the dubious inspiration of many a seaside chorus and the even more doubtful legitimation of the use of all manner of snares, lures, coercions and enticements which litter and disfigure the history of Christian mission. Jesus deserves better than the dishonest, domineering forms of evangelism sadly so often practised in his name. In the invitation to fish for people we again meet words which have a significant past; here are specific Old Testament texts which speak of fishing:

The prophet Jeremiah reports,

'I shall send for many fishermen', says the Lord, 'and they will fish for them. After

that I will send for many hunters and they will hunt for them in every mountain and hill and from crevices in the rocks. For my eyes are upon all their ways; they are not hidden from my sight, nor is their wrongdoing concealed from me.'
(Jeremiah 16:16-17)

Jeremiah is censuring Israel, calling the people to judgement for their sins. It is the fishermen who are the agents of the Lord's ingathering.

Amos speaks of judgement on the rich,

Listen to this, you women of Samaria, who grow fat like the well-fed cows of Bashan, who ill-treat the weak, oppress the poor, and demand that your husbands keep you supplied with liquor! As the Sovereign Lord is holy, he has promised, 'The days will come when they will drag you away with hooks; every one of you will be like fish on a hook.'
(Amos 4:1-2)

Ezekiel speaks of judgement on the powerful,

I am going to put a hook through your jaw and make the fish in your river stick fast to you. Then I will pull you up out of the Nile, with all the fish sticking to you. I will throw you and all those fish into the desert.
(Ezekiel 29:4-5)

These are powerful statements of judgement. When Jesus calls the fishermen, he invites them, as representatives of ordinary folk, to be the citizens of the Messiah's new order, the bearers of God's word of judgement to an old and weary earth. They are to establish in their new community, centred on Jesus, a new way of relating to one another, based on trust, faith and sharing. This is how the disciples, in their common life in Christ, will announce the coming of the new order. It is the quality of their common life which will be an act of creative subversion of the way things are in the world. In recent years there have been many hopeful and inspiring stories of Basic Christian communities and House Churches in Eastern Europe and in Latin America displaying just such qualities of the common life.

For the disciples are not merely the original four fishermen, Peter and Andrew, James and John. The call to follow is addressed to all who 'hear' Jesus. Here is the beginning of the radical challenge of the gospel, the inviting voice which bids us follow. Jesus' voice is insistent, but never coercive, our response to him is always of our own free choice, a choice requiring continual renewal. Here are two quotations to encourage us on our way. Listen to Jim Wallis again:

To leave their nets was no light choice for these Galilean fishermen. Their fishing nets were their means of livelihood and the symbol of their identity. Now Peter and the others were leaving not only their valued possessions; they were leaving their former way of life.

Four simple fishermen heard the call of Jesus. They were the first to obey and follow. They would not be the last. Others too would forsake all previous commitments to join Jesus' band. They would become disciples and share his life. From then on they were bound to Jesus and his kingdom; nothing would ever be the same for them again. They had made a real choice with very real consequences. (Wallis 1981 p2)

We can also revisit Albert Schweitzer's famous words about life choices:

He comes to us as one unknown, as of old he came by the lakeside to those who knew him not. He speaks to us the same words, 'Follow me'. And to those who obey him, whether they be wise or simple, they will learn in their own experience, in the toils and conflicts they pass through in his fellowship, Who He Is. (Schweitzer 1952 p. 86)

STUDY

BY YOURSELF
- Who introduced you to the invitation to follow Jesus?
- What does being a follower of Jesus mean to you?
- Has your understanding of following Jesus changed through your life's journey?
  You may like to draw a timeline of your life and doodle your thoughts on it. e.g.

| 1972 | 1978 | 1982 | 1985 | 2002 |

FOR GROUP WORK
Share in the group whatever personal reflections you feel able to offer and ask these questions.
- What was risky and costly for the first disciples in answering Jesus' call?
- What is risky and costly for us today?

Recommended resource: *Jesus and Peter* by John Bell and Graham Maule (Wild Goose Publications 1999) offers a series of humorous and stimulating imaginary conversations between Jesus and Peter on the theme of discipleship.

A BRIEF LOOK AT THE STRUCTURE OF MARK 1-3

On our journey through Mark's gospel we have taken considerable time to negotiate the opening verses. Now the pace begins to pick up. Our careful beginning has been necessary because so many of the gospel's major themes are announced and introduced in the opening verses and we need to have them clearly before us. We are about to meet another major theme, the stories of healing which occur frequently through the gospel.

However, before we look at healing and then return to the text, let us step back for a moment and consider where we are in terms of the gospel's basic structure. The framework of Mark's story is complex and fascinating. We have already seen that the gospel divides into two halves. The first half is largely concerned with Jesus' Galilean ministry, centred in, around and across the Sea of Galilee. The second half, pivoted round Peter's confession that Jesus is the Messiah and Jesus' own announcement of the way of the cross, is the story of the journey to the cross and, at the last, beyond it.

Each gospel half has a structure and a shape. What is most interesting is that the structure of the story of the Galilean ministry is mirrored and reinforced in the story of the journey to the cross told in the second half. Where we are now (here you need the text of Mark in front of you), is at the beginning of a section which runs from Mark 1:16 to 3:35. We could call it, 'The Capernaum Campaign', since that lakeside town is prominent throughout.

The section begins with the call of the disciples and goes on to describe an exorcism in a synagogue. In the story there is mention of an indirect clash with the Scribes. After the exorcism, Jesus is found in the home of Peter, one of the members of his new family, the family of the disciples. There he heals Peter's mother-in-law of a fever. Moving on to the middle of Chapter 3 (verse 13), the same pattern recurs. The section begins with the disciples; this time not only the original four but the twelve, symbolically representing the Twelve Tribes of Israel. Like the four, they are individually named to show their importance. What happens next? There is another story of an exorcism, but this time there is a very direct clash with the Scribes - the language is, to say the least, robust. Then follows another domestic scene, much less happy than the healing of Peter's mother-in-law, where Jesus' own mother and brothers come to rescue him from the 'trouble' into which they see him plunging. They, the old family, are summarily dismissed.

That is the pattern - the disciples, exorcism and the Scribes, the old and new family. They are like book-ends to this section of Mark. Next there are two slim yet significant volumes. First, 1:39 'And Jesus went throughout all of Galilee, preaching in their synagogues and casting out demons'. Second, 3:7-11, beginning, 'Jesus and his disciples went away to Lake Galilee, and a large crowd followed him'. (Mark then goes on to describe the various places from which people had come to see Jesus and the pressure on Jesus to teach, heal and cast out demons.) These two terse sets of verses remind us of the public nature of Jesus' ministry. They tell how his reputation spread throughout the region and of the way the sick, the disturbed, the poor, the broken, the outcast were drawn to him. They remind us of the way he makes time and room for all sorts and conditions of humanity.

These verses paint a picture of Jesus' dynamic, costly involvement with the people of the land in their hopes and pains. Lurking in the background lies perhaps the thought that in a troubled and politically volatile country, and Galilee was deeply troubled, gathering crowds as Jesus did was likely to be viewed by all in authority with the utmost suspicion. As the poet W H Auden says in 'City without Walls',

> In states unable
> To alleviate Distress
> Discontent is hanged.
> (Auden 1966 p51)

Finally we come to the centre, the main campaign narrative, from 1:40 to 3:6. On either side stand the ministries of compassion to the people, in the centre three stories of healing. Each story challenges the roots of the Jewish Law as it was practised in Jesus' time. In turn, the Purity Code, the Debt Code and the Sabbath Code are confronted and called into question. There are also other challenging words and actions which we will come to later.

PAUSE ───

HEALING IN THE GOSPEL OF MARK

Healing looms large, particularly in the first half of the gospel. Commentators reckon that around 40 per cent of the verses of the first ten chapters of Mark relate directly or indirectly to the theme of healing. So we face the question, how are we to explain and understand the healing miracles? By way of introduction, here are a few words from a great missionary figure of our time, Lesslie Newbigin, who in his own life and ministry straddled the worlds of East and West, India and Britain. Newbigin wrote,

> If one has lived at different times in different places, one becomes aware of the relativity of all "explanations". One of the first things I did when I arrived in India was to be involved in a bus accident which laid me off for two years. How to "explain" it? The Indian pastor said, 'It is the will of God'. A Hindu would have said, 'The Karma of your former lives has caught up with you'. In some cultures the explanation would have been that an enemy had put a curse on me. If I, as an "enlightened" European, so called, had said it was because the bus brakes were not working properly, that would have been, for the others, no explanation at all. It would have been simply a re-statement of what had to be explained. To speak of an explanation is to speak of the ultimate framework of axioms and assumptions by which one 'makes sense of things'.
> (Newbigin 1983 p 11)

Newbigin goes on to show how, in our world, we are dominated by scientific, historicist 'explanations' of how things work. He then argues convincingly that to accept such explanations is simply to exchange one set of 'explanations' for another. The gospel healing miracle stories have suffered from being a battlefield of differing 'explanations', ancient and modern, and often the battle has led far from the original point and place of the story on the gospel record. It is clear from the gospel narrative that Jesus was involved in many more healings than the evangelists report in detail. So we need to pay attention to the ones that are selected for detailed reporting and think about why they are chosen.

First, one of the least contestable facts of Jesus' life is that he was a healer. He made people well and, just as importantly, he restored them to a place of meaning and acceptance within their community. Sickness and disability, then as now, meant social dislocation as well as physical or mental illness. While we can, I hope, agree that Jesus was a healer, and a skilled and powerful one at that, fully in tune with the healing power of God's spirit, he was not the only one in his time. The ancient world was full of healers who used skills and techniques ranging from considerable knowledge of natural remedies to something approaching what we would call 'magic'. Jesus avails himself of ways of healing known to and used by others in his use of touch, soil and spittle. We recognise Jesus as a healer among others, although his powers are considerable, and his vision and compassion great.

Secondly, in Jesus' time, talk of and belief in 'signs and wonders' were commonplace. People's attitude to the miraculous could scarcely be more at odds with the atmosphere of scientific scepticism in which we now live. Miracles were expected to surround the lives of particularly holy and seriously powerful people. A holy man like Jesus was expected to be a healer and the telling of his healing powers was a part of the establishment of such a person's 'credentials'.

Today we are much more ambivalent about the miracles and wonders in the gospels. However, the gospels themselves, and particularly Mark, share that ambivalence. Mark is quite clear that the real meaning of Jesus is not to be found in his wonder-working but in his willing suffering, not in his power but in his renunciation of power. Here's an irony. Over the last two hundred years, scholars have been arguing and tying themselves in knots over the so-called gospel miracles, trying to explain them. Today we have become more familiar with other writings of Jesus' time including the non-canonical gospels - the other early accounts of Jesus' life and ministry which didn't make it into the New Testament. When we compare the non-canonical gospels with the four gospels we have, it is striking how comparatively little of the fantastic and miraculous there is in the biblical gospels, and particularly in Mark.

Thirdly, we can say that Jesus' healings point to his closeness and intimacy with God his Father. They are chinks in the curtain of the Son of God's hiddenness through which the healing light of the Father flashes. 'Hiddenness', 'the secret' is a central theme for Mark, therefore in Mark the so-called healing miracles have a particularly ambiguous status. To reiterate, only the cross in Mark's story reveals unambiguously who Jesus is.

Fourthly, there is limited value in persistent historicist questioning of each gospel event, i.e. what actually happened? This type of questioning has dominated our culture's approach to the healings. We feel quite clever if we deduce from scant evidence that such and such an incident describes a clear case of what our scientific medicine would diagnose as epilepsy or schizophrenia or whatever. For example, the boy with the evil spirit (Mk 9:14-24) is often described as epileptic, yet we rarely have enough evidence for such detailed diagnosis. There are clear limits to our abilities to 'demythologise' these healings. On the other hand, there are also real dangers in a superficial, literalist understanding of these stories. Both the historicist and the literalist fall into the same trap, they fail to attend sufficiently to the wealth of symbolic meaning in these stories and to their wider context.

Healing in our world (alternative medicine notwithstanding) is dominated by our biomedical understanding. A biological model of sickness and cure is the one we work with most of the time. It has worked wonders, even if we are sometimes painfully aware of its limitations. However, today we are rediscovering our need to pay more attention to the social networks which surround illness. How we react to the AIDS epidemic and how we treat people with chronic disabilities in our society, provide two disparate contemporary examples. When we come to look at the way people understood their world at the time of Jesus, we see that this social dimension is vitally important. For example, what the Bible describes as leprosy may not always be the disease of leprosy as defined from a modern biomedical perspective. What the Bible calls 'leprosy' may have included a number of different skin disorders. All of them placed the sufferers outside the Levitical purity code - they were forbidden contact with others and became outcasts. It is necessary to have in mind the distinction between our view of the modern physician who 'cures' a person's biological pathology and the New Testament world view of a healer who operates more holistically, and may do as much to restore relationships and a person's place in society as to heal the body.

Finally, when we look at the healing stories in their gospel context, what is most striking and unexpected about them, particularly in the case of the early healings in Mark, is their close relationship to conflict, potential or actual. Almost every time Jesus heals anyone, there is trouble. That is true in two out of the three healings in the passage to which we are about to turn. Why? Because, in bringing wholeness, Jesus is involved in a battle with all that disables and demeans the fullness of people's living. These 'powers', are sometimes described as the power of demons or Satan. Often they assume the more recognisable earthly form of the authority of Scribes, Pharisees or Caesar whose dominant 'law and order' did as much to disempower and marginalise people as physical illness.

chapter 4

Health and Healing

MARK 1:21-45

A Man with an Evil Spirit
(Lk 4:31-37)

Jesus and his disciples came to the town of Capernaum, and on the next Sabbath Jesus went to the synagogue and began to teach. The people who heard him were amazed at the way he taught, for he wasn't like the teachers of the Law; instead he taught with authority.

Just then a man with an evil spirit in him came into the synagogue and screamed, 'What do you want with us, Jesus of Nazareth? Are you here to destroy us? I know who you are - you are God's holy messenger!'

Jesus ordered the spirit, 'Be quiet, and come out of the man!'

The evil spirit shook the man hard, gave a loud scream, and came out of him. The people were all so amazed that they started saying to one another, 'What is this? Is it some kind of new teaching? This man has authority to give orders to the evil spirits, and they obey him!'

And so the news about Jesus spread quickly everywhere in the province of Galilee.

Jesus heals many People
(Matt 8:14-17; Lk 4:38-41)

Jesus and his disciples, including James and John, left the synagogue and went straight to the home of Simon and Andrew. Simon's mother-in-law was sick in bed with a fever, and as soon as Jesus arrived, he was told about her. He went to her, took her by the hand, and helped her up. The fever left her and she began to wait on them.

After the sun had set and evening had come, people brought to Jesus all the sick and those who had demons. All the people of the town gathered in front of the house. Jesus healed many who were sick with all kinds of diseases and drove out many demons. He would not let the demons say anything, because they knew who he was.

Jesus preaches in Galilee
(Lk 4:42-44)

Very early the next morning, long before daylight, Jesus got up and left the house. He went out of the town to a lonely place, where he prayed. But Simon and his companions went out searching for him, and when they found him, they said, 'Everyone is looking for you.'

But Jesus answered, 'We must go on to the other villages round here. I have to preach in them also, because that is why I came.'

So he travelled all over Galilee, preaching in the synagogues and driving out demons.

Jesus heals a Man
(Matt 8:1-4; Lk 5:12-16)

A man suffering from a dreaded skin-disease came to Jesus, knelt down, and begged him for help. 'If you want to,' he said, 'you can make me clean.'

Jesus was filled with pity, and stretched out his hand and touched him. 'I do want to,' he answered. 'Be clean!' At once the disease left the man, and he was clean. Then Jesus spoke sternly to him and sent him away at once, after saying to him, 'Listen, don't tell anyone about this. But go straight to the priest and let him examine you; then in order to prove that you are cured, offer the sacrifice that Moses ordered.'

But the man went away and began to spread the news everywhere. Indeed, he talked so much that Jesus could not go into a town publicly. Instead, he stayed out in lonely places, and people came to him from everywhere.

THE PATTERN OF THE DAY AND THE WEEK

Central to this passage are accounts of two healings and an exorcism. Before we look at the healings, note two other significant patterns in these verses. 'After the sun had set and evening had come, people brought to Jesus all the sick and those who had demons.' (1:32) The pattern of the Hebrew day begins in the evening, not the morning. The day runs from sunset to sunset. It is in the evening, after the sun has set and therefore the Sabbath has ended, that the people gather with the sick and the possessed for Jesus' ministry to them. It is worth noting that the only Sabbath healing in this passage takes place at home behind closed doors. (The exorcism in the synagogue comes into a slightly different category.) Jesus does not yet provoke trouble by openly healing on the Sabbath, very soon he will.

THE PATTERN OF ENGAGEMENT AND WITHDRAWAL,
ACTION AND PRAYER

The substance of the second pattern has been met already in the temptation incident. 'Very early the next morning, long before daylight' (1:35) Jesus left the house, left the town and went to a lonely place and prayed. The pattern to note here is the rhythm of withdrawal and engagement, engagement and withdrawal which we see in the life and ministry of Jesus. Jesus goes to work only after he has been to prayer. He goes apart to be steeped in the reality of God before he plunges himself again into the reality of the world. Before he lays hands on, he lets go. How important the pattern of Jesus' life is for our Christian lives here and now. In a world filled with beguiling and bewildering, deafening and discordant voices we need to make time and space for the still place where we can wait in the silence for the living word. Jesus himself sets the rhythm of our Christian living before us; no prayer without action, no action without prayer.

Jesus is rarely pictured at prayer in Mark's gospel. He is shown at prayer before crucial times of engagement and trial; supremely in the Garden of Gethsemane immediately before the cross (14:32-42). This comparative silence does not reflect a lack of prayer in Jesus' life. Mark's first readers would simply take it as read that Jesus would be frequently at prayer. In addition to the regular, three-times-a-day praying of the *Shema* (Deuteronomy 6:4 *RSV*) - 'Hear, O Israel: the Lord our God is one Lord; and you shall love the Lord your God with all your heart, and with all your soul, and with all your might' - and the blessing of God at meals, Jews, like most of the people of the Ancient World, instinctively turned to prayer whenever they began any task or undertook any journey. They had a sense of their whole lives as lived before God and would seek blessing and protection on all their endeavours. They would also return thanksgiving whenever their tasks were accomplished or a danger or trial was successfully negotiated. Life in the time of Jesus was much more fragile and dangerous than it is for modern, apparently self-sufficient Westerners. To turn to God in prayer was a natural response. Unlike our secular times, Jesus lived and the gospel was written in a climate and culture of prayer.

DISRUPTION IN THE SYNAGOGUE

We turn now to our three stories; two healings and the exorcism. Jesus is introduced in the first story as teaching in the synagogue at Capernaum on the Sabbath Day, the heart and high point of the life of the village community. Those who have gathered are astonished at the authority of his teaching, in contrast to the teaching of the recognised authorities, the Scribes or teachers of the Law. The potential for trouble is there already. Jesus, in speaking out in the synagogue, has penetrated the sphere of another authority. So the loud voice of the demon rings out, 'Why do you meddle with us? Have you come to destroy us?'(1:24)

On whose behalf does the loud voice speak? It speaks in the name of all the powers whose authority is challenged by the new presence and power of Jesus in their midst. In the gospel, Jesus is frequently portrayed as in conflict with 'demons' and 'evil spirits'. These elemental powers 'possess' both individuals and groups - they wield power over them. The exorcism stories in the gospel are not so much about the specifics of cure, rather they serve to throw light on Jesus' struggle with the powers. Here the community of the Scribes, teachers of the Law, first comes under pressure from Jesus. The 'demon' in the synagogue represents the baneful power the Scribes could wield over Jewish social order, a power which Jesus will confront again and again. The crowd are amazed now not only at the authority of his teaching but also the directness of his challenge. The picture is of people open-mouthed, awe-struck in panic and excitement before the new power in the land which they meet in Jesus of Nazareth (1:27).

A MOMENT OF DOMESTIC PEACE AND QUIET

After the drama and tension of the exorcism in the synagogue, the healing of Peter's mother-in-law is quietly domestic. It stands as a sign of the wholeness Jesus brings to those in his new family, the extended disciple community. We can rest for a moment in the safe place of the disciple's house.

THE POWER OF TOUCH, THE COST OF INCLUSION

Rest is only given for a moment. Enter the leper of the third story. This man was ritually unclean. The essence of the rules regarding leprosy and uncleanness (see Leviticus 13 and 14) was that since the disease was communicable, all human contact was forbidden. Only a priest could preside over ritual cleansing, release a person from quarantine and so restore him or her to ordinary human community. Jesus breaks through these rules. His compassion will not let him stand with his hands by his side. Our text of 1:41 says of Jesus, 'He was filled with pity'. He reaches out and touches the man. This makes Jesus technically unclean in the eyes of the Law. Jesus also declares the man clean in contravention of an authority which belonged to the Scribes alone.

Other manuscript versions of 1:41 read, 'Jesus was filled with anger'. Let's take both readings here and see Jesus 'inspired by love *and* anger' as John Bell and Graham Maule's song says (Bell and Maule 1987 p126). It is also possible to translate the beginning of 1:43 'Jesus snorted with indignation', instead of 'spoke sternly to him'. How are we to understand Jesus' anger and indignation? One explanation is that the leper may have applied to the priest already and the priest, for some reason, had not declared him clean. Jesus' anger is kindled by the system which gives such priestly power to include or exclude; it is directed at the priest who refuses to allow this man back into ordinary society. To be unclean meant not only to be bearing physical illness, it also meant being outcast and isolated. It further involved having to make special payments to the priest in return for a declaration of wholeness. It is against this triple burden that Jesus takes action to set the man free, indignant at the injustice of it all.

Jesus' action backfires. He asks the man to tell no one of what has happened between them and to go straight to the priest. Instead, the man, ecstatic about his new healing and freedom, shouts about his cure far and wide. Jesus, now publicly declared unclean from the leper's touch, has to stay out of town until the furore has begun to die down.

The implication is clear - healing and liberation involve considerable cost. To set people free from whatever burdens them will very often mean conflict. It is already crystal clear that, in the company of the disciples, life with Jesus is anything but quiet. The pace is about to get even more hectic. We end this passage, like the crowd in the synagogue at Capernaum, simply amazed, and give God the glory.

STUDY

BY YOURSELF

A prayer for healing.
God of life, you are always at work in our lives and the life of the world, bringing healing, renewal and reconciliation. Help me to see in a new way through the healing ministry of Jesus the breadth and depth of your work among us. Day by day, make me whole and enable me to be source of healing in our world, in Jesus' name. *Amen.*

• Reflect on your own experiences of healing, and be thankful.

chapter 5

New Cloth from Old?

MARK 2

Jesus heals a Paralysed Man
(Matt 9:1-8; Lk 5:17-26)

A few days later Jesus went back to Capernaum, and the news spread that he was at home. So many people came together that there was no room left, not even out in front of the door. Jesus was preaching the message to them when four men arrived, carrying a paralysed man to Jesus. Because of the crowd, however, they could not get the man to him. So they made a hole in the roof right above the place where Jesus was. When they had made an opening, they let the man down, lying on his mat. Seeing how much faith they had, Jesus said to the paralysed man, 'My son, your sins are forgiven'.

Some teachers of the Law who were sitting there thought to themselves, 'How does he dare to talk like this? This is blasphemy! God is the only one who can forgive sins!'

At once Jesus knew what they were thinking, so he said to them, 'Why do you think such things? Is it easier to say to this paralysed man, "Your sins are forgiven," or to say, "Get up, pick up your mat, and walk"? I will prove to you, then, that the Son of Man has authority on earth to forgive sins.' So he said to the paralysed man, 'I tell you, get up, pick up your mat, and go home!'

While they all watched, the man got up, picked up his mat, and hurried away. They were all completely amazed and praised God, saying, 'We have never seen anything like this!'

Jesus calls Levi
(Matt 9:9-13; Lk 5:27-32)

Jesus went back again to the shores of Lake Galilee. A crowd came to him, and he started teaching them. As he walked along, he saw a tax collector, Levi son of Alphaeus, sitting in his office. Jesus said to him, 'Follow me'. Levi got up and followed him.

Later on Jesus was having a meal in Levi's house. A large number of tax collectors and other outcasts were following Jesus, and many of them joined him and his disciples at the table. Some teachers of the Law, who were Pharisees, saw that Jesus was eating with these outcasts and tax collectors, so they asked his disciples, 'Why does he eat with such people?'

Jesus heard them and answered, 'People who are well do not need a doctor, but only those who are sick. I have not come to call respectable people, but outcasts'.

The Question about Fasting
(Matt 9:14-17, Lk 5:33-39)

On one occasion the followers of John the Baptist and the Pharisees were fasting. Some people came to Jesus and asked him, 'Why is it that the disciples of John the Baptist and the disciples of the Pharisees fast, but yours do not?'

Jesus answered, 'Do you expect the guests at a wedding party to go without food? Of course not! As long as the bridegroom is with them, they will not do that. But the day will come when the bridegroom will be taken away from them, and then they will fast.

'No one uses a piece of new cloth to patch up an old coat, because the new patch will shrink and tear off some of the old cloth, making an even bigger hole. Nor does anyone pour new wine into used wineskins, because the wine will burst the skins, and both the wine and the skins will be ruined. Instead, new wine must be poured into fresh wineskins.'

Jesus was walking through some cornfields on the Sabbath. As his disciples walked along with him, they began to pick the ears of corn. So the Pharisees said to Jesus, 'Look, it is against our Law for disciples to do that on the Sabbath!'

Jesus answered, 'Have you never read what David did that time when he needed something to eat? He and his men were hungry, so he went into the house of God and ate the bread offered to God. This happened when Abiathar was the High Priest. According to our Law only the priests may eat the bread - but David ate it and even gave it to his men.'

And Jesus concluded, 'The Sabbath was made for the good of human beings; they were not made for the good of the Sabbath. So the Son of Man is Lord even of the Sabbath'.

THREE BIG QUESTIONS

If the early verses of Mark's gospel can be likened to a trip on a roller-coaster, up and down and up in bewildering close succession, the second chapter is like stepping on an express train. This must be one of the most exciting chapters in the whole Bible, as Jesus rushes headlong into his Galilean ministry.

There are three main incidents in the chapter: the healing of the paralysed man; the call of Levi and its aftermath; and the confrontation in the cornfield. Each of the three incidents raises a major question. 'Why does this man dare to forgive sins?' 'Why does this man eat and drink with publicans and sinners?' 'Why does this man allow his disciples to break the holy Sabbath Law?' Let us look at the incidents and questions (slightly out of sequence).

'Why does this man dare to forgive sins?'

First comes the graphic story of the paralysed man and his four friends. It is an excellent story for a group Bible study. Take all the different groups of people involved in the story, and consider what each group or individual would be thinking and feeling. There is the man on the bed, helpless, hoping, despairing, hoping again. For years people have walked past him - suddenly he's at the centre of the picture. There is the group of four friends who come to Jesus with three things; their loving concern, their willingness to bear the burden of their friend, their hope. There is the crowd at the door, eager to get as close to Jesus as possible. How would they react to this guy who jumps the queue? There are the teachers of the Law, already on their guard, watchful and suspicious of this man Jesus, outraged by what he says. There are the disciples, in the background yet not in the background, in their own way deeply involved, concerned about yet more trouble. Last, but by no means least, there is Jesus himself.

We can marvel at the faith, devotion and ingenuity of the four friends; we can note that it was at a poor man's house that Jesus was healing (otherwise the roof would not have come off quite so easily); we can rejoice over the excitement of the crowd and, above all, over the joy of the man who folded up his blanket and walked home; we can wonder at the way Jesus finds just the right word to say to release him from his disabling burden. Wait, though. Is it the right word? What we certainly see is Jesus walking bang into controversy again. Sometimes, the way our Bible is divided up into chapters and verses hinders us from seeing the continuity of an argument or the development of a theme. Here we note that there is no break between Chapters 1 and 2; the second chapter simply takes up and off from the theme of the first.

Mark 1 ends with Jesus healing the leper and, in so doing, challenging the prevailing Law of Purity. Chapter 2 begins with Jesus healing this paralysed man and challenging the existing Debt Code. He says, 'My son, your sins are forgiven' (2.5). We can note with gratitude each of the words of that short sentence. 'My son' is a greeting of warmth, familiarity and affection. Such a greeting is typical of Jesus' living word of address to the sick and the sinner, the poor and the outcast. Later in Mark's story, in Jesus' encounter with the woman with chronic bleeding, we hear the greeting with equal warmth, 'Daughter'(5:34).

'My son, your sins are forgiven you.' These words are central, not only to this story, but to the whole meaning of Jesus Christ. The action of the paralysed man is telling. He acts out the meaning of the forgiveness of sins, and the release it brings. He takes up his bed, symbolic of the whole burden of his guilt, of his past, disabled life, and walks on, whole and free. 'I have come that you may have life, life in all its fullness', says Jesus (John 10:10).

A disabled man is restored to health so, what's the row all about? Once again Jesus is at loggerheads with the Scribes. They said, 'Who is this man to dare to forgive sins, to cancel debts? Only God can cancel debts. The man Jesus is a blasphemer!' (2:7) The Scribes were being disingenuous. They fell into the trap which perpetually awaits the religious now as then, confusing upholding their own power and position with safeguarding the honour of God. It was true that Jesus claimed a radical authority in forgiving sins, the prerogative of God alone. The Scribes, however, as teachers of the Law, had a considerable role in determining sins and indebtedness. Within the Debt Code of the existing law, the Scribes had annexed to themselves just such a power and role. Jesus takes aim again at their authority; once again it is a case of 'not as the Scribes'. It is no wonder that the reaction of the crowd is, 'We never saw anything like this!' Not only is the man restored, Scribal authority is roundly shaken. It is worth noting that the Greek word which Mark uses to describe the crowd, *ochlos*, means the mass, the poor, the unimportant, those without power, influence or rights. They would be the very ones who felt most acutely the weight of the authority of the Scribes.

'Why does this man allow his disciples to break the holy Sabbath Law?'

Next in the firing line come the Pharisees. Out of sequence, we go to the end of the chapter and turn to the story of the cornfield on the Sabbath Day (Leviticus 19:9), bearing in mind that wayfarers were allowed to pick grain from the edges of every cornfield. This incident has nothing to do with property rights but everything to do with the thousand and one regulations with which the Pharisees had hedged around the Fourth Commandment. Keeping the commandment had become a real burden for ordinary people and an impossibility for the poor. Therefore poor people, in addition to their poverty, had the added stigma of being despised by the Pharisees as lawbreakers. The particular fault here was that technically, to pluck corn was to engage in the activity of reaping, and reaping, as a form of work, was strictly forbidden on the Sabbath Day.

Jesus obviously did not deter or forbid his disciples' activity, indeed he is quick in their defence. He is somewhat cavalier in his quotation of scripture - in the incident of David and the bread offered to God in the sanctuary, Abiathar was not the High Priest at the time, it was Ahimelech. Jesus argues that sacred rules can be put aside in times of necessity. The question remains, 'What is a time of necessity?' The whole Sabbath question will be continued at the start of the next chapter when a Sabbath healing intensifies Jesus' challenge to the Sabbath Law. The two stories go powerfully together.

We can note here is that this is a story about bread. Jesus makes this a controversy about bread by raising the matter of David and the sacred bread. Bread will feature prominently in the gospel. Perhaps Jesus is saying that not just the Sabbath, but bread itself, is made for the feeding of humankind.

'Why does this man eat and drink with publicans and sinners?'

Finally, there is the story centred on the call of Levi. Levi is a very different character from the four original disciples, the fishermen. Levi is a tax-collector, a thoroughly shady and despised character in his society, considered a collaborator, a crook. He too is called. He too leaves his old way of life behind him and follows Jesus. It is of interest, however, that Levi's name does not appear on the list of the twelve disciples. It is obvious that there were a number of different disciple groups around Jesus, of whom the twelve formed an inner core. There is also an important group of women who, surprisingly in terms of the culture of the times, are found close to Jesus. They have not received the attention they deserve from centuries of predominantly male commentators on the Bible. There is a wider group of disciples and there is the group of common people, the crowd, who heard and followed as they were able.

Levi's first action is to invite Jesus and his disciples into his house. In the eyes of those who watched Jesus' every move, this was all wrong. It was out of order for Jesus to accept Levi's invitation. Here is where he first draws to himself the condemnation of the Pharisees. With curled lip and superior self-righteousness they ask, 'Why does this man eat with outcasts and tax-collectors?' (2:16) Why indeed? Why is he prepared to forfeit his reputation for respectability and holiness in their eyes? What is it in the Pharisees' view of the world that he calls into question by his action? Once again, what Jesus attacks with the Pharisees as with the Scribes, is the way in which they have taken and used the law of Moses - abrogated the faith of Israel to prop up their own position and prestige. The Pharisees look disdainfully at those who cannot attain their strict standards of rectitude and purity. They were perfect examples of those who live by the dubious maxim, 'You can tell a man by the company he keeps'. They kept a very strict and exclusive company indeed.

The choice of eating companions still matters to us even in our freer society. It was much more significant in Jesus' time and was an obsession with the Pharisees. Jesus cuts right through their exclusive view of the world, 'I have not come to call the righteous, but sinners'. We can delight in that phrase - it opens up for us the door into the Kingdom. Yet we do not always see the radical consequences for Jesus. It meant that his group, his company, was available to the last, the lost and the least, and his followers must have been a motley and unsettling crowd. We also have to ask ourselves, to what extent does our keeping company with Jesus open us up to keeping company with those whom we usually ignore, or shut the door uncaringly in their faces?

We might pause to note all those whom Jesus has already drawn to himself: the sick, the sinner, the unclean, the poor, the crowd, the disreputable, the deranged, the debtor. They are invited into the company of Jesus, with whom we should expect to sit down at the table of our Lord. We have already been introduced to the connection of Jesus with bread. That theme will develop. We are now introduced to Jesus at table with all sorts and conditions of humanity, for Jesus has come to bring a new society where old barriers, old ways, old fears, old privileges, old prejudices are broken down and dissolved.

It was all too much for the Pharisees. Their suspicions were quickly confirmed when Jesus' disciples were found breaking a fast day. (2:18) Jesus says nothing negative about fasting as such; indeed, a fresh look at the spiritual discipline of fasting (as distinct from 'slimming') would be no bad thing in our overfed and ill-divided western world. Once again, Jesus' concern is not to be bound by old rules which limit and diminish. Jesus takes the Pharisees' question and applies it to himself - 'There will be plenty of time left for fasting after I've gone.' (2:20)

Last in this chapter we come to the gospel's first two parables, brief and explosive, offered as a comment on all that has gone before.

> Nobody puts a patch of new cloth on an old coat, unless they want to tear it to bits. Nobody puts new wine into old wineskins, unless they are determined to have an explosion and waste an awful lot of wine.
> (2:21-22 paraphrased)

Watch the hackles of the Scribes and Pharisees rise, the atmosphere of tension visibly tighten. Jesus cannot really be much more explicit. This kingdom he announces, this kingdom present in his own person, this kingdom that is near, that is now, shakes the old order to its very roots, whether the old order is formed in the structure of thinking in people's minds, or framed in the regulations and institutions that govern the way people relate within society. 'The new wine, heady and explosive, is here.' This is the sum and substance of the words and works of Jesus as they are offered to us in these two opening chapters of Mark. A colleague and friend says that in preparing people for church membership he spends most of his time with them exploring these early chapters of Mark. With their excitement and their depth, we can see why.

STUDY

BY YOURSELF

'Your imagination can become the place where the world of Gospel reality and the world of daily life meet.' (Margaret Silf 1999, p.128)

Use your imagination to enter into the world of the Gospel stories. Choose one of the scenes from this section.

- What can you see, hear, smell, taste, feel as you imagine being present at the scene?
- What is the weather like? Warm, cold, windy, peaceful, wet, dry?
- What kind of atmosphere is there? Inviting, threatening, lively, solemn?
- Does anything about the scene particularly grab your attention?
- Where are you in the scene? One of the crowd? One of the disciples? Are you an outsider or an insider?
- How are you feeling? Disturbed? Attracted? Curious? Afraid? Eager?
- Do you feel you want to speak to anyone there? What do you want to say? What is being said to you? Can you enter a conversation with Jesus?
- If you noticed earlier one part of the scene drawing you more powerfully than any other, let yourself follow that leading now. In your imagination go to that part of the scene. Without forcing anything, see if you can identify what is attracting you.

FOR GROUP WORK

- Since eating together is a key feature of life with Jesus as a disciple, now might be a good first time for the group to plan and share a meal together. Perhaps the meal should include a real or imaginary bottle of new wine!
- Either adapt the personal imaginative exercise described above and exchange personal insights you feel able to share comfortably (remembering that there are no 'right' or 'wrong' answers), or use the Bible Study technique described on p.36 to explore the healing of the paralysed man. (*Note for Group Leaders:* If you decide to put people into different groups to explore this story, let each member of the study decide which group they want to join. Some people do not like being Pharisees, etc.) Either method can lead into discussion of the following questions.
  - What is it like to be long-term sick or disabled in our society?
  - What symbolic meaning does sickness and health have for us?
  - What do you think is a 'holistic approach' to health?
  - What questions and insights does this section raise about the church's role/ministry in healing?

chapter 6

Sabbath Shocker!

MARK 3:1-6

The Man with a paralysed Hand
(Matt 12:9-14; Lk 6:6-11)

Then Jesus went back to the synagogue, where there was a man who had a paralysed hand. Some people were there who wanted to accuse Jesus of doing wrong; so they watched closely to see whether he would heal the man on the Sabbath. Jesus said to the man, 'Come up here to the front'. Then he asked the people, 'What does our Law allow us to do on the Sabbath? To help or to harm? To save someone's life or to destroy it?'

But they did not say a thing. Jesus was angry as he looked round at them, but at the same time he felt sorry for them, because they were so stubborn and wrong. Then he said to the man, 'Stretch out your hand'. He stretched it out, and it became well again. So the Pharisees left the synagogue and met at once with some members of Herod's party, and they made plans to kill Jesus.

He gaed again intil a synagogue. The' war a man there wi' a shirpit airm, an they tentit him gleglie tae see gin he wad hail him on the Sabbath, sae at they micht hae a faut tae chairge him wi.

Jesus said til the man wi the shirpit airm, 'Staund up an come forrit intil the bodie o the synagogue.' Syne tae the lave o them he said, 'Hou think ye? Is it leisome tae dae guid on the Sabbath, or tae dae ill - tae sauf life, or tae tak it awa?' But the ne'er a wurd spak they.

Than, glowrin round at them wi bruindin een, for he wis sair vexed wi their waukitness o hairt, he said til the man, 'Rax out your airm'; an he raxed it out, an it wis made haill an sound aince mair.

An that the Pharisees liftit an immedentlie begoud tae collogue wi the Herodians: an thegither they socht hou they micht hae him pitten tae deith.

(Lorimer *The New Testament in Scots,* p.65)

SETTING THE SCENE, PRIMING THE CHARGES

John Taylor, author of that rich book on the Holy Spirit, *The Go-Between God*, likened the first half of this gospel to an explosion. He says, '... no other word will do to describe the onrush of power and challenge that floods the story of the gospel'. Perhaps early Mark is not so much a single explosion as a series of explosions. We come now to the biggest bang so far.

Remember where we have come from. Jesus has already been in conflict with both the Scribes and the Pharisees. In healing the leper he has challenged the prevailing Law of Purity, in healing the paralysed man he has challenged the existing Debt Code. Twice he has provoked the Scribes. By sitting down at table with the outcast and disreputable he has attracted the disapproving scrutiny of the Pharisees and he is now in deeper trouble with them through his cavalier reinterpretation of the holy Sabbath Law.

In most of these instances, apparently in a quite calculating and deliberate way, Jesus has made himself the focus of attention. He draws to himself both those who come to feed on his words, to hear his unauthorised teaching with authority, and those who come to find through him healing of body, mind and spirit. He draws also, like a magnet, those who would criticise and oppose, those whom he would challenge, those whose interests he most powerfully threatens.

The scene here is the synagogue on the Sabbath Day. The congregation have come to worship as was their weekly custom, but it is clear that the atmosphere is much more highly charged than usual. People were waiting, watching, expecting something to happen. A sense of crisis pervades the air. No doubt there were those in the congregation who felt that their usual Sabbath peace was being wantonly disturbed, no one likes disturbance when they come to worship. No doubt there were the curious, drawn in by the drama circling around Jesus. Certainly there were the disciples, maybe unsure again about what would happen next in their eventful walk in the company of Jesus. Certainly also there were the critics, waiting to pounce, waiting for this upstart to step so far out of line that they could make a case against him once and for all.

By the time of Jesus, the Sabbath Law was hedged around with literally hundreds of regulations. The root of the conflict in the synagogue was this: on the Sabbath it was permitted to do all that was possible to prevent sick persons getting worse but it was not legitimate to help them get any better. Healing was considered on this day to be a forbidden work. The argument is, 'You've got to draw the line somewhere'. This type of casuistry is a good example of what one professor always referred to as 'the nuttiness co-efficient of religion', where law overwhelms spirit and trivial regulations block a wider general principle. In the eyes of the Pharisees, the authors of the nutty regulations, the Sabbath was no longer the day of life and re-creation, it had degenerated into the day of restriction. Like much of the 'celebration' of Communion in Presbyterian Scotland until recent years, the festival had been converted into a funeral. Until, that is, Jesus with his unauthorised authority comes on the scene.

EXPLOSION!

In the synagogue, on a not-so-sleepy Sabbath, they watch and wait. Jesus is there, and a man with a withered arm. A withered arm is a chronic rather than an acute condition. It could have waited at least until the Sabbath sun's setting for Jesus' attention. It was not urgent, until Jesus makes it so. 'Come out here,' he says, 'out into the body of the kirk where everybody can see you. Now, here's a question for you all, What's the Sabbath law really about, what is it for, is it allowed to do good or to do evil, to save life or to kill on the Sabbath day? Let's get down to basics. What do you say?' Not a word is said, neither a 'yes' nor a 'no.' There is a tense and sullen silence. The Greek used to describe Jesus' anger - *met orges* - is strong. Lorimer, in his translation of the New Testament into Scots, says that Jesus looked round the crowd, 'wi brundin e'en', 'with eyes blazing'. He is angry at their obstinacy, their sheer hard-heartedness, their stubborn clinging to principles which frustrate the way of love and healing. Just in case we get smug and become quite pharisaic about the Pharisees, we will soon see that Jesus finds the same obstinate blindness in his own disciples. None of us has any monopoly of virtue.

Jesus is angry. To the man he says, 'Stretch out your hand'. He stretches it out, blood flows into withered and wasted tissue, muscles and sinews flex again, the man is made whole. Immediately (one of Mark's favourite adverbs, count how often it appears in these hectic chapters), the Pharisees and the Herodians, a most unlikely and cynical combination of religious and political opponents, come together in an unholy marriage of convenience. At once they begin to plot Jesus' death - BANG!

THE FIRST SHADOW

At this point, early in the gospel, the shadow of the cross falls across the path of Jesus. The freedom Jesus brings is not cheap. The challenge he offers to the tyranny of the old law, the warfare he makes on the powers of darkness which bind and disable God's children through the liberation of the leper, the debtor, the poor, the outcast, the sinner, the disabled, has a very real cost. Here is no mindless rebellion. This is deadly serious. The freedom which Jesus is and brings will cost him everything. Our healing and salvation comes at the price of the shedding of his own blood. The way of costly freedom continues; it is the way of discipleship, our way, now.

In addition to the Good News Bible translation, the full translation from W L Lorimer's *New Testament in Scots* is given above. It has been good in recent years to have the gospel translated into our vivid northern speech. It is a reminder that the whole of the first half of the gospel takes place in the context of the rough northern speech of Galilee, the speech that blew Peter's cover in the courtyard of the High Priest on the eve of the crucifixion(14:66-72). Inclusive language is an issue frequently discussed in relation to gender, but it is also about those whose speech is looked down on and dismissed - usually the poor and people on the margins.

PAUSE

THE MAIN GROUPS IN MARK'S GOSPEL

We have just heard how some Pharisees and Herodians are beginning to plot to kill Jesus. It is worth looking briefly at the groups who are ranged in opposition to him. Opposition forces don't get the best of presses in the gospel. We need to understand them in the particular circumstances of their time and society, although they also demonstrate attitudes which are all too discernible in our own church and world. We also note throughout the gospel the subtlety of Mark's story of the opposition to Jesus. That opposition comes not only from the obvious sources, it also lies in the blindness and faithlessness which is at the heart of the community of the disciples. No one, past or present, has any reason for smug superiority, according to Mark. Here are the main opposition groups.

TEACHERS OF THE LAW/SCRIBES

These people were entrusted with the task of interpreting the scriptures. The Law, the *Torah*, was the glue which held Jewish society together. The teachers of the Law were therefore an important group. They were concerned not only with the right practice of the Law in religious ritual, but in every part of life. They wielded considerable influence and power. In their work of interpretation they recognised both the written scriptures and the considerable body of oral tradition which had grown up around those scriptures. They had been and were a positive force in society. However, with the power and status they held, many showed undue conservatism, group self-interest and corruption. They were a strong professional trade union.

Scribes were to be found throughout the land, though it seems from the gospel that the Scribal community in Jerusalem carried particular weight. Twice the Scribal 'heavies' from the capital are portrayed as coming to Galilee to cast a more than critical eye on Jesus. We see similar excesses today in a clericalism which stands on its rights and disempowers lay members of the church. The Scribe castigated in the gospels stands in the continuing tradition of the over-zealous official who is, alas, alive and proliferating in our world.

PHARISEES

Pharisees were members of a lay reform movement in Judaism. A Pharisee could be a Scribe, and many were, though Scribes were not necessarily Pharisees. Like the Scribes, Pharisees recognised both the written scriptures and the oral traditions which had grown up around them. Scholars today think there were distinct groupings of Pharisees but all had in common a commitment to live lives of holiness by the exact keeping of the Law. They saw this not as a duty, but as a delight. They often met for fellowship meals where they scrupulously observed the food rules. These rules governed not only preparations for the meal, but also eating companions. The Pharisees' name derives from *perushim* meaning 'separate'. In thought and belief they were the group closest to Jesus himself, though that cannot be deduced from the gospel. Politically they were patriots but were quietist; they looked for the renewal of Israel through moral and spiritual regeneration. The gospel's dispute with them concerns their separatism and the strictness of their observance of the Law - it was so detailed that the ordinary people, the poor of the land, simply could not keep it. 'Pharasaism' has entered our language to describe condescending self-righteousness, tinged with hypocrisy.

SADDUCEES

Sadducees were upper-class conservatives. 'They represented the wealthy priestly and lay Jewish aristocracy from whom the high priests and the elders were chosen. In religious matters they were conservative, accepting only the written Law and rejecting new beliefs such as oral Law and the resurrection.' (Weber 1989, p.14) High priests and elders, together with some pharisaic Scribes, made up the Sanhedrin, the law court for dealing with Jewish affairs under Roman authority. 'In the time of Jesus they had more contact than most Jews with the Roman government, because of their role as religious leaders of the nation, and some supported peaceful co-existence, if not active co-operation, with the Romans for the sake of peace and security.' (Rowland 1985, p.68 - cf John 11:48f)

The Sadducees shouldered the burdens and bore the temptations of power. Their role in Jesus' story is marked by cynicism and expediency.

HERODIANS

This loose grouping supporting the dynasty of Herod was largely made up of his court followers. Herod the Great had died in CE6; his territories were divided among his sons. In the time of Jesus, Herod's son Herod Antipas (beheader of John) ruled Galilee. Philip (who married Salome) ruled the area to the north east of Galilee. Judea, Idumea and Samaria had been under the sway of a third son, Archelaus (Matt 2:22) until they were taken under Roman procuratorship in CE6. The dynasty of Herod ruled uneasily and often brutally.

The Roman Empire

Judea and the capital, Jerusalem, were under Roman rule during the period of Jesus' ministry. Pontius Pilate was the appointed Procurator (governor) from CE26-36. The whole area, including the domains of Herod and his family, held under Roman guardianship, was turbulent at the time of Jesus and even more so at the time when Mark was writing (see comments on Mk 13). The Jews greatly resented and resisted the Roman presence. Rome dealt with dissidents firmly and brutally. The behaviour of Pilate and his soldiers, described at the end of the gospel, is all too credible as the typical action of a colonial power throughout history.

Study

By yourself

Where are they now? Using the above descriptions of the main groups in the world of the gospel, where in today's society/church/world might we find these characters?
• Teachers of the Law/Scribes
• Pharisees
• Sadducees
• Herodians
• The Roman Empire

chapter 7

Comings and Goings

MARK 3:7-19

A Crowd by the Lake
(Mk 3:7-12)

Jesus and his disciples went away to Lake Galilee, and a large crowd followed him. They had come from Galilee, from Judaea, from Jerusalem, from the territory of Idumea, from the territory on the east side of the Jordan, and from the region round the cities of Tyre and Sidon. All these people came to Jesus because they had heard of the things he was doing. The crowd was so large that Jesus told his disciples to get a boat ready for him, so that the people would not crush him. He had healed many people and all those who were ill kept pushing their way to him in order to touch him. And whenever the people who had evil spirits in them saw him, they would fall down before him and scream, 'You are the Son of God!'

Jesus sternly ordered the evil spirits not to tell anyone who he was.

Jesus chooses the Twelve Apostles
(Matt 10:1-4; Lk 6:12-16)

Then Jesus went up a hill and called to himself the men he wanted. They came to him, and he chose twelve, whom he named apostles. 'I have chosen you to be with me,' he told them. 'I will also send you out to preach, and you will have authority to drive out demons.'

These are the twelve he chose: Simon (Jesus gave him the name Peter); James and his brother John, the sons of Zebedee (Jesus gave them the name Boanerges, which means 'Men of Thunder'); Andrew, Philip, Bartholomew, Matthew, Thomas, James son of Alphaeus, Thaddaeus, Simon the Patriot, and Judas Iscariot, who betrayed Jesus.

BESIDE THE SEASIDE

The first few verses of this passage sound, after the tense excitement of the incident in the synagogue, like a fill-in. In a sense they are, since they link what has gone before with what comes after. They speak of a strategic withdrawal, showing Jesus leaving the confines of the town for the open space of the lakeside. Jesus moves out of the centre to the edge, back to the beginning. These verses serve as a reminder of the larger context of the Galilean ministry, punctuated by the key incidents which Mark describes. They depict the presence of the ubiquitous, demanding crowd, from (in Burns' phrase) 'a' the airts', hungry for words, hungry for healing, crowding in on Jesus. The list of places from which people were drawn to him could easily be described as, 'from... all points of the compass' (3:7,8). Here is a snapshot of the busy-ness and intensity of Jesus' life and ministry in Galilee, the costly ministry among urgent human hunger and need.

Having spent my own formative years on the shores of the Firth of Clyde, the image of Jesus standing on a boat half in the blue water and half on the sandy shore, with the crowd standing attentively around, is a very strong, early childhood picture. Such a picture adorned the wall of many Sunday School rooms. Sunny, serene and peaceful, like so many childhood images, it is a very idealised picture. Always it was summer: 'God's in his heaven, all's right with the world', and there's that nice man Jesus saying nice words and being nice and kind to people.

The adult reality is that God has come to earth and in the establishment of the kingdom, things are a lot more dusty, earthy, sweaty, bloody and tumultuous.

The sea and the shore are important locations and symbols at many key places in the gospel narrative. Already we have met the lakeside as the place of the first call to discipleship, at the gospel's end we will hear echoes of that call. We will also travel back and forward across the lake more than once before journey's end.

High calling

There is a clear link between the call to Peter and Andrew, James and John, the first disciples, and what happens next. Disciples are the focus of the final incident in these verses. The scene changes again; for the naming of the twelve we climb to a high place, a hill or a mountain. High places have long been regarded as holy in many traditions. The great temple stood on Mount Zion in Jerusalem; Assisi is dominated by its monastery; the homes of Orthodox monasticism are to be found in impossibly precipitate places in Greece and its islands. Older than any monastery or temple is Mount Sinai itself, the place of Moses' encounter with God and the establishment of the Covenant with Israel.

Jesus climbs the mountain as Moses did, and chooses twelve men, symbolic of the twelve tribes of Israel. Here is a picture of the new community being forged. This community contrasts with the old community, whose ways have already been thoroughly threatened. In verses coming shortly, Jesus will subject yet another fundamental way of human belonging to challenge and scrutiny. He gets involved in lively disagreement with his mother and brothers, and he makes it very clear that the old ways and ties of family and kinship will change in the new kingdom of 'right relations' he brings (3:31-35). This new community is broader and deeper than any grouping of family or nation.

Here is the symbolic naming of an inner core of twelve disciples (3:16-19). We must remember they are not the only disciples. There are others, particularly the women, who form part of the larger discipleship group. To the twelve is given a special place and task, a task of proclamation and the authority to cast out demons. They are called and named. Calling by name was very significant in the Ancient World. Names spoke of a person's identity, character and familial relationships. Jesus still calls and names disciples. He calls your name and mine, speaking to us in the present tense. 'Will you come and follow me?'

Low humour

Not only are the disciples called by name, some are given new names, symbolic of new identity and purpose within the new community Jesus creates around him. The names themselves raise for me what has always been a fascinating question. Can we speak of Jesus' sense of humour? I think we can, for a number of reasons. Much of humour thrives on a sense of the ridiculous, the unexpected or the grossly contrasting. The sayings and parables of Jesus contain many examples of such contrasts - the struggling camel in the needle's eye is perhaps the most obvious (10:25). We have much to answer for in reading the Bible in a sepulchral voice which deadens the word of life. How can we recover in our faith communities the necessary distinction between the serious and the solemn? Serious truths need not be presented in a heavy-handed way, serious occasions need not be pompous and stuffy.

So, is there humour in the naming of the disciples? Rural communities have a tradition of nicknaming. I think of a brawny house painter on a Hebridean island, called 'Picasso'. Jesus called Simon and named him 'the Rock'. The Rock? As the story unfolds, he seems more like a slippery, unstable stone in the middle of a swift-flowing stream. Maybe Jesus' tongue was slightly in his cheek? To James and John he gives the name *Boanerges* - 'Sons of Thunder'. Does this mean they had a short fuse, or were rather fond of the sound of their own voices? The same two brothers will later claim the best seats in the Kingdom(10:37). It sounds as though the lads had a 'guid conceit' of themselves. Maybe the 'voice of thunder' was a sly dig against those in the disciples' community who liked to shout the loudest. The naming of the disciples becomes even more intriguing if there is the hint of a smile on the face of Jesus.

Such an interpretation bursts the bubble of those who build up a high doctrine of the Apostolic Succession, portraying the original disciples as a row of plaster saints. Mark portrays them as a group of ordinary mortals who frequently reveal feet of clay. The last-named of the twelve bursts the bubble anyway, Judas Iscariot, 'who betrayed him'. The twelve disciples represent no superior elite, they are simply the group closest to Jesus in the flesh and blood struggles of discipleship, where they will display ignorance, faithlessness, obstinacy, intolerance, fear, desertion and betrayal.

Yet these are the ones who, religiously speaking, represent the new priesthood and in social and political terms represent the new order. They sound very ordinary, very accessible, very like us, sometimes faithful, often doubtful, sometimes successful, often painfully aware of their own powerlessness and failure, sometimes very close to Jesus, sometimes unable to stand the heat of his call to follow. What remains constant is not their great faith, achievements, or moral stature, it is Jesus' call and Jesus' presence. That call and that promise of presence remain the 'bottom line' of the way of discipleship.

STUDY

BY YOURSELF
'The disciples sound very ordinary, very accessible, very like us, sometimes faithful, often doubtful, sometimes successful, often painfully aware of their own powerlessness and failure, sometimes very close to Jesus, sometimes quite unable to stand the heat of his call to follow.' There is a long history of Christian biographical literature which paints the saints and heroes of our faith in the most glowing colours. It is designed to be inspirational, but sometimes its effect is paralysing rather than liberating, as we fail to measure up to impossible standards of sainthood.
• Keeping in mind the more realistic description quoted above, muse over your own life-story. In humility, and perhaps with repentance, offer it to God, warts and all …

FOR GROUP WORK
• What is the effect of emphasising the humanity and fallibility of the disciples rather than their sainthood?
• What difference might it have made to the unfolding history of Christianity if the twelve named apostles had all been women?

chapter 8

Breaking and Entering

MARK 3:20-35

Jesus and Beelzebul
(Matt 12:22-32; Lk 11:14-23, 12:10)

Then Jesus went home. Again such a large crowd gathered that Jesus and his disciples had no time to eat. When his family heard about it, they set out to take charge of him, because people were saying, 'He's gone mad!'

Some teachers of the Law who had come from Jerusalem were saying, 'He has Beelzebul in him! It is the chief of demons who gives him the power to drive them out'.

So Jesus called them to him and spoke to them in parables: 'How can Satan drive out Satan? If a country divides itself into groups which fight each other, that country will fall apart. If a family divides itself into groups which fight each other, that family will fall apart. So if Satan's kingdom divides into groups, it cannot last, but will fall apart and come to an end.

'No one can break into a strong man's house and take away his belongings unless he first ties up the strong man; then he can plunder his house.

'I assure you that people can be forgiven all their sins and all the evil things they may say. But whoever says evil things against the Holy Spirit will never be forgiven, because he has committed an eternal sin.' (Jesus said this because some people were saying, 'He has an evil spirit in him'.)

Jesus' Mother and Brothers
(Matt 12:46-50; Lk 8:19-21)

Then Jesus' mother and brothers arrived. They stood outside the house and sent in a message, asking for him. A crowd was sitting round Jesus, and they said to him, 'Look, your mother and your brothers and sisters are outside, and they want you'.

Jesus answered, 'Who is my mother? Who are my brothers?' He looked at the people sitting round him and said, 'Look! Here are my mother and my brothers! Whoever does what God wants him to do is my brother, my sister, my mother'.

'OFF HIS HEAD'

'Then Jesus went home.' (3:20) After such hectic activity, there is no doubt that the poor man was sorely in need of a rest, which is exactly what he didn't get. Such a large crowd gathered that Jesus and the disciples did not even have time for a bite to eat. Here is yet another picture of Jesus drawing people to himself - all sorts of people, folk in need of healing, folk desperate to hear his teaching. In a very few words, Mark again creates an atmosphere of pressure and excitement.

There was too much pressure and excitement for some people. The news of Jesus' activity had reached his family, embellished and distorted along the way. What was reported to the family was, 'Your son, your brother, he's gone way over the top now, he's mad'. (3:21) That is the first charge laid against him in this passage - 'He's off his head'. The response is as would be expected from a caring and protective family; they come to rescue him from the heat, to take him out of the limelight. They arrive to take him home.

'THE VERY DEVIL'

Just as the family appears on the scene there is an interruption. Mark uses a device in his story-telling which will occur again in the gospel. He introduces some characters and an incident, claims our attention, but before the incident reaches its climax, he introduces another story-line with fresh characters and a new theme which acts either to reinforce the first story or to work in tension with it.

Here the second story reinforces the sense of Jesus' having to work against a background of misunderstanding and opposition from many different quarters. Enter yet again some Scribes/teachers of the Law. This time they are not the local representatives but some of the 'heavy' team from Jerusalem. This upstart provincial has become a genuine threat. The charge the Scribes make is not that of insanity, but that he is the very Devil. 'Pay no attention to him, he's an agent of Satan, he's in the grip of Satan, Beelzebul! He's demon possessed!' (3:22) The insults are flying.

ABOUT MYTH-MAKING

It's worth stopping here to think about the importance of myths in any society or culture. The first mistake many people make when thinking about 'myth' is to suppose that it belongs to a primitive, old-fashioned view of the world. If we say we want to 'demythologise' ancient writings, we mean to reinterpret them for the benefit of enlightened, abstract-thinking, rational, modern *homo sapiens*. The main problem about such a project is that 'enlightened, abstract-thinking, rational, modern *homo sapiens* is itself a mythological creation. It 'ain't that simple'. We can describe 'myth' as an overarching story or image whose power is other than rational and whose 'truth' is often assumed or accepted uncritically. In that sense, every society has its myths, although it is more accurate to state that most societies have undergone one or more 'wars of myths'. Today, a 'war of myths' might be called a 'battle of ideologies'.

In Britain in the 1980s, we witnessed the war of myths raging fiercely in the political sphere. For example, the attack by the new Right on the public sector, the nationalised industries and utilities contained many mythological elements. The simplistic equating of the public sector with waste and inefficiency and its juxtaposition against the wonders of private sector efficiency is a good example of the coincidence of myth, symbol and propaganda. On the other side of the political agenda, change within the Left has been hindered by an inability to examine and discard some cherished myths about the so-called working class. Move from the sphere of politics to the omnipresent world of advertising, and we find a treasure trove of potent myths, symbols and archetypes, so often used to manipulate us. Consider car advertising, full of seductive images of speed, freedom and the wide open spaces, while the reality of our road experience is more often fume-filled frustration in an urban traffic jam. Take the constant images of conviviality and sexual attractiveness in alcohol advertising and set them against the misery of many for whom alcohol is not the door to freedom but the prison gate. Reality is that the car and the bottle are the two greatest causes of premature death in Western societies. But still we cherish our myths.

The second mistake is to think that myth belongs largely to the world of religion. On the contrary, as we have seen, myth operates at every level of people's social, political and cultural life. We find our mythologies in all forms of human communications; painting, film, stories, jokes, songs, speeches, newspaper articles, academic papers, and so on.

Many people say of all this mythical/symbolic talk, 'I don't believe in all that airy fairy stuff, I only deal in reality, I believe in hard facts, I look for cash values'. Look again at a banknote. What is a banknote but a piece of paper with some fancy pictures and a little writing on it which we as a society agree has a specific value? It is *all symbol*, just as flags, handshakes and the peculiar ecclesiastical furniture and raiment of our sanctuaries and clergy are - and so are jeans and trainers.

Symbols and myths are the stuff of life and language. As well as the negative power of symbols and myths, often they enhance our discussions, providing vital aids to communication and consensus within society. They can be aids to truth, both common and profound. But in the hands of a skilled communicator, they can be used to manipulate and obscure.

What is of particular interest to us in relation to the bad-mouthing of Jesus by the Jerusalem Scribes is how a dominant social order uses the language of myth to discredit those who challenge its authority. Here are two examples. *Disturbing the Peace*, the title of a book by Vaclav Havel, who became President of the Czech Republic, is his ironic comment on the way he was labelled a 'hooligan' and imprisoned by the powers-that-be in the old days of State Communism. In South Africa, for many years the white regime was strident in the way it regarded all opposition to apartheid as part of an international Communist conspiracy. Whenever authority is in trouble it will not hesitate to play the 'bogey-man' card, heavy with mythology.

'A KINGDOM AND A HOUSE DIVIDED'

That is what happens here in Mark 3:22. The Scribes use two titles for Satan - Beelzebul and the Prince of Demons. 'Don't pay any attention to that Jesus,' they say, 'He's the very Devil.' The level of discourse has hit the gutter, but Jesus won't take the insult lying down. Listen carefully. He will match fire with fire.

> 'How can Satan drive out Satan?
> Should a kingdom be divided against itself that kingdom cannot stand;
> Should a house be divided against itself that house cannot stand;
> Thus if Satan has revolted against himself and is divided,
> He cannot stand and is coming to an end.'
> (3:23-26 *RSV*)

Here is a series of intricate, tightly argued parallelisms. They sound more than a little cryptic. What do they mean? These words have been interpreted as Jesus saying to the Scribes, 'Come off it, lads, I'm really on your side or, at least, on the side of the angels.' They can also mean something much stronger. It can be argued that here Jesus is saying that if the Scribes' argument and accusation of devilment against himself fails, it rebounds on themselves. The charge lands on the heads of the accusers; it is they, not Jesus, who are the very Devil. The text speaks of 'a kingdom and a house divided'. 'The kingdom divided' may well refer to the centralised power of Jerusalem, 'the house divided' to the symbolic centre of that power, the temple itself. That is certainly the context in which the final battle of the gospel will be played out.

The word used for Satan, 'casting out,' 'exorcising', is exactly the same word that will be used of Jesus' activity in 'casting out' from the temple those who have 'divided' or diluted its purpose as 'a house of prayer for all nations' (11:17). It is not that Jesus in any way denies or diminishes the reality of Satan or the power of the forces of evil, rather he sees that reality and these forces at work in the very structures of society, structures which the Scribes represent and will use all manner of power games to keep and conserve.

'BINDING THE STRONG MAN'

Jesus then compares himself to a burglar breaking and entering into 'the house of a strong man', which here represents the home territory both of Satan and the earthly powers-that-be. John the Baptist has already announced the coming of the 'stronger one' (1:7) in the advent of Jesus himself. Remember also the cry of the demon in the Capernaum synagogue which attributes no little strength to Jesus, 'What do you want with us, Jesus of Nazareth? Are you come to destroy us?' (1:24)

Here is the heart of the symbolic battle, a terse summation of all that has gone before and a preparation for what will come after. Jesus is God's strong one, come to bind all the forces of evil and darkness, to bring release to all who are now in bondage to these forces. These words from Isaiah 49 sum up the promise being fulfilled and yet to be fulfilled,

> Can the prey be taken from the mighty
> or the captives of a tyrant be rescued?
> But surely, thus says the Lord:
> Even the captives of the mighty shall be taken,
> and the prey of the tyrant be rescued;
> for I will contend with those who contend with you,
> and I will save your children.
> I will make your oppressors eat their own flesh,
> and they shall be drunk with their own blood as with wine.
> Then all flesh shall know
> that I am the Lord, your Saviour,
> and your Redeemer, the Mighty One of Jacob.
> (Isaiah 49: 24-26 RSV)

It is a battle indeed, and the victory shall be won.

THE SIN AGAINST THE HOLY SPIRIT

Jesus then underlines what he has just said. With all due solemnity, he begins with the assurance 'This is the truth, my word on it,' and then promises again that sins will be forgiven (3:28). Radically, he says all manner of sins will be forgiven, the captives released. The debt system, which was the Scribes rationale for their status and function, is comprehensively flattened. All manner of sins will be forgiven, with one exception, speaking evil against the Holy Spirit, i.e. binding the work and activity of the spirit. What is the sin against the Spirit? It is for a person to be so bound by their own experience, attitudes and dogma that they deny all freedom, creativity and the possibility of new insights and fresh truth. The freedom Jesus is and brings is condemned by the Scribes as the Devil's work. From the perspective of Jesus, they are decrying and miscalling the work of the holy, present and living spirit. On the Scribes the tables are turned, metaphorically, at this time.

The sin against the Holy Spirit continues today. People are still in thrall to the way things are and 'have always been'. It is all too human to resist criticism and change, suppressing efforts towards freedom and full human life. Such blinkered thinking shuts us off from the grace and forgiveness of God. The challenge is constantly before us to work hard to ensure that we are never the ones who are blind to the presence and promptings of the Holy Spirit. We are called to be open to the life-giving breath of the Spirit in all manner of places at all sorts of times. The Spirit always remains the Lord of the Unexpected.

THE NEW FAMILY OF GOD

Now, at the end of the passage, we can 'go home', or return to the family. Our world is very different from the world of Jesus. The family is under unprecedented attack from many forces at work in our society. In Jesus' day the family and the extended kinship system formed the bedrock of society. To the family belonged primary human obligation. It is a serious matter when the family of Jesus turn up in numbers to take him home. Word is sent in to him that they are waiting. Once more the unexpected happens. It looks as though they will have a long wait.

Jesus asks, 'Who is my mother? Who are my brothers?' He looks round at the eager, disparate group crowding round the door. With an inclusive wave of his hand he announces, 'Here are my mother and my brothers. Whoever does what God wants is my brother, my sister, my mother.'(3:33-35) Yet another taboo has gone, another barrier has been broken. In the new community Jesus comes to create, the ties of blood no longer dominate and exclude, the rigid tightness of the family circle is breached. Here there is space and room for all sorts and conditions, for new and liberating relationships. The only test of admission remains, 'Do you hear and do you follow?'

Study

By yourself

- List the people and groups you have seen bad-mouthed and demonised in recent years, e.g. 'Teenagers are trouble', 'Muslims are dangerously fanatical'.
- Thinking in stereotypes is lazy and dangerous. Reflect on how Jesus treats each person he meets as a person and pray for the compassionate wisdom to do the same.

For group work

There are three diverse themes in this section:
- the ways in which we and our society (particularly the media) stereotype and demonise people
- the sin against the Holy Spirit
- the question about the family, 'Who is my mother?' 'Who are my brothers?'

The group could explore each theme in turn, or choose one to look at in depth. One way to involve all group members would be to ask each person, 'After reading this section, what question does it raise for you about our world today?' The questions raised will form the basis for the ensuing discussion. A final, important question to focus upon is, 'How inclusive are you/is your church, both in thinking and in practice?'

chapter 9

The Sower Sermon

MARK 4:1-34

The Parable of the Sower
(Matt 13:1-9; Lk 8:4-8)

Again Jesus began to teach beside Lake Galilee. The crowd that gathered round him was so large that he got into a boat and sat in it. The boat was out in the water, and the crowd stood on the shore at the water's edge. He used parables to teach them many things, saying to them:

'Listen! Once there was a man who went out to sow corn. As he scattered the seed in the field, some of it fell on the path, and the birds came and ate it up. Some of it fell on rocky ground, where there was little soil. The seeds soon sprouted, because the soil wasn't deep. Then, when the sun came up, it burnt the young plants; and because the roots had not grown deep enough, the plants soon dried up. Some of the seed fell among thorn bushes, which grew up and choked the plants, and they didn't produce any corn. But some seeds fell in good soil, and the plants sprouted, grew, and produced corn: some had thirty grains, others sixty, and others a hundred.

And Jesus concluded, 'Listen, then, if you have ears!'

The purpose of the Parables
(Matt 13:10-17; Lk 8:9-10)

When Jesus was alone, some of those who had heard him came to him with the twelve disciples and asked him to explain the parables. 'You have been given the secret of the Kingdom of God,' Jesus answered. 'But the others, who are on the outside, hear all these things by means of parables, so that,

'They may look and look,

yet not see;

they may listen and listen,

yet not understand.

For, if they did, they would turn to God,

and he would forgive them.'

Jesus explains the Parable of the Sower
(Matt 13:18-23; Lk 8:11-15)

Then Jesus asked them, 'Don't you understand this parable? How, then, will you ever understand any parable? The sower sows God's message. Some people are like the seeds that fall along the path; as soon as they hear the message, Satan comes and takes it away. Other people are like the seeds that fall on rocky ground. As soon as they hear the message, they receive it gladly. But it doesn't sink deep into them, and they don't last long. So when trouble or persecution comes because of the message, they give up at once. Other people are like the seeds sown among the thorn bushes. They are the ones who hear the message, but the worries about this life, the love for riches, and all other kinds of desires crowd in and choke the message, and they don't bear fruit. But other people are like the seeds sown in good soil. They hear the message, accept it, and bear fruit: some thirty, some sixty, and some a hundred.'

A Lamp under a Bowl
(Lk 8:16-18)

Jesus continued, 'Does anyone ever bring a lamp and put it under a bowl, or under the bed?

Doesn't he put it on the lampstand? Whatever is hidden away will be brought out into the open, and whatever is covered up will be uncovered. Listen, then, if you have ears!'

He also said to them, 'Pay attention to what you hear! The same rules you use to judge others will be used by God to judge you - but with even greater severity. Those who have something will be given more, and those who have nothing will have taken away from them even the little they have.'

The Parable of the Growing Seed
(4:26-29)

Jesus went on to say, 'The Kingdom of God is like this. A man scatters seed in his field. He sleeps at night, is up and about during the day, and all the while the seeds are sprouting and growing. Yet he does not know how it happens. The soil itself makes the plants grow and bear fruit; first the tender stalk appears, then the ear, and finally the ear full of corn. When the corn is ripe, the man starts cutting it with his sickle, because harvest time has come.'

The Parable of the Mustard Seed
(Matt 13:31-32; Lk 13:18-19)

'What shall we say the Kingdom of God is like?' asked Jesus. 'What parable shall we use to explain it? It is like this. A man takes a mustard seed, the smallest seed in the world, and plants it in the ground. After a while it grows up and becomes the biggest of all plants. It puts out such large branches that the birds come and make their nests in its shade.'

Jesus preached his message to the people, using many other parables like these; he told them as much as they could understand. He would not speak to them without using parables, but when he was alone with his disciples, he would explain everything to them.

'PAUSE AND CONSIDER'

'A sower went to sow ...' Time to reflect. We are invited to step back from hectic activity and think. Remember that Mark's gospel has two roughly parallel halves; in each of them, after a spell when the pace of events is breathtaking, there is a space for reflection. This space is created in the form of what has been called the two great Marcan sermons, that is, this passage in Mark 4 and another in Mark 13. In each there is a key word summoning us to attention; in Chapter 13 the call is to 'watch', here in Chapter 4 the invitation is to 'hear', to 'listen' (4:3,9,23).

Let's briefly recap. The theme of the gospel has been announced, 'The Gospel of Jesus Christ - the Good News of Jesus Messiah'. We were then thrown into a melee of ups and downs, climaxes and dis-locations. The story begins not at the centre of things, in proud Jerusalem, but at the edge, in despised Galilee, out of the very wilderness. Whenever Jesus moves into the centre, even, in Galilean terms, into the synagogue, there is confrontation and struggle. Jesus is brought to us as the strong man, one who speaks with authority, yet not as the Scribes. He takes one tilt after another at the prevailing systems of authority and social control, the Purity Code, the Debt Code, the law of the Sabbath. He is indeed the one who heals and saves, yet he is able to effect this work only by calling into question the existing order in which others put their trust and find meaning, status and belonging. He is also busy building the new community, calling the disciples, agents of God's justice and judgement, symbolic of the twelve tribes of Israel, the community of the old covenant. The disciples, however, are twelve ordinary men and they are only the core of a much larger and looser community of men and women which already includes the sick, the unclean, the publican, the sinner. The crisis created by his ministry has swiftly mounted, Jesus' death has begun to be plotted, he has been called the 'very Devil' and he has just made a break with that most vital and entrenched support system, his own family. After all that, we are bidden to 'listen'.

ABOUT PARABLES

'A sower went to sow.' We begin with this long parable which is in two halves, with connecting verses which have always been a real conundrum (4:11,12). In the first half, the parable is spoken to the crowd; in the second, it is interpreted to the disciples. To introduce the parable, here are five general points.

First, teaching by way of parable (Hebrew *mashal*) was a well-recognised and frequently used form of communication within the tradition of Jesus' people. Both prophets and teachers in the Wisdom tradition often spoke in parables. Parables could take many forms: a saying, often snappy and memorable; a taunt; a riddle; a prophetic oracle; a longer story making a single point; a longer story which was allegorical throughout. The common thread running through all parabolic speech was that it pointed to a meaning beyond the obvious. Such meanings could be very diverse. It is a particularly rich and allusive form of speech, inviting the hearer to consider the 'hidden' meaning of the words. Because parables point to a 'hidden' meaning, the history of the interpretation of parables is long and confusing.

Second, the parables in Mark invite reflection on the surrounding action at a level deeper than the literal. Attention also needs to be paid to the context of the parables.

Third, Jesus resorts to parables in Mark when conflicts become intense. In so doing, he is using a tradition found in both prophetic and apocalyptic writing in the Old Testament and of which the supreme example in the New Testament is the Book of Revelation. This tradition uses parable or extended metaphor to say indirectly what is too dangerous to say directly. This is parable as religious, societal or political criticism, a genre with which modern readers are familiar. We need look no further than Eastern Europe in the time of totalitarianism to find such writing of considerable currency and validity. On the Western side of the old Iron Curtain, Arthur Miller's *The Crucible* is an important example of extended parabolic writing. Witch-hunting in seventeenth-century New England forms the vehicle for Miller's trenchant criticism of the anti-Communist witch-hunt (associated with Senator Joe McCarthy) in Cold War America in the years following World War 2.

Fourth, as an intensification of this theme, we come to the difficult words of verses 11, 12 and 13 of Chapter 4, with their quotation from Isaiah 6 about people on the outside 'hearing and not understanding'. At first sight, these words suggest that Jesus is saying that his parables are there not to clarify, but to confuse all but his own inner circle. This sounds less than just, and unlike the Jesus we have met so far in the gospel. There is a simpler explanation. Mark here is taking up that ancient tradition which states that the word of God can divide, or polarise. He is struggling with the problem, 'How is opposition to Jesus, resistance to God's word, to be explained?' He goes back to an understanding as old as the stories in the Old Testament which speak of God 'hardening the heart' of Pharoah. From the time of Moses, prophets are as likely to be pelted as praised. Those 'outside' will not hear because they have already 'hardened their hearts' against hearing. If we think back to our last passage, we remember the Scribal Establishment characterised there as those determined not to 'hear'. Jesus has already said they sin against the Holy Spirit by their blindness, deafness and lack of openness (3:29,30). But watch out! Mark will soon give a subtle, radical twist to this whole situation. Before the end of this chapter, not only those 'outside' will be accused of blindness, the inner core of disciples will also be criticised for their lack of faith. The theme of the disciples' failings will develop. It will be made clear that even the faithful do not see the fullness of the meaning of the One who has come. Mark makes no simple division between insiders and outsiders, 'goodies' and 'baddies'.

Finally, we look to these parables themselves, the parables of growth. What is immediately striking is their down-to-earth nature. In a peasant society, they would speak to people's everyday experience. The parables have been called 'earthly stories with heavenly meanings'. The danger with that expression is that it invites us to look in the wrong direction, focusing our attention away from the earth. The truth is the other way round; the parables speak of the mystery of the Kingdom among us. They are earthly intimations of a heavenly presence - they bring heaven to earth, rooting God's activity in our midst, here and now.

THE PARABLE OF THE SOWER

Jesus says that God's activity is like the work of the sower. Jeremias, one of the greatest commentators on the parables, reminds us,

In Palestine sowing precedes ploughing. Hence, in the parable, the sower is depicted striding over the unploughed stubble ... he sows intentionally on the path which the villagers have trodden over the stubble, since he intends to plough the seed in when he ploughs up the path. He sows intentionally among the thorns standing withered on the fallow, because they too, will be ploughed up. Nor need it surprise us that some grains should fall on rocky ground; the underlying limestone, thinly covered with soil, barely shows above the surface until the ploughshare jars against it. (Jeremias, 'The Parables of Jesus', in Myers 1988, p. 176)

On the paths, on the stony ground, among the thistles, the seed is sown. Here are the obstacles to the kingdom's taking root, the stumbling blocks on the path to discipleship. On the path, by the way, Satan makes sure the way of discipleship never gets started. The seed on the path signifies the crowd who hear but never follow and the social leaders whose opposition, we have just seen, is attributed to the reign of Satan. Satan's work is not confined to the 'opposition', however, soon it will penetrate the inner circle, as we will hear in Jesus' words to Peter at Caesarea Philippi (Mark 8).

The seed falling on the stony ground speaks of the obstacles of trouble and persecution which cause disciples to defect. Mark makes it clear elsewhere that the fruits of the Messiah come only to those who endure through tribulation. This tells us something significant about Jesus' original parable and also about Mark's readers. This gospel is written for a struggling community who know hard times and are tempted to give up. The perennial temptation of the church is to trim its message, to produce a gospel which has no depth, a fair-weather religion.

The next group gets slightly further. Their faith is choked by thorns and thistles, 'worldly cares and the false glamour of wealth and evil desires of all kinds' (4:19), as the Revised English Bible translates. Mark underlines the specific temptations of affluence. The one person who, throughout the whole gospel, rejects the call of Jesus is the rich young ruler (10:17-22).

All these obstacles to discipleship reappear from generation to generation. They crop up in the context in which the believing community lives and works and they occur in each believer's struggle to keep faith. It has been wisely said that we hear the gospel with ears conditioned by the space we occupy in life. If we 'listen', but do not 'attend' or 'hear', it is not due to the obscurity of the word, it is because we are loyal to other 'goods and gods'.

Yet it is not with a series of hurdles that the story ends, but an abundance, with the seed that multiplied, thirty-, sixty- and one hundred- fold. The story comes to a climax in wonder, in the mystery of the growth of faith, the glory of creative grace, which Jeremias describes as, 'the final overflowing of divine fullness, surpassing all human measure'. We have been thinking frequently of the social implications of this gospel; with a harvest like this, a peasant farmer could not only feed the family and pay all his tithes and rents, there would be enough left over to buy the land for himself and thus win freedom. It is a wonderful picture we are left with, of freedom and plenty. Let the light of that freedom and plenty flood in upon us. What is told to the crowd baldly and explained to the disciples in private, is now there for any who will pause to read and reflect. See and hear. The kingdom is on its way. (We have arrived at 4:23.)

The next two verses (4:24,25) present a problem. 'Pay attention to what you hear! The rules you use to judge others will be used by God to judge you - but with even greater severity. Those who have something will be given more, and those who have nothing will have taken away from them even the little they have.' They contain a proverb about measuring and a corollary about giving and getting. Their interpretation has always been difficult. On the surface they exude an atmosphere of cynical commonsense. Try this. The verb translated by the Good News Bible (GNB) as 'pay attention' can also be rendered 'beware'. 'Beware of what you hear.' 'Be on your guard against the prevailing cynicism of the popular world view, which claims that the rich get richer and the poor poorer because such is the natural order of the way God made the world.' These verses can be read as a warning of what not to believe, set in counterpoint against the last two parables in this passage (4:26-34). Read them as ironic comment on what not to believe.

MORE ABOUT SEED

The last two short parables open up the way again into the new Kingdom (4:26-34). Jesus offers another parable of the scattering of seed (4:26-29).This time he focuses our attention on the sower's inactivity once the seed is sown. He sows and waits ... and waits. He sows but he neither makes the crop grow nor understands the mystery of growth. This parable is a lesson about the slowness of the growth of the seed of the word, but also its sureness. It is a lesson in what Dorothy Soelle has well called 'revolutionary patience'. The task of the disciple is to sow the seed and then leave to God the growth and the increase. To be sowers of the seed is the individual and corporate calling of the Christian.

Remember the story of the Vietnam anti-war protester who, as he was being hauled away from his sit-in by a large policeman, was told by the officer with world-weary cynicism, 'You don't think you're going to stop this war, do you?' To which the protester replied, 'I'm not trying just to stop this war, I'm trying to stop the war after the war after this war'. We are called to witness as slowly and surely and steadily as water dripping on a rock - eventually it will carve out a channel in the most impervious material.

This parable also directs our attention to the end, 'when the corn is ripe, the man starts cutting it with his sickle, because harvest time has come' (4:29). Harvest is a metaphor for judgement, the reminder that in the end, the judgement is sure, and God's justice will prevail.

That theme is strengthened in our final story, the famous picture of the tiny grain of mustard seed growing into a great tree, big enough to give sanctuary to the birds for their nesting (4:30-34). The mustard seed parable reinforces the parable of the sower. At the last, there will be 'disproportionate abundance'. From tiny beginnings, the seed of faith, the wonder of the kingdom, will grow and grow. Mark's picture of the mustard seed tree would be familiar to his hearers, since in late biblical literature the sheltering tree was often a symbol of power and rule. Look at Daniel 4, and particularly Ezekiel 31 where the prophet paints a picture of the kingdom of Egypt as the growth of a magnificent cypress tree, higher and greater than all other trees. That magnificence is ironic, for the power of Egypt is corrupt, and the end of the tale is that the great tree is felled and the kingdom shattered. 'Upon its ruin will dwell the birds of the air, and upon its branches will be all the beasts of the field.' (Ezekiel 31:13 *RSV*) It is the mustard seed of faith which will produce the plant which will endure while the might of Rome will end, like Egypt's cypress, as a fallen log. Frail beginnings notwithstanding, the Kingdom of God will grow and endure. The message is, 'Have courage, see beyond the immediate, faith will endure and multiply miraculously'.

It is not in the power and pretensions of the great, but in the daily wonders of life and growth, seen all around, that the secret and the way of the Kingdom of God lies.

STUDY

BY YOURSELF
A Meditation
With a bit of work, all soil can be good soil.
Spend some time considering yourself as soil.

- The trampled soil on the path, packed down, hardened by many feet, closed to feeling and the lives of others...What will it take to soften the hard soil... to allow the seed to penetrate?
- The thin soil, littered with rocks, both on and below the surface... What are these stones? What commitment will it take to begin to remove these stones? What back-breaking determination?
- The thorn-infested soil, choking the new growth unless weeded out... time-consuming, careful sifting is needed... What are the thorns? How can they be identified and dealt with, repeatedly, if necessary?

The task of keeping the soil prepared is ongoing. In our lives we need regular, daily, weekly, spiritual practice to clear the good soil, for the seed to sink in, survive and flourish.

chapter 10

Symbols and Storms:
'Peace, be still!'

MARK 4:35-41

Jesus calms a Storm

(Matt 8:23-27; Lk 8:22-25)

On the evening of that same day Jesus said to his disciples, 'Let us go across to the other side of the lake'. So they left the crowd; the disciples got into the boat in which Jesus was already sitting, and they took him with them. Other boats were there too. Suddenly a strong wind blew up, and the waves began to spill over into the boat, so that it was about to fill with water. Jesus was in the back of the boat, sleeping with his head on a pillow. The disciples woke him and said, 'Teacher, don't you care that we are about to die?'

Jesus stood up and commanded the wind, 'Be quiet!' and he said to the waves, 'Be still!' The wind died down, and there was a great calm. Then Jesus said to his disciples, 'Why are you frightened? Have you still no faith?'

But they were terribly afraid and said to one another, 'Who is this man? Even the wind and the waves obey him!'

The time for reflection is over very quickly. 'On the evening of that same day', the way of discipleship beckons again. 'Way' is too earth-bound a word here, the disciples move out on to the sea of faith, and run straight into a storm. As we look now at the story of the stilling of the storm, we reflect on not one but two storms which this story raises.

The first storm concerns our modern debates about how we should interpret ancient texts in general and biblical texts in particular. Mark tells us this story simply as a realistic narrative. The disciples are out on the sea, a sudden squall blows up, Jesus is wakened by his terrified friends, he stands up in the boat, tells the wind to, 'Be quiet' and the waves, 'Be still'. They do so. That's that, end of story. Underneath this surface story, however, lurks a whole host of symbolic meanings to which we will turn in a moment.

Our problem with this story is that we have never met anyone who can calm a physical storm. What is told is totally beyond our experience, so the question immediately arises, 'What is the meaning of this story?' Here are the two extremes of interpretation: 'This story must be taken literally' and 'This story is no more than ancient myth, given to bolster our belief in Jesus the wonder worker. Any major religious figure in Jesus' time would have attached to it signs and wonders.' I find neither extreme satisfactory. The literalists in the first camp miss the symbolic content and marvel at a story which has little present-day relevance, while the myth school in the second camp interprets the story in the limited light of the norms and views of our own time. Is it too difficult to 'see' Jesus as one who had an altogether deeper relationship with the natural world than we alienated, estranged and (increasingly) urban people can ever imagine? This story, as it comes to us through the written gospel, had already been told and retold through two generations, so there is no sure way back to answering the question about what actually happened.

In terms of letting this story speak to us, however, the words of an interview on BBC Television's *Late Show* are relevant. Peter Brook, the distinguished theatre director, once said something like this, 'Tragically, there is only one religion truly alive and well in the world today, that is the religion of rational thought. Anything that does not submit easily to rational analysis is labelled primitive, ancient, barbaric'. The result of such a narrow view, mistakenly dubbed rational and progressive, is to dismiss truths and feelings, experiences and values out of hand. Life is diminished. Rationalism and its close relation, empiricism, encompass only a small segment of human searching and striving. Instead of being dominated by the sort of historicism which narrows everything down to the question, 'What actually happened?', or being satisfied by a thoroughly modern (smug and superior) 'I don't believe it!', let us allow Mark's account of the stilling of the storm to speak to us in all its force and subtlety. These words by Vincent Donovan from his book, *The Church in the Midst of Creation*, will lead us:

> The 'nature miracles' of Jesus are sometimes dismissed as being unworthy of belief. If they are looked at as special effects tricks or super wonderworks, perhaps they are unbelievable. But if they are seen as portraying a person, Jesus, completely in

consonance with the world of things and the earth from which he came; if they are seen as a sign of the presence of the creating, saving God whose domain extends beyond the souls of men and women to their bodies and to the whole world of creation in which they are immersed; if they are viewed as extending to that 'creation groaning and travailing even until now', as Paul describes it, 'waiting for the revelation of the children of God' - Romans 8:19,22 - then the actions of Jesus flow naturally and without violence to our faith.

(Donovan 1989,1991 p. 122)

THE STORM OF DISCIPLESHIP

We move back to the text to find a second storm. Jesus and the disciples are moving on. It is the close of the day but there is no time for rest yet; the road of discipleship gives little time for rest while the kingdom is near and its proclamation urgent. A journey across the lake looms. We have already seen how the gospel describes the way of Jesus and the path of discipleship as an *ex-cursion*, a going out, outside the old law, outside the familiar, acceptable, respectable limits of community. The journey across the lake represents a new phase in the journey outwards for Jesus and the disciples. Now, for the first time, they step outside Israel and the Jewish community. In face of this new step, it is not difficult to imagine a storm already brewing in the minds of the disciples. With all their notions of chosenness and exclusiveness which were so central to their Hebrew hopes and identity, this journey outwards must have raised radical questions. The external storm on the lake springs up when an internal storm is already raging.

In the background of this story are a number of significant Old Testament themes. In the Old Testament, the sea, much feared by the Hebrews, was seen as a place of God's continuing struggle with the forces of chaos and evil - a place of primal struggle. The ability to control the sea was seen as one of the characteristics of God's divine power, while the human ability to remain calm in the face of a storm was seen as a sign of true faith. In this story, therefore, Jesus is true to his calling as the one who brings the divine presence; the disciples, who are asked only for a calm faith, are found wanting.

What are we to make of the picture of Jesus asleep in the boat while the storm shrieks and the disciples wail? Two Old Testament pictures are relevant. First, at a human level, sleeping in peace in spite of the threatening surrounding circumstances is shown as a sign of faith, of trust in the never failing providence of God. Jesus here demonstrates that spirit of utter trust and calm. Second, from the Old Testament comes a picture of God seemingly asleep as his people were being confronted by personal or national disaster. From both the Book of Psalms and Isaiah, at a time of peril comes the cry, 'Wake up, God!' In Mark's story, Jesus does wake, eventually. In Jesus, God does indeed awake, and speak peace.

Once again, Mark offers a story of contrasts. He is saying that the same Jesus who calls us out on to the stormy waters of the sea of faith, in the midst of the storm will bring to us calm and peace, if we but see, hear and attend to him. All the way through the parables earlier in the chapter, Jesus invites people to 'Listen'. In the stilling of the storm, even the wind and the waves 'listen', and 'obey' him. The question arises, 'Will the disciples show the same obedience?' Are their lives truly formed by an open, trusting faith grounded in Jesus alone? For the first but by no means the last time in the gospel, they are shown here in a negative light. This is important as it signals the start of another developing theme - the disciples' own lack of faith. Already the Scribes have been exposed as those who neither listen or see because their minds are already made up and closed. Now the disciples have neither seen nor heard as they should. The question is obviously addressed to you and me, 'What faith have you? Is it also pretty small?'

The question is not a put-down. There is a real difference between a little faith and no faith at all. However little and meagre our faith seems, there is no call to despair. We have just come from the parable of the grain of mustard seed which promised that faith, no matter how small, can grow. In face of this whole chapter our prayer is very clear, 'O Lord, increase our faith'.

STUDY

BY YOURSELF
Imagine yourself in the boat with Jesus, you could perhaps use some music to set the scene.
• What sights, sounds, tastes, smells, feelings are there?
• Where in the boat are you? Who else is there?
• Look on Jesus' face as he lies asleep. What do you want to say to him?
• When he wakes up, what will he say to you?
Whatever storms you are currently facing, and whatever grain of faith you have, offer the prayer to God, 'Lord, increase my faith'.

FOR GROUP WORK
• In reading the Bible, we all bring our own understanding of the nature of its truth. Imagine a scale with literal and symbolic at either end of a line, and mark where you would be on it.
• Can you explain your view? What are your reasons for it, for example, a concern to maintain the authority of Scripture or a desire to give a rational explanation for seeming 'miracles'?
• Share your views together. The point is not to try to change one another's minds but to understand different points of view, so listen carefully as each group member speaks.
• What do you gain or lose by being open to a symbolic reading, as outlined on p.68?
• Spend some time in prayer together, either silent or open, praying for one another. Don't leave a discussion raw where there may have been real disagreement.

 Outsiders

MARK 5:1-20

Jesus heals a Man with Evil Spirits

(Matt 8:28-34; Lk 8:26-39)

Jesus and his disciples arrived on the other side of Lake Galilee, in the territory of Gerasa. As soon as Jesus got out of the boat, he was met by a man who came out of the burial caves there. This man had an evil spirit in him and lived among the tombs. Nobody could keep him chained up any more; many times his feet and hands had been chained, but every time he broke the chains and smashed the irons on his feet. He was too strong for anyone to control him. Day and night he wandered among the tombs and through the hills, screaming and cutting himself with stones.

He was some distance away when he saw Jesus; so he ran, fell on his knees before him, and screamed in a loud voice, 'Jesus, Son of the Most High God! What do you want with me? For God's sake, I beg you, don't punish me!' (He said this because Jesus was saying, 'Evil spirit, come out of this man!')

So Jesus asked him, 'What is your name?'

The man answered, 'My name is "Mob" - there are so many of us!' And he kept begging Jesus not to send the evil spirits out of that region.

There was a large herd of pigs near by, feeding on a hillside. So the spirits begged Jesus, 'Send us to the pigs, and let us go into them'. He let them go, and the evil spirits went out of the man and entered the pigs. The whole herd - about two thousand pigs in all - rushed down the side of the cliff into the lake and was drowned.

The men who had been taking care of the pigs ran away and spread the news in the town and among the farms. People went out to see what had happened, and when they came to Jesus, they saw the man who used to have the mob of demons in him. He was sitting there, clothed and in his right mind; and they were all afraid. Those who had seen it told the people what had happened to the man with the demons, and about the pigs.

So they asked Jesus to leave their territory.

As Jesus was getting into the boat, the man who had had the demons begged him, 'Let me go with you!'

But Jesus would not let him. Instead, he told him, 'Go back home to your family and tell them how much the Lord has done for you and how kind he has been to you'.

So the man left and went all through the Ten Towns, telling what Jesus had done for him. And all who heard it were amazed.

A MAN POSSESSED

One mighty work follows another. After the stilling of the storm on the lake comes the stilling of the storm raging in and around the wild man living in the place of death. We have now moved outside Israel, as the presence of the pigs, regarded as ritually unclean animals by the Jews, makes very plain. We have moved to the borderlands between life and death. The man in the graveyard in the country of the Gerasenes was in very bad shape, he was in dreadful internal turmoil and also a complete social outcast.

The story begins in an atmosphere of dirt and death. There are the 'unclean' pigs; there's the graveyard, a place of symbolic uncleanness and the dwelling of the power of death; and there's the man himself, a walking no-man's land, fragmented, breaking up, driving himself to destruction. What a graphic description is given of him, spending his considerable strength in futility, keeping up an incessant, tormented monologue, rejecting and defeating all who would control him. He has no real name, for he has no value, no worth. His only name is 'Mob', or 'Legion,' the name of the host of demons who possess and control him so that he is split asunder. 'Legion' of course was the name of a unit of the Roman army, the forces of occupation. One interpretation of this story is that it represents, in symbolic form,

Jesus' challenge to the power of the Roman occupation which colonised and oppressed all under its sway. Clues here suggest such a possibility, among others. This man was 'occupied territory', colonised, invaded and bound in mind and heart .

In the place of death, the man meets Jesus. The demons in him are quick to recognise Jesus but, after a real struggle, they are cast out of the man and he is released from his torment. The demons enter the pigs, the pigs rush down the hillside to the lake and are drowned. The man sits quietly and placidly, in his right mind. Then the conflicts begin. The pig-keepers and the pig-owners are not happy. The folk of the neighbourhood beg Jesus to go away and get lost. The man himself has to struggle with his new identity and his vocation as a whole and integrated person.

TENSIONS AND CONTRASTS

We can look at this story from a number of different points of view in order to explore the tensions within it. Start with the point of view of the outcast man. 'I'm on my own, quite isolated, outside society, nobody wants me, I'm dangerous, frightening, useless ... They try to chain me up, but I can break their chains, ... but there are other chains, chains inside me, chains I can't break. I'm out of control, my own control, I'm bound and driven at the same time.'

Think of the same man, healed. 'I'm all right now. I've got my head together. I'm in control. I'm no threat to anybody but nobody seems to want me. They're all still frightened of me. I'm all right now, but nobody seems very happy about it. I think they'd prefer me the way I was, at least then they had something to complain about. I'd like to get right out of this place and leave the whole lot of them behind. I'd really like to go with this man who's restored my sanity, who's straightened me out. He says, "No, you've got a job to do right here, where you've always been."'

Look at the pig-keepers. They say, 'OK, so this guy is well now, we're sure that's a good thing. What about us, we've lost our jobs! We've got families to feed! Is it worth it, is he worth it?'

Take the pig-owners and the general public. They say, 'There goes our money, there goes our dinner. Bang goes our livelihood. How dare this stranger say that this wretch's sanity is worth two thousand pigs? Who is this stranger who's caused all this trouble anyway? We'd be better off if he went right back home where he came from. Healing you call it? We don't want the kind of healing that he brings. We weren't happy when that man was raging among us out of control, but we're prepared to live with our fears and demons. To be honest, the cost of getting rid of them is altogether too high.'

PRESENT DAY RELEVANCE: TRUE FREEDOM

We can also look at the story in relation to contemporary issues. It raises plenty. Here are three. First, we can take this story as a tale about freedom. Here is this man - his neighbours try to bind and chain him, but they cannot contain him. He bursts their bonds, he is beyond their restraint. So, he's free, is he? He owes no allegiance or obligation to anyone. For him 'there is no such thing as society'. He is the ultimate individualist. The truth is that he is not free at all, for he is totally rootless, dislocated and disconnected, unresponsive and irresponsible. Ultimate individualism is not complete freedom but living death, inhabiting a graveyard. The siren voices of the myth of individualism are powerfully seductive today. The truth is that there is no true freedom unless there is a balancing sense of obligation to the other and to the community. We are made not for splendid isolation, not for freedom for the indulgence of our own drives, desires and whims, not to inhabit only our private world. We are made for mutuality, sharing, community. We are given freedom for the willing acceptance of the bonds of mutual obligation and the interdependence of service.

The man in his original state wasn't free anyway. He was bound and driven by malevolent forces within his head, until he meets in Jesus a presence and a power which brings freedom and release. The very name 'Jesus' means 'he who saves', 'he who brings freedom'. The saving, freeing action marks the journey from a narrow, confining place - a prison, a dungeon, a coffin - out into a wide, open place of spaciousness and room to grow, live and breathe, as in the words of the modern hymn.

> The love of God is broad like beach and meadow,
> Wide as the wind and our eternal home.
> (Anders Frostensen, 1974)

Jesus sets the man free. The man has still to realise his freedom, make it real, walk it out. What enormous challenges he faces. Previously, his life may have been hell but at least it was a familiar hell. He had a role as the scapegoat, the outcast, one from whom nothing was expected. Now he has a new life to make, after many years in limbo, a life for which he himself is responsible. Jesus brings healing and responsibility to us in his works of healing and the result is that we cannot hide any more. As he said earlier in the gospel to the paralysed man on the stretcher, 'Your sins are forgiven, now rise up, stand on your feet and walk'. This present story ends when the possessed man accepts his freedom and picks up the burden of his vocation, his calling.

PRESENT DAY RELEVANCE: CONTEMPORARY DEMONS

This is also a story about demons, about possession. In the New Testament a very important distinction is drawn between people and demons. People have their sins forgiven and are themselves accepted. They are treated with compassion and hope, as the man is here. In contrast, demons are fought and driven out. If we have eyes to see we will easily recognise some at least of the demonic forces at work in our world. It is a mistake to believe that demons belong mainly to the world of the individual. The issue of demons invites us to face up to the questions, 'What are the forces which keep us and our world in bondage?' 'What makes us less free and able for the service of God and one another?'

Take an example of one contemporary demon of enormous destructive power, racial prejudice. None of us is untainted by that demon, one which prevents us loving our neighbour fully. How do we deal with this demon, confront it and cast it out? First, we need to become more self aware, more self critical about how we respond to people face to face, and how we respond to events around the world. We begin by acknowledging the plank in our own eye. We continue by approaching the religion, values and culture of others with openness, humility and a willingness to learn. We eschew hasty judgements. We freely acknowledge our ignorance and partiality.

We must also recognise that the struggle with racial prejudice is not only an inner, personal battle. There is also a war raging in society at large. Here we have to pick our ground and tactics with care. On the one hand it is no good simply blaming folk for attitudes picked up unthinkingly from their upbringing and environment. Here in Britain we still struggle with perverse attitudes of superiority inherited from the old days of the British Empire, from which we need to pray to be delivered. It's no good blaming people but equally it is not right to continue tolerating a destructive spiritual force, which is what racial prejudice is, in us and in our society. Here is a force which destroys and diminishes people, tears them apart from one another, colonises their minds, legitimates many forms of oppression and exploitation. There is a war to be fought, beginning with ourselves, in the name and following the example of Jesus, against contemporary demons which bind and estrange and render worthless. Racial prejudice is only one demon, there are plenty of others around.

PRESENT DAY RELEVANCE: THE COST OF HEALING

Finally, this is a story about the cost of healing. At one level we are very aware of the cost of healing in financial terms (think of the continuing debate over the funding of the UK National Health Service). This story speaks to us about the cost of healing at another level altogether. In a world forever searching for instant magic pills, it is good to be reminded that healing is often a costly business. There is always a price to be paid in the struggle against evil; in this story a lot of disruption has occurred before its end and many people have suffered loss. Think of the story again. Until the man met Jesus, he was outcast. To make him whole, the demons are cast out. As an exercise in damage limitation, the pigs are expendable. To prevent any more disturbance in the neighbourhood, Jesus is asked to leave, *He* is outcast.

The insane man's worthlessness doesn't come to rest only on the pigs, it ends up being laid on Jesus too. For setting the man free he is told to go. He is prepared to carry the cost, to be thrown out. He will bear the disorder himself, he will be the new scapegoat. We hear an echo of the words, 'Here is the Lamb of God who takes away the sins of the world'. He takes them away by shouldering their burden himself. Works of healing, peace-making and reconciliation often carry with them burdens of vulnerability and ambiguity. Are we prepared to take Jesus' costly way of healing which will involve us in all the ambiguities heaped on him here?

At the very end of the story, we have a picture of the man, healed and restored, asking if he too can join the disciples' community and go with Jesus. Very often just such a following is exactly what Jesus asks. Not here. To the man he says, 'Your place is where you are. You are not being called to be a dependent follower, but to be an evangelist among your own people, to tell them by the living witness of your changed life of the work and mercy of the Lord. Go among this people with all their manifest dis-ease as living evidence of the new order, the new state of things. It is a formidable challenge. The story has been acted out once and people rejected it - go and tell it again.' 'The man is bidden to go and evangelise in that most difficult of all environments, home.' (Vincent and Davies 1986, pp. 54-57)

STUDY

BY YOURSELF
• Much in this section is relevant to our world . With self-awareness and humility, ponder over the questions it raises for you under the headings of true freedom, contemporary demons, the cost of healing.
• 'Your place is where you are ... living evidence of the new order, the new state of things ...'. What does this call mean for you in the places which are 'home' to you, in your own household, neighbourhood, workplace, church?

chapter 12

Daughter Of Privilege,
Daughter Of Poverty

MARK 5:21-43
Jairus' Daughter and the Woman who touched Jesus' Cloak
(Matt 9:18-26; Lk 8:40-56)

Jesus went back across to the other side of the lake. There at the lakeside a large crowd gathered round him. Jairus, an official of the local synagogue, arrived, and when he saw Jesus, he threw himself down at his feet and begged him earnestly, 'My little daughter is very ill. Please come and place your hands on her, so that she will get well and live!'

Then Jesus started off with him. So many people were going along with Jesus that they were crowding him from every side.

There was a woman who had suffered terribly from severe bleeding for twelve years, even though she had been treated by many doctors. She had spent all her money, but instead of getting better she got worse all the time. She had heard about Jesus, so she came in the crowd behind him, saying to herself, 'If I just touch his clothes, I will get well'.

She touched his cloak, and her bleeding stopped at once;

and she had the feeling inside herself that she was healed of her trouble. At once Jesus knew that power had gone out of him, so he turned round in the crowd and asked, 'Who touched my clothes?'

His disciples answered, 'You see how the people are crowding you; why do you ask who touched you?'

But Jesus kept looking round to see who had done it. The woman realised what had happened to her, so she came, trembling with fear, knelt at his feet, and told him the whole truth. Jesus said to her, 'My daughter, your faith has made you well. Go in peace, and be healed of your trouble'.

While Jesus was saying this, some messengers came from Jairus' house and told him, 'Your daughter has died. Why bother the Teacher any longer?'

Jesus paid no attention to what they said, but told him, 'Don't be afraid, only believe'. Then he did not let anyone else go on with him except Peter and James and his brother John. They arrived at Jairus' house, where Jesus saw the confusion and heard all the loud crying and wailing. He went in and said to them, 'Why all this confusion? Why are you crying? The child is not dead - she is only sleeping!'

They laughed at him, so he put them all out, took the child's father and mother and his three disciples, and went into the room where the child was lying. He took her by the hand and said to her, '*Talitha, koum,*' which means, 'Little girl, I tell you to get up!'

She got up at once and started walking around. (She was twelve years old.) When this happened, they were completely amazed. But Jesus gave them strict orders not to tell anyone, and he said, 'Give her something to eat'.

A STORY FOR CHILDREN - AND ADULTS

This story tells of the healing of Jairus' daughter - a young girl in the midst of a life and death crisis. How old were you when you first heard this story? Children can easily identify with it. It's a compelling story - the movement of the crowds, the sense of urgency in Jairus' plea for help, then the diversion of the woman with the bleeding. Mark builds up the tension as we watch the action unfold - we want to say, 'Hurry up, Jesus, get on with it, the wee lassie's very ill, see this other woman tomorrow, she can wait'. Then the awful moment of apparent tragedy, 'You've left it too late, sir, the girl is dead'. That is followed by the contrasting paid despair of the professional mourners and Jesus' insistent promise that the girl will live - before the last moment of privacy, intimacy and joy where she is raised up and, with all the vigour of the young, bounces back to life so quickly that Jesus' parting shot to her parents is, 'You'd better give her some breakfast'.

It certainly is a tale with which a child can identify, but it is not simple. This isn't one story at all, there are two stories, the healing of Jairus' daughter and the healing of the woman with the chronic bleeding. The healing of the woman is a story within a story, a device met before in Mark, and much of the point of the setting of the two stories together is the tension between them, the contrasts and the connections to which Mark points us.

CONTRASTS AND TENSIONS: JAIRUS AND THE WOMAN

To examine the contrasts and tensions in the stories, compare Jairus and the woman with the bleeding. First we meet Jairus, ruler of the synagogue. We know he is an important person because we are told his name. He is a man of religious authority and position, in a place of privilege and responsibility. According to the values of his society, Jairus is also extremely socially secure. He is male, a father, surrounded by his family - also a sign of God's blessing.

Contrast the woman. She is the victim of the same religious system which gives Jairus his place of honour and whose authority he upholds. Obviously, her chronic bleeding had made her physically weak, but that weakness was compounded by religious laws which labelled her ritually 'unclean' and condemned her to social isolation. She could touch no one - everything she touched would be tainted by her 'uncleanness'. She has no name, a reflection of her perceived status and value. She is anonymous, outcast, female, isolated, living a wretched life with no family around her and no visible means of support. It seems as if she were under the curse of God.

While Jairus comes with all the confidence of his position to ask Jesus for attention, she is voiceless and has to make her claim on him by stealth. We are presented with an upside-down situation. Jairus, the public person, makes a public request for healing, yet for him the healing takes place in private. The woman, an intensely private person, makes her approach in secret, yet her healing takes place in public.

Between Jairus and the woman the contrasts are great, yet they have much in common. In this encounter they are both shown as falling down before Jesus, Jairus imploring, the woman (after her healing) in fear, confessing. Also, they both have something to lose. Jairus is a prominent, establishment figure, a person of position and orthodoxy. Jesus is seen as unorthodox, unconventional, not respectable, already deeply suspect because of his undermining of the very law Jairus is charged with upholding. It must have cost Jairus a great deal to go to Jesus. Yet *in extremis*, out of his need and for the sake of the daughter whom he loves, he is prepared to sacrifice his dignity, venture his reputation, and go. We might think that the woman had little to lose compared with Jairus, she had lost everything already. Her illness and its social consequences had made her turn into herself. For her healing, all that has to go. Her secrecy, intimately connected with her sense of herself, is quite blown away.

There is another profound link between them. After her healing, the woman confesses that she has touched Jesus. In this story, touch is highly significant. Jairus says to Jesus concerning his daughter, 'Just touch her, and she will be well'. The woman touches Jesus without asking - she is afraid to ask because for her, touching is against the law which it is Jairus' professional duty to uphold. We will return to this matter of touching which is at the heart of the story.

CONTRASTS AND TENSIONS: THE TWO WOMEN

First, we'll look at the contrasts between the two women. They are bound together by the number twelve. The young girl is twelve years old, in her society that was on the threshold of womanhood. She is the hope and promise of her family's future, and everything has led up to this moment. She is about to come to her physical and social fullness. The woman has endured twelve years of losing her lifeblood, of being continually menstrual, her physical rhythms disrupted, her social relationships dislocated.

Now the young girl's life is in danger of being wasted in a flash while, for the older woman, wasting is a slow, dreary, daily process. All her resources have been expended already. For both, the situation seems beyond help.

Healing help comes through the action of Jesus, and there the contrasts continue. The young girl is the centre of attention, surrounded by the wailing mourners. The woman's healing occurs when everybody's attention is focused on someone else. Jesus, however, reduces the public attention being paid to the young girl. He throws everyone out and attends to her with only her parents and his closest companions at hand. With the woman it is quite different; Jesus focuses public attention on the one who has approached him anonymously. He makes her the centre of the scene.

While Jairus pleads for his daughter, Jesus calls the older woman by that same name of honour and promise, 'Daughter'. He tells her that her faith has healed her, while the daughter of privilege has to wait yet a little while for her healing, given in the words, *talitha koum*, which mean, 'arise', or 'be resurrected'. The girl, the privileged one, sits down at the breakfast table; the woman, the outsider, is given her new place in the peace and justice of God.

The contrasts between these two women illustrate the difference between their situations. The older woman in all her hopelessness has been excluded and disinherited during the years in which Jairus' daughter has been growing up to a comfortable, honourable place in the society - until this crisis.

CRISIS!

Jairus is obviously a man in desperate straits, with whom we can all identify. His daughter is suddenly acutely ill. He needs Jesus NOW. And yet, at the very moment when her life hangs in the balance - in today's world we would hear the approaching ambulance sirens wailing wildly - there is an interruption. Jairus, important leader, has to wait while Jesus attends to a woman who could - couldn't she? - easily wait a little longer.

Worse, Jesus not only allows himself to be interrupted by the 'inferior', he is touched by her, and thus himself becomes 'unclean'. How does he react? Instead of the formal rebuke she was obviously expecting and dreading, he commends her, restores her and gives her a new life in which the old laws of exclusion have no more authority. Then, unclean as he now is, he goes in to touch Jairus' daughter and Jairus is so desperate that he makes no protest. The touch of the 'unclean' man brings resurrected life, new life which is no mere continuation of the old. Having first brought salvation to the dispossessed, Jesus brings salvation to the child of privilege.

TOUCHED

Mark has turned the screw one notch tighter. We have already seen how Jesus has been prepared to take 'uncleanness' or disgrace upon himself, (with the leper, with tax collectors and outcasts, with the demonic in the last story). Here we are shown an incident in which it is only by the touch of one who has made himself 'unclean,' that the one who is apparently secure, privileged and 'righteous', can be given new life. It's a kind of holy 'tig' or 'tag', shocking and delightful at the same time. We see that the new life Jesus brings is contagious, and marvel that only when Jairus allows his daughter to be touched by the man who was touched by the woman whose 'uncleanness' he, Jairus, was appointed to guard against, that the new life comes.

People always ask why Jesus allows himself to be diverted. The gospel is saying that for Jesus, the woman's chronic state is as important as the acute state of the young girl. If he had not stopped, the woman would not have reached out and discovered, to her amazement and delight, that her unlawful, secret action is the defiance of convention which Jesus needed to enable healing to take place. She is commended and praised, as well she should be - if she had not touched Jesus, we would not have this clear evidence of Jesus' approval of her action and, as a corollary, his disapproval of the system which disinherited and denied her. We would not have the authority in his name to make war on the whole mythology of female 'uncleanness' represented here. This is one of the many places in the gospel where Jesus gives a new and distinct place to women. Here he destroys a taboo which still has lingering power where religion is dominated by a male world view.

At the end of Jesus' encounter with the older woman, the young girl is dead. There is no nick of time rescue. The one who is secure in her place in religion and society is allowed to die while the one who has no security, is marginalised, has nothing, is healed. Only on the other side of a real death does the call to rise up come. Out of that extremity comes new life for the secure, a true rebirth.

The number twelve may hold even more symbolic meaning. 'Twelve' stands for the tribes of Israel, it represents the nation. Mark is saying here that new life will come to the people of God only through the painful process of death and resurrection; only by dying to the old ways of privilege could there be the possibility of God's effecting new life. He is also saying that new life for all *must* include the poor, the broken, the disregarded and, particularly, those whom the old law disempowered and disinherited.

This is a profound story. At its heart is Jesus, who awakens and encourages faith among very different people and brings healing and life. Where he is there is life, where he is, healing happens. He is in the world, accessible, trailing the hem of his garment which people can touch, find life, and discover the kingdom.

Mark wrote his gospel for a young church immersed in a struggle where Jewish Christians, the privileged insiders, had to find a way to accept Gentile Christians, the outsiders. According to Mark, Jesus promises a place for all, but the secure and privileged will come to new life only when they recognise the mission and activity of Jesus outside and beyond them. As it was, so it is. Here we are being asked, 'In what ways, if we are to be true to our calling, must we, as insiders, die to old ways?'

This great story of healing, hope and life speaks of the touch that heals. We are reminded of the central place which Jesus gave to women, against the stream of the culture of his world. We are recalled to the central place he gives and calls us to give to all outsiders. Before us is the demonstration of that essential truth for us and for Jesus himself, as will later be unfolded, that new life comes only through a process of dying.

STUDY

BY YOURSELF
Use your imagination to get into this story.
- What can you see, hear, smell, taste, feel?
- What is the weather like? Warm, cold, windy, peaceful, wet, dry?
- What seems to be happening? Who is there?
- What kind of atmosphere is there? Inviting, threatening, lively, solemn?
- Does anything about this incident particularly attract your attention?
- Where are you in this scene? One of the crowd? One of the disciples? Are you with Jairus or the untouchable woman? Are you an insider or an outsider?
- How are you feeling? Disturbed? Attracted? Curious? Afraid? Eager?
- Do you feel drawn to speak to anyone there? What do you want to say? What do you hear being said to you? Can you enter into a conversation with Jesus?

If you noticed earlier one part of the scene drawing you powerfully, let yourself follow it. In your imagination go to be part of that scene. Without forcing anything, see if you can identify what it is that is attracting you.

- Let each person in the group take the role of one of the main characters: Jairus, his daughter, the poor woman, one of Jairus' friends, a mourner, a disciple, a member of the crowd, Jesus. If you need to, work in pairs or groups. Prepare an eye-witness account of the events of this story, focusing on what you saw, heard and felt. You might want to write some notes but, preferably, start with discussion and reflection then try speaking in 'your' character, e.g. *Jairus*: I was desperate. I have no son, only this one daughter and she is precious to me. I knew that Jesus was suspect, but I didn't care what people thought, or what the rule book said, I only knew ...
- Once you have shared your ideas and the story from the point of view of your character, look at these questions together.

    - What do you think are Jairus' thoughts and feelings in the course of this incident? Remember, he is both a person of privilege, and someone who has laws and standards to uphold.
    - Why do you think the woman tried to touch Jesus in secret?
    - Why did Jesus make her healing public?

- This is a liberating story for people who are disempowered and marginalised. Can you think of a similar kind of story in today's world?

chapter 13

The Big Bad World

MARK 6:1-29

Jesus is rejected at Nazareth
(Matt 13:53-58; Lk 4:16-30)

Jesus left that place and went back to his home town, followed by his disciples. On the Sabbath he began to teach in the synagogue. Many people were there; and when they heard him, they were all amazed. 'Where did he get all this?' they asked. 'What wisdom is this that has been given to him? How does he perform miracles? Isn't he the carpenter, the son of Mary, and the brother of James, Joseph, Judas and Simon? Aren't his sisters living here?' And so they rejected him.

Jesus said to them, 'Prophets are respected everywhere except in their own home town and by their relatives and their family.'

He was not able to perform any miracles there, except that he placed his hands on a few sick people and healed them. He was greatly surprised, because the people did not have faith.

Jesus sends out the Twelve Disciples
(Matt 10:5-15; Lk 9:1-6)

Then Jesus went to the villages round there, teaching the people. He called the twelve disciples together and sent them out two by two. He gave them authority over the evil spirits and ordered them, 'Don't take anything with you on your journey except a stick - no bread, no beggar's bag, no money in your pockets. Wear sandals, but don't carry an extra shirt'. He also said, 'Wherever you are welcomed, stay in the same house until you leave that place. If you come to a town where people do not welcome you or will not listen to you, leave it and shake the dust off your feet. That will be a warning to them!'

So they went out and preached that people should turn away from their sins. They drove out many demons, and rubbed olive-oil on many sick people and healed them.

The Death of John the Baptist
(Matt 14:1-12; Lk 9:7-9)

Now King Herod heard about all this, because Jesus' reputation had spread everywhere. Some people were saying, 'John the Baptist has come back to life! That is why he has this power to perform miracles.'

Others, however, said, 'He is Elijah.'

Others said, 'He is a prophet, like one of the prophets of long ago.'

When Herod heard it, he said, 'He is John the Baptist! I had his head cut off, but he has come back to life!' Herod himself had ordered John's arrest, and he had him chained and put in prison. Herod did this because of Herodias, whom he had married, even though she was the wife of his brother Philip. John the Baptist kept telling Herod, 'It isn't right for you to be married to your brother's wife!'

So Herodias held a grudge against John and wanted to kill him, but she could not because of Herod. Herod was afraid of John because he knew that John was a good and holy man, and so he kept him safe. He liked to listen to him, even though he became greatly disturbed every time he heard him.

Finally Herodias got her chance. It was on Herod's birthday, when he gave a feast for all the chief government officials, the military commanders, and the leading citizens of Galilee. The daughter of Herodias came in and danced, and pleased Herod and his guests. So the king said to the girl, 'What would you like to have? I will give you anything you want'. With many vows he said to her, 'I swear that I will give you anything you ask for, even as much as half my kingdom!'

So the girl went out and asked her mother, 'What shall I ask for?'

'The head of John the Baptist,' she answered.

The girl hurried back at once to the king and demanded, 'I want you to give me here and now the head of John the Baptist on a dish!'

This made the king very sad, but he could not refuse her because of the vows had made in front of all his guests. So he sent off a guard at once with orders to bring John's head. The guard left, went to the prison, and cut John's head off; then he brought it on a dish and gave it to the girl, who gave it to her mother. When John's disciples heard about this, they came and took away his body, and buried it.

DOWN TO EARTH AGAIN - A STRANGER AT HOME

What does it mean to be a disciple? We have seen this question is crucial to Mark's purpose. Remember it as we join the roller coaster again. We have just witnessed Jesus raising Jairus' daughter from death, or apparent death - a most impressive event on two counts. Not only was it a marvel because of the seeming hopelessness of her condition; her father seeking help from Jesus is also a wonder. Jairus, we remember, is head of the local synagogue, representative of the powers that up to this point have consistently opposed Jesus. This looks like the moment of Jesus' greatest power, influence and acceptance so far.

But then Jesus goes home and takes his place in the familiar synagogue at Nazareth, among the community where he grew up. As the well-known Scottish put-down says, 'I kent his faither'; here it's, 'This guy can't be serious, he used to be one of the local joiners. Who does he think he is?' Here is Jesus, a stranger in his home town: among his own people, rejected and treated with suspicion and cynicism. In the face of such unbelief, he finds his attempts at ministry largely fail. Remember the earlier encounter with his mother and brothers, who came to rescue him from himself; the hardest mission sites may be at home, among those who may have a vested interest in denying the possibility of change and growth. They may be determined, for what they believe are good reasons, to keep us where they think we should always have been. Once again the way of discipleship leads us out of our primal, familial communities into a wider world experience, into relationships not determined by the demands of kith and kin.

THE JOURNEY OUTWARDS - AT HOME WITH STRANGERS

Jesus and the disciples find themselves strangers at home, so Jesus sends the disciples out to be at home with strangers! Now the disciples are equipped to teach and heal. Out they go in pairs to strengthen, support and complement one another. Jesus builds into the ministry and mission of his disciples the support and discipline of collegiality. Is that true of our church, our ministry?

The first calling of the disciples, as their name implies, is to be 'learners', companions on the way with Jesus. Now they are called 'apostles' (6:30), 'those who are sent out'. They are set on their way to witness and to heal, to drive out demons and to proclaim the Kingdom's presence. Mark is not at all interested in the results of their mission. He doesn't tell us how they fared. He is interested in the instructions that Jesus gives them as he sends them outwards. It has been commented that the instructions given are remarkably like those given to a guerrilla army, but with important differences. Unlike guerrillas, they are sent out unarmed, physically defenceless, and they are sent into new territory to find lodging and hospitality quite without coercion. Instead of bringing terror, they offer peace. If they receive a welcome, they stay, if they do not, they shake off the dust and leave. Above all, they travel light. Here is the prerequisite for the disciple's journey. No excess baggage. Carry none of that (so descriptive) Latin word for baggage, *impedimenta*. No impediments, nothing to hold you back. How easily '*impedimenta*' can prevent us from following, from getting through the needle's eye. Often the mental and spiritual baggage we carry is a deadweight. The result is we lack the flexibility to respond with true openness to new situations and new people.

A TALE OF A TYRANT AND TERROR

We now move from one kingdom to another, to the kingdom of Herod Antipas, ruler of Galilee. The contrast between the kingdom which Jesus announces and the kingdom of Herod could scarcely be greater. In Herod's kingdom arbitrary power, fear, lust and murder rule. The background to the death of John the Baptist is as follows. Herod had 'put away' his first wife and married the wife of his brother, Philip. Marriages at that time in such circles were about power rather than human relationships. They were used to forge dynastic alliances with neighbours or act as the means of making peace with enemies. The Herodian dynasty ruled uneasily in Judea and Galilee. On the one hand they owed allegiance to Roman power which would remove them summarily if they stepped out of line or their subjects got out of control; on the other, they were not native Jews either, they were hybrids, keeping the Jewish law only when it suited them and so prone to fall foul of prophetic figures like John the Baptist.

Naturally, John's following alarmed Herod. John's insistence that Herod's second marriage was unlawful alarmed him even more. Herod feared that John could turn the people against him. It appears that Herod's new wife, Herodias, was even more angered than Herod by John's outspoken criticism - certainly she had little of Herod's fear of and respect for the holy man. Eventually, John became so much of a threat to the tyrant's peace of mind that he was flung in gaol while Herodias began to plot his death.

The story of John's execution is like a Hollywood epic - a gross caricature of political, courtly intrigue. At a drunken orgy, Herod lustfully makes a reckless promise to Herodias' daughter, Salome, who is dancing for him. At the prompting of her mother, the daughter exacts her due - 'Bring me the head of John the Baptist.' Herod, instead of observing the demands of justice, gives in to the dancing girl's whim. Thus John meets his end, victim of the capricious exercise of power. This is also, paradoxically, a story about the powerlessness of power. Herod is trapped into doing the wrong thing through the public nature of his foolish boasting. Because he is frightened to lose face, John loses his head. As a ruler, Herod is unable to exercise one of his prime functions as a ruler, dispensing justice.

What has this to do with being a disciple? Isn't this story a bit of a distraction from the main action - Mark, having introduced John into his story at the start of the gospel, needing to get him off-stage by relating his subsequent fate? No indeed. By the narration of John's death Mark foretells the lengthening shadow which falls across the whole gospel story. Before the story ends, there will be another death, through which the meaning of the gospel will be made plain. The death plot against Jesus has already been announced in Mark Chapter 3. Very soon, Jesus will announce his own death and spend much of the second half of the story seeking to make his disciples aware of its reality, a reality which they will consistently deny and seek to evade.

We can well understand their denials and evasions, since Jesus will make it clear that before them lies not only his own death but their surrender. 'If anyone wants to come with me,' he says, 'he must forget self, carry his cross, and follow me.' (8:34) Mark makes it clear that in following Jesus there is deadly risk and seriousness in the face of the forces of evil. To be a disciple is to take up the way of the cross, to try to live out the meaning of Christ's death in constant self-surrender, as we live out the gospel in a dangerous and risky world.

STUDY

BY YOURSELF
A reflection about yourself
- Reflect on the baggage you carry in your own life. It might help to visualise your backpack. What does it look like? What colour? Shape? Is it in good condition or travel worn?
- Now picture yourself opening the backpack. Taking your time, and in as relaxed a way as possible, reach into the bag and take out anything which is acting as an impediment to you. Spend some moments examining each item, and then put it down, or give it away, so that you are ready to travel lighter.

A reflection about our world
'The powerlessness of power'
- What examples can you think of from history or current affairs where leaders have shown themselves apparently powerless to act with justice?
- What were the forces that have seemed to defeat them?
- Can you also think of examples when people have acted with integrity and justice, and perhaps had to leave behind some of the trappings (or baggage) of power?

chapter 14

feeding the People

MARK 6:30-44

Jesus feeds a Great Crowd

(Matt 14:13-21; Lk 9:10-17; Jn 6:1-14)

The apostles returned and met with Jesus, and told him all they had done and taught. There were so many people coming and going that Jesus and his disciples didn't even have time to eat. So he said to them, 'Let us go off by ourselves to some place where we will be alone and you can rest for a while'. So they started out in a boat by themselves for a lonely place.

Many people, however, saw them leave and knew at once who they were; so they went from all the towns and ran ahead by land and arrived at the place ahead of Jesus and his disciples. When Jesus got out of the boat, he saw this large crowd, and his heart was filled with pity for them, because they were like sheep without a shepherd. So he began to teach them many things. When it was getting late, his disciples came to him and said, 'It is already very late, and this is a lonely place. Send the people away, and let them go to the nearby farms and villages in order to buy themselves something to eat'.

'You yourselves give them something to eat,' Jesus answered.

They asked, 'Do you want us to go and spend two hundred silver coins on bread in order to feed them?'

So Jesus asked them, 'How much bread have you got? Go and see.'

When they found out, they told him, 'Five loaves and also two fish.'

Jesus then told his disciples to make all the people divide into groups and sit down on the green grass. So the people sat down in rows, in groups of a hundred and fifty. Then Jesus took the five loaves and the two fish, looked up to heaven, and gave thanks to God. He broke the loaves and gave them to his disciples to distribute among them all. He also divided the two fish among them all. Everyone ate and had enough. Then the disciples took up twelve baskets full of what was left of the bread and the fish. The number of men who were fed was five thousand.

'How?' and 'Why?' questions

People have always been interested in 'How?' questions, such questions dominate in our modern world. 'How does it work?' 'What's the technique?' 'How did it happen?' It's a basic question of the scientific mind. We live in a world of cause and effect. We are very interested in connections, explanations, root causes.

Often, however, the 'How?' question can leave us stuck. There is another very important three-letter word around - 'Why?' If 'How?' is the question of science, of function, 'Why?' is the question of meaning, of religion. When we read the gospels we must guard against becoming so ensnared in our modern 'How?' questions that we fail to understand the gospel's 'Why?' answers.

Few stories have suffered more from an over-concentration on 'How?' questions than the story of the feeding of the five thousand. In part this is because of the way it is narrated - feeding five thousand people out of almost nothing is hard to believe. We are either awed by Jesus the great wonder-worker or, if we are of a more sceptical turn of mind, we use our ingenuity to produce a matter-of-fact, historicist explanation of 'what actually happened'. One example is to suggest that rather than multiply loaves miraculously, Jesus persuaded people to open their hearts and their sandwich bags and share what they had with one another.

The gospel account is reticent in describing 'what actually happened'. In answer to the question 'How were these people fed?' there is no mention either of a miraculous multiplying of loaves in their material substance, or of a miraculous opening of human hearts. Over a distance of two thousand years and a considerable divide of understanding and ideas, we cannot conclusively answer the 'How?' question. What we have is what the gospel tells and what the gospel tells is 'Look, here is a story of great importance to faith in Jesus Christ', and that faith includes our faith, now.

THE STORY: BACKGROUND

The evangelists put a good deal of weight on this story; it appears in some form in all four gospels. Indeed, the story appears twice in Mark's gospel - there is a variation of it in Mark 8:1-10. When we look at these accounts of desert or wilderness meals, it is important to see them against the background of a wider scriptural context. There are many descriptions of meals taken together in the story of Jesus and they have a place within the context of the broader biblical witness to the Messianic feast.

Beginning with the wider sweep of the biblical panorama, the great words of Isaiah 25 provide a foundation:

> Here on Mount Zion the Lord will prepare a banquet for all the nations of the world, here he will remove the veil, the cloud of sorrow, here he will destroy death for ever, here he will wipe away the tears from all faces and take away all their shame.
> (Isaiah 25:6-9, author's paraphrase)

In time, these words came to be understood as a description of the coming Messianic banquet. This feast was as much one of the marks of the coming of the Messiah as the bringing of sight to the blind or hearing to the deaf. For the gospel writers, the desert meals are signs of the Messiah's coming, indications that Jesus is indeed the Christ. At the end of the Bible, in the book of Revelation we find John of Patmos' great description of the marriage feast of the Lamb when, at the end-time, all humanity and all creation are restored and recreated (Rev 19:5-10). The desert meal not only has a reference backward into the prophecies of Isaiah, it points forward. It stands as a foretaste of that last great feast of joy and love.

MANY MEALS, ONE MEAL

Within the gospels, Jesus is present at many meals. He eats with outcasts and tax collectors, with the woman who brings the ointment in Mark (14:3-9) and with folk as different as lepers and Pharisees in the other three gospels. His presence at table is always a sign of the breadth of the fellowship he makes; of the hospitality he receives and offers. The meals all point forward to those meals just before and after Jesus' death. The feeding of the crowd leads us to that central table when, 'on the night he was betrayed, Jesus took bread ...' (1 Cor 11:23) There are very close connections between meals with the crowd and the table of the Last Supper. Look at this comparison:

The Feeding of the 5000	*The Last Supper*
he took the loaves	he took the bread
he blessed the loaves	he blessed the bread
he broke the loaves	he broke the bread
he gave the loaves	he gave the bread
he took the fish	he took the cup
he divided the fish among them	he gave the cup
they all ate the fish	they all drank the cup

We can clearly see that these stories of the five/four thousand belong within the tradition of Jesus' taking, blessing, breaking and giving which finds its focus in the Last Supper. Yet taking, blessing, breaking and giving are not confined to that central moment of Communion; they are at the very heart of the life of Jesus and indeed at the heart of the lives of those who would be his disciples.

At the Last Supper, where he is the host, Jesus freely shares the gifts of God's creation with his people. He then goes out immediately to share with all through the giving of his own life, of himself. We receive the benefits of his giving in many rich and different ways. At the table of the communion which he makes with us, his people, he puts his life in us and invites us in turn to be taking, blessing, breaking, giving people, with his own open-handed compassionate lack of discrimination and reserve. 'You are my body', he says, 'the continuation of my life in the world'.

JUST BREAD FOR HUNGRY FOLK

In the two feedings of the five and four thousand, we see Jesus meeting human need in all its ordinariness. These random crowds, with no special attributes of holiness or obedience, with only their hunger and their hope, become connected to the giving of Christ himself. They become part of his mission; he has come to bring them life by sharing with them himself. The way of mission remains the same for Christ's people now. The Greek word used in both the stories to describe Jesus' feeling for the crowds, *esplangchnisthe*, translated as, 'he felt sorry, his heart was filled with pity', is a very strong word, literally describing a tearing of the gut, indicative of a deep and visceral emotion. Jesus is deeply *moved* with compassion. A similar movement is called forth from us on our way of discipleship.

Here also, a new order of sharing is announced as the heart of the economics of the kingdom. We are given this clear picture, not once but twice, of the whole crowd being organised and provided for from within the resources of those present, under the blessing of God. In the 'hippie' world of the 1960s and 1970s, 'bread' was a synonym for 'money'. Had they stumbled on gospel truth?

The feeding of the five thousand shows Jesus feeding his own people. Again we meet the common Marcan theme of contrast between Jesus and his disciples. The disciples are shown struggling in vain with a problem which is too big for them, 'How can we ever feed that lot?' (6:37) They are helpless and uncertain - Mark would say 'faithless'. In startling contrast is Jesus' supreme confidence and faith. The contrast here makes two points. On the one hand, Jesus is able to use the offerings of the disciples, even if they are brought in a spirit of confused faithlessness. This is a vital truth for us to hang on to, that though our offerings may be made out of our acknowledged imperfection and inadequacy, Jesus will make them perfect. We are released and set free. In the words of the poet T S Eliot, '... for us there is only the trying, the rest is not our business.' ('East Coker', *Four Quartets*.)

Here also the real difficulties and weaknesses of the disciples are transformed and overcome when they bring their burdens before their Lord. Making Jesus part of all our deliberations and our counsel, admitting him to the problems of our lives and our faith as Master and Lord as a matter of daily practice, can make all the difference in the world.

THE CROWD

Finally, a word about the crowd, whatever its size. What would it have been like to be among that crowd? And what would the authorities think of such crowds - far too many for comfort, for security reasons? This story occurs immediately after the beheading of John the Baptist, where political authority is shown to be both capricious and fearful. Remember that Jesus lived in a territory ill at ease with its rulers. Authoritarian governments fear and discourage crowds, they routinely forbid the meeting of large assemblies. When news of these crowds reached Herod and Pilate, as it undoubtedly would, what would they think?

Alan Dale was one of the great Bible translators of our time. He was also a missionary in China at the time of the Japanese invasion of Manchuria in 1933. Listen to his words,

> Several times I had to move in and out of an area which was occupied by Japanese troops. So, for the first time, I lived in occupied territory and saw the effect this had on the life and attitudes and conversations of ordinary Chinese people. Suddenly I realised that this was the situation in which Jesus grew up and in which he carried out his ministry. The conversation with every meal in which he shared must have been very like the conversation I listened to. There, whatever the subject, the Japanese presence forced its way into the talk.
>
> I began to read Mark's story of Jesus in a quite different way. What Jesus had to say, his stories, remarks and sayings, took on a new liveliness and bite. The impression deepened when I read Josephus' Jewish War and also some Israeli accounts of the freedom fighters, the Zealots, and the story of Masada.
> (Alan T Dale, quoted in Davies and Vincent 1986 pp. 66-7)

The desert meal of the five thousand can look like a mob searching for a way to become an effective resistance movement. The tragedy of Jewish resistance was that it was always fragmented, no single leader could count on total support. Do we have here the five thousand looking to Jesus to lead a revolt against Rome? Remember, one popular expectation of the coming Messiah was that he would set his people free in the most literal of senses. 'Sheep without a shepherd' (6:34) had a long history of meaning an army without a general or a nation without a leader. The 'many things' which Jesus taught could represent his struggling to teach the crowd how he could not be the leader they wanted. John's gospel is quite specific; after the feeding the crowd sought to make him king and Jesus had to take avoiding action (John 6:15). At the end of the story, Jesus goes apart to pray, suggesting that he had been through a real ordeal.

The story of Jewish resistance to Rome is a sad and tragic tale. It ended with the destruction of the Temple in Jerusalem which had such far-reaching consequences for subsequent Jewish history. It also resulted in the destruction of one particular community, the community of resistance at Masada, in CE73. There is the powerful picture of this dedicated but introverted community sharing resources together before they committed mass suicide. What a contrast there is between the meal at Masada and the feeding of the five thousand! Here are four obvious points:

Masada	Jesus and the 5000
a defiant wastage	gathering up to avoid waste
a closed community	an open community, especially for those with nowhere to go
fellowship for the 'in'	fellowship especially for the outsider
a meal to say 'goodbye' to the world and one another	the sign of the new, a community of all sorts, shaped only by the call of Jesus, and a new order of mutual sharing

(Davies and Vincent 1986, p.68)

Here are two quite distinct ways of relating to the worlds of people and power. The contrast is between an exclusive, fiercely single-minded sect committed to armed resistance, and an open fellowship, no less committed to the way of service and non-violence. Christ's people are called to the Banquet of the Messiah, to belong at his table and, in their worship and their living, to displace and disempower Caesar without bloodshed or despair.

JESUS ALONE

In the unfolding of Mark's witness to Jesus, these great desert meals are almost the last times everyone is around Jesus. Time and again in the first half of the gospel we are shown scenes of crowds thronging around him. From now on, the crowd begins to thin out, opposition mounts, supporters fade away, until Jesus hangs on the cross quite alone. The waning of his 'supporters' will make no difference to him, for he will not be compelled by others. He will work out his own revolution. Let's end this section with three questions for Christians which arise out of these pivotal stories.

First, are we aware every time we come to the Lord's table, to the breaking of bread together, what a challenge this table presents to the way things are, in ourselves and in our world? In the words of St Paul, 'When anyone is in Christ Jesus, he is a new creature, there is a new world.' (2 Cor 5:17, *NEB*)

Secondly, are we aware, as the church, as Christians, that we are part of a movement which has implications for every part of our lives and the world's life? Questions such as 'How do we feed a hungry world?' 'How do we participate in the sharing of the "bread"?' take us into many areas of work, society, politics and economics.

Thirdly, are we aware that at the heart of the movement, the new order is of the pattern and rhythm of taking, blessing, giving and sharing?

Jesus rejects one kind of revolution, the all-too-common revolution of force and naked power; he substitutes another. He brings a new way which has sharing and giving at its very heart. The feedings of the five and four thousand show us Jesus meeting people's need with total disregard for names and labels, levels and abilities. Our calling today is clear; to feed people now with similar openness and generosity of spirit. Pray for the Spirit that we might be so caring and so bold.

STUDY

BY YOURSELF

- Reflect on the three questions above. They clearly require individual commitment, but they also require collective action. What do they mean for you?
- Reflect on the rhythm of taking, blessing, breaking, giving and sharing in your own life.

FOR GROUP WORK

- Perhaps this is another good opportunity for your group to eat together - a potluck supper of course!
- It can well be argued that globalisation and the domination of the superpowers, or consumerism and materialism, are our modern equivalents of occupation by the Roman Empire.
- What are the signs of occupation?
- In what ways is the Church responding by retreating like the people of Masada?
- What sorts of positive resistance should we as Christians be developing? Should it be involvement in local justice and community initiatives, with fair trade ventures, with the debt relief campaign?
- What might the model of taking, blessing, breaking, giving, sharing, look like and involve? What are the costs (not necessarily financial) and what are the gains?

chapter 15

Off Course, On Course

MARK 6:45-56
Jesus walks on the Water
(Matt 14:22-33; Jn 6:15-21)

At once Jesus made his disciples get into the boat and go ahead of him to Bethsaida, on the other side of the lake, while he sent the crowd away. After saying goodbye to the people he went away to a hill to pray. When evening came, the boat was in the middle of the lake, while Jesus was alone on land. He saw that his disciples were straining at the oars, because they were rowing against the wind; so sometime between three and six o'clock in the morning he came to them, walking on the water. He was going to pass them by, but they saw him walking on the water. 'It's a ghost!' they thought, and screamed. They were all terrified when they saw him.

Jesus spoke to them at once, 'Courage!' he said. 'It is I. Don't be afraid!' Then he got into the boat with them, and the wind died down. The disciples were completely amazed, because they had not understood the real meaning of the feeding of the 5,000; their minds could not grasp it.

They crossed the lake and came to land at Gennesaret, where they tied up the boat. As they left the boat, people recognised Jesus at once. So they ran throughout the whole region; and wherever they heard he was, they brought to him sick people lying on mats. And everywhere Jesus went, to villages, towns, or farms, people would take those who were ill to the market places and beg him to let them at least touch the edge of his cloak; and all who touched it were made well.

AGAINST THE WIND

The journey is resumed. Mark here narrates the second crossing of the lake in some detail. (6:45-52) This time there is no raging storm, rather a persistent head wind which frustrates their intended landfall. Instead of arriving at Bethsaida they end up off course at Gennesaret.

The symbolism at work here is important. For Mark, storms and sea spell danger. The sea crossing itself stands for the journey of faith and this occasion again illustrates the intensity of that journey. Here Mark stresses how easy it is to be side-tracked from our destination by the counter-winds with which we have to struggle. It is so easy to become lost and faithless when we forget the light we have been given, the signs and wonders we have seen. This is the clear meaning of 6:51 and 52. 'The disciples were completely amazed, because they had not understood the real meaning of the feeding of the five thousand.'

UNEARTHLY POWER

Two other points are worthy of brief notice. In the strange incident when Jesus comes across the water towards the disciples' boat and the gospel says 'he was about to pass them by' (6:48), we should not think that he did not notice them or was indifferent to their plight. Once more Mark is alluding to the Old Testament. The reference here is to the way the Old Testament describes the signs of God's presence, notably in the story of Moses (Exodus 33:19-23; 34:6) and in the story of Elijah in the cave (1 Kings 19:11). In both cases God the Saviour appears as the one who passes by; yet whose tangential, hidden presence is enough for his servant.

There is another echo from the Old Testament. Jesus says to the disciples, 'Don't be afraid, it is I'. The translation, 'It is I', could equally well be rendered, 'I am'. The Greek is '*egw eimi*' and both translations are possible. 'I am' reminds us of the great 'I am' sayings of Jesus in John's gospel; 'I am ... the bread of life' (Jn 6:35), '...the light of the world' (Jn

8:12), '...the door' (Jn 10:9), '...the good shepherd' (Jn 10:11), '...the resurrection and the life' (Jn 11:25), '...the true and living way' (Jn 14:6), '...the true vine' (Jn 15:1). Moreover, 'I am' is the self-revealing name of God offered to Moses in their encounter before the burning bush in Exodus 3. 'Who are you?' asks Moses, 'Living and hidden one, tell me your name'. The mystery answers, 'I am that I am' (Ex 3:14). Here is an allusion to Jesus' divine nature and origin, to the truth enshrined in all the gospels that, in meeting Jesus, we meet none other than the living God. These two points together give strong intimations of divinity. Joel Marcus comments,

> When Jesus quells the power of the sea, strides in triumph over the waves, and announces his presence to the disciples with the sovereign self-identification formula 'I am he' (4:35-41, 6:45-52), he is speaking and acting out the language of the Old Testament divine warrior *theophanies* (self-disclosures), narratives in which Yahweh himself subdues the demonic forces of chaos in a saving, cosmos-creating act of holy war.
> (Marcus 1992, p.144-5)

POLES APART

One strong impression which comes from this story of the disciples at sea is that of the space between Jesus and the disciples. Three references are made to physical distance: Jesus orders the disciples to go on ahead of him while he dismisses the crowd; he leaves them to go apart to pray; and Mark comments that the boat was far out at sea while Jesus was alone on land. In addition, Jesus leaves the disciples to their own devices until the fourth watch of the night, i.e. early morning just before dawn, the darkest hour.

The physical space also emphasises the chasm between Jesus and the disciples in terms of faith. There is scarcely a more graphic picture anywhere in the gospels. What a contrast there is between the sure and complete confidence of Jesus' approach over the water and the disciples' timidity within the safe confines of their boat! Mark is clear about the reason for the disciples' fear. They do not 'know' the one in whose company they have been travelling; they have not understood what they have seen and heard (6:52). In particular, they did not understand the real significance of the feeding of the five thousand - that they were standing in the presence of the Messiah. They do not recognise that they have together witnessed an unfolding of the signs and wonders of God. In the story of the first lake crossing, Jesus has to be wakened to deal with the disciples' fears (4:35-41), here he is diverted. Twice on the stormy voyage of discipleship, Jesus has to intervene as his followers' faith gives way to doubt and fear.

BELIEVING NOW

Think for a moment of the context - not of the original event, but of the writing down of this story. Mark is writing for a community of believers who share a common experience with us, in contrast to the original disciples. Neither the original readers of the gospel nor any subsequent readers know the flesh and blood Jesus of Nazareth. We and they have not seen, heard, shared, touched Jesus directly. There is a space between us. How do we come to faith, how do we continue in faith? How do we become those 'blessed' who have not seen and yet have believed? Mark is saying here through this story, and Jesus is saying, through Mark, that faith is possible without his actual physical presence. 'You can have faith, you must, you will. Just remember what you have seen and known, just trust the witnesses. You can do it without my physical presence. I send you out to live in the eye of the storm, to battle against the head winds. Don't be frightened. Don't ever think that you are on your own. Have faith. Remember, "I AM".'

At the end of this second story of sea and faith, we acknowledge that our experience of the sea of faith is not so much of stormy waters as of a receding tide in a society living under the pressure of relentless secularism. In a different context we, on our faith journey, can share the disciples' experience of being alone, abandoned and in the dark. R S Thomas' poem, 'The Moon in Lleyn', with its Celtic consciousness of Christ, hidden yet alive in creation, offers us courage for our uncertain times.

> *The Moon in Lleyn*
> The last quarter of the moon
> of Jesus gives way
> to the dark; the serpent
> digests the egg. Here
> on my knees in this stone
> church, that is full only
> of the silent congregation
> of shadows and the sea's
> sound, it is easy to believe
> that Yeats was right. Just as though
> choirs had not sung, shells
> have swallowed them; the tide laps
> at the Bible; the bell fetches
> no people to the brittle miracle
> of the bread. The sand is waiting
> for the running back of the grains
> in the wall into its blond
> glass. Religion is over, and
> what will emerge from the body

of the new moon, no one
can say.
But a voice sounds
in my ear: Why so fast,
mortal? These very seas
are baptised. The parish
has a saint's name time cannot
unfrock. In cities that
have outgrown their promise people
are becoming pilgrims
again, if not to this place,
then to the recreation of it
in their own spirit. You must remain
kneeling. Even as the moon
making its way through the earth's
cumbersome shadow, prayer, too,
has its phases.
(Thomas 1993, p. 282)

STUDY

BY YOURSELF

I grasp thy strength, make it my own,
My heart with peace is blest;
I lose my hold, and then comes down
Darkness, and cold unrest.
Let me no more my comfort draw
From my frail hold of thee,
In this alone rejoice with awe -
Thy mighty grasp of me.
(John Campbell Shairp, *CH3* 675)

- Think of a time when you felt 'all at sea'. Recall the circumstances. Were you aware of the presence of God - at the time, later? What difference does it make to follow the hymn writer's advice and 'rejoice in God's grasp of me'? Picture yourself held in God's hands, and give thanks.
- Read R S Thomas' poem, 'The Moon in Lleyn' several times, underlining key words and phrases. Is the poem optimistic or pessimistic about faith? Do you share the poet's perception?

chapter 16

Breaking the Bonds

MARK 7:1-23

The Teaching of the Ancestors
(Matt 15:1-9)

Some Pharisees and teachers of the Law who had come from Jerusalem gathered round Jesus. They noticed that some of his disciples were eating their food with hands that were ritually unclean - that is, they had not washed them in the way the Pharisees said people should.

(For the Pharisees, as well as the rest of the Jews, follow the teaching they received from their ancestors: they do not eat unless they wash their hands in the proper way; nor do they eat anything that comes from the market unless they wash it first. And they follow many other rules which they have received, such as the proper way to wash cups, pots, copper bowls, and beds.)

So the Pharisees and the teachers of the Law asked Jesus, 'Why is it that your disciples do not follow the teaching handed down by our ancestors, but instead eat with ritually unclean hands?'

Jesus answered them, 'How right Isaiah was when he prophesied about you! You are hypocrites, just as he wrote:

"These people, says God, honour me with their words, but their heart is really far away from me.

It is no use for them to worship me, because they teach human rules as though they were God's laws!"

You put aside God's command and obey human teachings.'

And Jesus continued, 'You have a clever way of rejecting God's law in order to uphold your own teaching. For Moses commanded, "Respect your father and your mother," and, "Whoever curses his father or his mother is to be put to death". But you teach that if a person has something he could use to help his father or mother, but says, "This is Corban" (which means, it belongs to God), he is excused from helping his father or mother. In this way the teaching you pass on to others cancels out the word of God. And there are many other things like this that you do.'

Things that make a Person Unclean
(Matt 15:10-20)

Then Jesus called the crowd to him once more and said to them, 'Listen to me, all of you, and understand. There is nothing that goes into a person from the outside which can make him ritually unclean. Rather, it is what comes out of a person that make him unclean'.

When he left the crowd and went into the house, his disciples asked him to explain this saying. 'You are no more intelligent than the others,' Jesus said to them. 'Don't you understand? Nothing that goes into a person from the outside can really make him unclean, because it does not go into his heart but into his stomach and then goes out of the body.' (In saying this, Jesus declared that all foods are fit to be eaten.)

And he went on to say, 'It is what comes out of a person that makes him unclean. For from the inside, from a person's heart, come the evil ideas which lead him to do immoral things, to rob, kill, commit adultery, be greedy, and do all sorts of evil things; deceit, indecency, jealousy, slander, pride, and folly - all these evil things come from inside a person and make him unclean'.

A PERSONAL CONFESSION

'My sins and faults of youth, do Thou, O Lord, forget.' says the hymn. We all remember incidents from our gauche young days which make us squirm. As an angry young divinity student, child of the revolting sixties, I once preached to a sleepy, midsummer seaside congregation. My text was from Mark 7:9 in the full might and majesty of the Authorised Version, 'Full well ye reject the commandment of God, that ye may keep your own tradition'. I am sure I addressed the congregation with impertinence, upbraiding the people for the 'sins' of conventionality and complacency and visiting on them my own ecclesiastical frustrations and prejudices. I wasn't asked back; I hope I now know when to bite my tongue!

DISABLING AND EXCLUDING TRADITION

And then I read again Mark's gospel, and from this passage before us, I wonder. Maybe my original instinct was not as bad as my performance? Here is Jesus, spoiling for a fight again. And yet again the fight is with the Pharisees, the issue is the Purity Code and the rules for table fellowship. Once more, the contrast is between an exclusive fellowship and a truly open community.

The story begins with the disciples' dirty hands (7:1 -5).They had been eating not merely 'food', as the GNB translates, but 'bread', as stated in the original Greek. Having lately come from the feeding of the five thousand, we remember the centrality of bread in the gospel. The disciples' dirty hands have nothing to do with hygiene but relate rather to the elaborate religious Code of ritual purification before eating. The Pharisees had built up this Code from instructions in the books of the Law. It had now become so demanding that ordinary poor folk, the people of the land, could not possibly keep it. They were therefore looked down on by the Pharisees and excluded, dismissed as careless in their religious practice and responsible for their own damnation. This is a well-used exclusion technique. The sequence is, first make so many demands that many people, especially the poor, cannot begin to meet them all, then when they fail to do so, blame them for their own folly and inadequacy.

It's an old and a continuing song. Donald C Smith in his book, *Passive Obedience and Prophetic Criticism: Social Criticism in the Scottish Church 1830-1945* tells of the nineteenth-century Scottish church's failure to produce any social ethic fit to cope with the situation created by the Industrial Revolution. So often the main response of the church to the urban underclasses created by that Revolution was to blame, disenfranchise and alienate them. We still reap that harvest. While there has been real improvement in our understanding of the relation of the gospel to society and in particular the gospel as good news to the poor, our church structures often fail to reflect our understanding. There is still no adequate strategy for confronting urban poverty, no real bias of resources, human and financial, towards the poor. Indeed, within the Church of Scotland, congregations struggling against great odds in urban priority areas are still assessed by the same criteria as their more affluent suburban neighbours. All too often, the lifestyle of these neighbours sets the norm - an inappropriate norm which is a denial of their own costly witness and service and inhibiting to the exercise of their gifts, insights and creativity.

Returning to the text, the protests of the Pharisees rouse Jesus to anger. 'Why,' they say, 'do your followers not keep the traditions of our ancestors?' (7:5) The Pharisees had two sources of tradition, the written Hebrew scriptures and the extensive oral traditions, the *Halakah*, which elaborated upon the scriptures. Jesus dismisses these oral traditions as sophistry, mere human-made rules. He gets quickly to the central theme of his teaching here, that outward observance is not primary. What matters is the heart, the devotion, the motivation within. 'This people honours me with their words, but their heart is far from me.' (Isaiah 29:13, quoted in Mark 7:6)

A QUESTION OF WILLS

Jesus then moves the discussion away from ritual eating. An explanation is necessary for the word *corban* in verse 11. *Corban* was a vow which a person could make, willing or consecrating their property and resources to the Temple. Having made this vow, no one could use the property and resource for any other purpose. This could mean in practice that someone who had made the vow of *Corban* would be unable to use their resources to help aged and dependent parents. The religious obligation they had undertaken could operate in an inhumane way by impoverishing elderly parents. The result would be in direct contradiction to the commandment, 'Honour your father and your mother'. Jewish society in the time of Jesus, like other ancient societies, was built on bonds of mutual obligation between husband and wife, parent and child, brother and sister. Here is an instance of religion obstructing the operation of a just society, of proper mutual obligation and caring. Jesus says that it is nonsense to claim to give to God directly what should be rendered to the Lord through the discharge of familial and societal obligations. True religion involves true humanism; the touchstone of any religious practice remains its humanity.

This whole incident was provoked by the Pharisees. Jesus has dismissed their elaborate oral teaching which discriminated against the poor. Now, by raising the issue of the vow of *Corban*, he has included the Jerusalem Scribes and the Temple itself in his attack. Very close to the end, Jesus will return to attack the Temple and the way it was used to exploit the poor and the old. The final attack will be launched, not from the safe distance of provincial Galilee, but from within Jerusalem, at the temple courts themselves.

TRUE RELIGION

We come to the last piece of teaching in this passage. Publicly to the crowd and privately to the disciples, Jesus makes it quite clear that it is not what goes in that makes a person unclean but rather what comes out. Neither dirty hands nor food from the banned list make any difference, the difference comes from the law of the heart, the fruits of a person's living. We would certainly agree, nothing seems more obvious to us. However, it is so obvious to us because we belong to a society and a culture which has been steeped for centuries in the teachings of the prophets and the words of Jesus. These combine to attack mere outward observance, to stress the inner springs of faith and obedience. They have combined so effectively that we can easily forget that Jesus brought revolution with his frontal attack on a religion of multifarious rules and manifold observances, interpreted and enforced by an elite.

Jesus came to abolish such a way of religion. In that sense it's true as it has been said, that Jesus came to destroy religion. He attacks with vigour any view of religion as either a set of rigid rules or an exclusive club for those who could afford the membership. The demands of faith and love and the obligation to God and neighbour are all that is important. The way to God is now open for the poor of Israel and, particularly important for us, the whole Gentile world.

The danger of misinterpreting these words of Jesus with their stress on the heart and our inner motivation is that we lapse into a religion of mere inwardness, piety for its own sake. It is good to remember how the reading ends, with its list of what can come out of the heart to degrade and defile our lives (7:21-23). It is no mere list of inner vices. It contains not only lust, but murder, greed and dishonesty, which pollute the market place and the body politic as well as our own homes and our own souls. This was ever the teaching of the prophets and the way of Jesus, for he is not only the light of our life, the inner light, but the light of all the world.

STUDY

BY YOURSELF

There is a difference between Jesus being lovingly critical of some of the practices of his own faith from within and a quick and smug dismissal of Jewish practice from outside. We need to be wary of unconscious anti-Semitism here. Was Jesus attacking the Jewish Purity Codes themselves, or the way in which some religious leaders observed them?

Sometimes Christians can be dismissive of the formal practice of religion, but another way to look at this is to see that regular attendance at worship or a daily prayer discipline can provide the framework underlying 'true religion'. One definition of *praxis*, a word very like our English word 'practice' and a term much used by liberation theologians, is 'action undertaken with reflection'. This offers a balance between inner motivation and the outward actions of our lives.

FOR GROUP WORK

We believe that the church is always in need of reform and renewal. Share together what you think needs to be changed today to make the church true to its calling and relevant to our times. Begin with the local. And be bold!

chapter 17

Real Mission

MARK 7:24-37
A Woman's Faith
(Matt 15:21-28)

Then Jesus left and went away to the territory near the city of Tyre. He went into a house and did not want anyone to know he was there, but he could not stay hidden. A woman, whose daughter had an evil spirit in her, heard about Jesus and came to him at once and fell at his feet. The woman was a Gentile, born in the region of Phoenicia in Syria. She begged Jesus to drive the demon out of her daughter. But Jesus answered, 'Let us first feed the children. It isn't right to take the children's food and throw it to the dogs.'

'Sir,' she answered, 'even the dogs under the table eat the children's leftovers!'

So Jesus said to her, 'Because of that answer, go back home, where you will find that the demon has gone out of your daughter!'

She went home and found her child lying on the bed; the demon had indeed gone out of her.

Jesus then left the neighbourhood of Tyre and went on through Sidon to Lake Galilee, going by way of the territory of the Ten Towns. Some people brought him a man who was deaf and could hardly speak, and they begged Jesus to place his hands on him. So Jesus took him off alone, away from the crowd, put his fingers in the man's ears, spat, and touched the man's tongue. Then Jesus looked up to heaven, gave a deep groan, and said to the man, '*Ephphatha*,' which means, 'Open up!'

At once the man was able to hear, his speech impediment was removed, and he began to talk without any trouble. Then Jesus ordered the people not to speak of it to anyone; but the more he ordered them not to, the more they spoke. And all who heard were completely amazed. 'How well he does everything!' they exclaimed. 'He even causes the deaf to hear and the dumb to speak!'

EVANGELISM AND MISSION

The run-up to the Millennium was designated by many mainstream churches as the 'Decade of Evangelism'. The call went out to engage in serious thought together about how we should make the gospel known in the world. 'Evangelism' is a word with which we are all familiar, although how to 'evangelise' in our increasingly secular world still raises as many questions as answers. 'Evangel' is the same word as 'Gospel'; both mean 'the Good News' of the coming into our world of Jesus Christ, Son of Mary, Son of God, our Saviour, Redeemer, Liberator.

Another word which belongs beside the word 'evangelism' is 'mission'. Mission means 'to be sent out'. It describes how the good news is made known in the world. Mission always begins with God, with the sending of his Son. It continues with the way Jesus sent out his disciples to be apostles, literally 'the sent out', during his earthly ministry. It becomes the task given to the apostles by the risen Christ when he says, 'Go out and teach all peoples, make all nations my disciples' (Matt 28:19). The apostolic task is passed down to us through the living community of faith, as the disciples of Jesus, now. Whatever we may think of particular forms of evangelism (there is room for a number of different, yet sincerely held, opinions), of the common task and obligation of mission there is no doubt. A church that is not missionary is not a church, in the New Testament sense of the word. A church that is not outward looking, out-going, outwardly directed in its thinking and action cuts itself off from the Lord of its own life. 'The church exists for mission as fire exists for burning.' The words of this well-known saying should be written on all our hearts.

So the question remains, 'How are we to be a missionary people, how are we to think, look and move outwards?' It is a question which is easier asked than answered. We are always in danger of settling for answers which are too quick, glib or narrow. If we settle for less, we trivialise the depths of the Good News, the gospel itself. The clues to the uncovering of the answer are to be found in the gospel itself. If we want to understand *our* mission, we begin with the mission of Jesus himself.

ON THE MARGINS

The two stories before us, the story of a woman with her possessed daughter and the story of a deaf and dumb man point to mission in Jesus' way. The obvious link is that they are both healing stories; the hidden link is the setting. Once again, the geography is significant. The setting is again the borderlands, the margins of the holy land and people. The first story takes place in Tyre, in present-day Lebanon. It is outside Israel, in Gentile territory. The second setting is near Decapolis on the fringes of Galilee, also outside Israel. Mark's narrative builds up as he shows over and over again that Jesus' own mission, his own journey, moves outward from the secure heartland of Israel, territory of established belief and practice and of pious, conventional respectability. He has to move beyond these boundaries which - as ways of thinking and as social forces - hinder and obstruct the fullness of God's mission. Again and again the 'Son of Man', 'the Human One' is to be found on the margins with the unacceptable, the untouchable. That is where the passion and the logic of mission leads and is why true mission is an outgoing, risky, costly business.

THE WOMAN WHO ANSWERED BACK

We move to our first story, Jesus' encounter with the Syro-Phoenician woman. As a woman and a Gentile she is doubly an outsider, a non-person. By all accepted standards she should not dare to speak to Jesus and Jesus should have nothing to do with her. It's quite an encounter they share. On the surface. their brief conversation is pretty awful. Here are the bare bones of it. The woman comes up to Jesus and asks him to heal her daughter. Jesus replies, 'We've got to feed the children first, it isn't right to take the children's food and give it to the dogs' (7:27). The children are the people of Israel, the dogs are the Gentiles, the outsiders. In Semitic society the dog was regarded as about the lowest form of animal life. Jesus' answer seems harsh, brutal, insulting, off-putting.

Quick as a flash, however, the woman comes back at him. 'Sir,' she says, 'even the dogs get the crumbs from the children's table'. Jesus says, 'Well said, because of your answer your daughter is well, go back home and see for yourself' (7:28-30).

Three points are worthy of consideration here. First, what is reported to us is only part of a larger conversation, as so often in the gospels. Through the demands of space Mark pares down the story. We are given a couple of key sentences out of a larger dialogue. Such condensed reportage is every reporter's stock in trade.

The second point is more important. It concerns the way we read our Bibles. Because of the seriousness of its subject matter, the habit lingers of reading the Bible with awful solemnity. Often, too, we are lazy or timid in using our imagination to try to feel, sense and visualise the living situation.

A LITTLE HUMOUR

If we have a little imagination, more so if we have a little humour, this story leaps to life. Imagine that the conversation between Jesus and the woman takes place with a glimmer in the eye of each person. The story is transformed! We all know people who excel at the art of the (usually) good-natured insult. Insults depend on facial expressions and tones of voice. We often trade our best jibes with those we know and love. In travelling to Tyre, Jesus had already put himself in a place where he was not meant to be. His words about the children and the dogs can be read as heavy with irony since he has already left the safety of the children to visit the land of the dogs. He has 'gone to the dogs'. It's not hard to imagine him relishing the woman's quick riposte, heavy both with humour and also real faith in Jesus. This interpretation would certainly be consistent with the picture of Jesus which Mark has been drawing up to this point in the gospel.

EDUCATING JESUS

There is another equally tantalising reading which I heard first from Bishop Richard Holloway at a University Mission in Glasgow. He raised the possibility that the woman here is an agent of Jesus' evangelisation, that she teaches him to 'see' a truth he had not known before. Her response to him in her quickness, need and anger makes him look at her with fresh eyes which 'see' her humanity and her claim on him, beyond the barriers of race, religion and gender. This incident would then be a turning, growing point in Jesus' own understanding and in his mission. It is a timely reminder that mission is as much about listening and learning as doing and speaking. John Taylor writes:

> I think it is possible to detect ... annunciation experiences in the gospels which were decisive turning points in Jesus' understanding of his own mission. Such was his encounter with the pagan woman of Syro-Phoenicia. When first she accosted him he believed that his vocation was strictly limited to the house of Israel; but in her gay, irrepressible importunity he saw a faith that outshone that of his own people, and his vision was enlarged.
> (Taylor 1972, p.92)

However we decide to interpret Jesus' decision to heal the woman's daughter, the bottom line of the story is that the girl was healed. Remember, we have just come from a passage where Jesus has been arguing for the importance of a clean heart rather than a ritually pure diet. If what matters is not what goes in, then ethnicity needs to be reconsidered. We can leave this story, rejoicing, as Jesus rejoiced, at the quickness of the woman's ready answer and the surprising measure of her faith. We can rejoice as she rejoiced that this stranger has made her daughter whole and well again. We are left with the picture of this woman and her daughter, doubly outsiders as females and foreigners, being touched and healed by the mission of Jesus. Once again he has upset the apple cart of accepted social relationships, he has broken the bounds.

TAKING THE PATIENT SERIOUSLY

The second story is of the healing of the deaf and dumb man, brought by his friends to Jesus. The way Jesus deals with this man is worth looking at very closely. Jesus' first action is to take the man away from everybody else, to extract him from the company (7:33). Is that significant? It would be if we were deaf. People with hearing difficulties find it particularly hard to communicate in a crowd. Jesus begins by recognising this man's real situation and responding appropriately to his needs. He takes him away from the babble of the crowd to give him a chance to concentrate and hear.

Jesus' next actions are to put his fingers in the man's ears, to spit and touch his tongue. Here Jesus uses the most visceral of sign language to communicate with the man what he is going to do next in ministering to him. Then he looked up to heaven, gave a deep sigh and said, (not to heaven, but directly to the man), '*Ephphatha*' which means, 'Open up!' Very occasionally the gospels give us the actual Aramaic words which Jesus spoke rather than simply their Greek translation. If the word is given in the original language, it is because the word itself has considerable significance. This is the case here. To catch the significance try saying the word aloud, attempt to get your tongue round it, '*E-PH-PHA-THA*' Its very difficulty in pronunciation makes the word a gift for lip reading. The English translation, 'Be opened' offers little; '*E-ph-pha-tha*' is just perfect. The pronunciation is all lips, tongue and teeth.

It is easy to think that the healings of Jesus are all much the same and that their main characteristic is an overpowering 'supernaturalism' in which a quick word or touch from the master is more than enough. A careful reading of the gospel makes plain that this is simply is not so. An important characteristic of Jesus' healings as described in the gospel is their diversity. Jesus takes each person's situation on its merits. That is made very clear here. Mark shows Jesus entering imaginatively, carefully, pastorally into the deaf man's situation. He shows him by touch and sign what he is going to do. Side by side with the spiritual is the tangible, the sacramental. Through Jesus' clear demonstration of his intent, the man is enabled to be fully present and involved in his own healing.

'OPEN UP!'

Then Jesus speaks the precise, necessary word, '*Ephphatha*', 'Be opened'. He attacks the man's closedness, his shut in-ness. The man hears and because he can hear, he can speak.

The people go away in amazement saying, 'He has done all things well, he makes the deaf hear and the dumb speak.' It seems the man was dumb because of his deafness, as is often the case. He was not dumb because of a disability in his speech organs, he spoke badly because he could not hear. Mark describes his speech impediment with a rare Greek word, *mogilalos*, meaning 'a stammerer, one with unclear speech'. The word appears in one other place in the Greek Old Testament, in Isaiah 35:6, 'Those who cannot speak will shout for joy.' Here is the extended passage telling of the healing and liberating effects of the Messiah's coming.

> Give strength to hands that are tired
> and to knees that tremble with weakness.
> Tell everyone who is discouraged, 'Be strong and don't be afraid,
> God is coming to our rescue,
> coming to punish your enemies.'
> The blind will be able to see and the deaf hear,
> The lame will leap and dance,
> and those who cannot speak will shout for joy.
> (Isaiah 35:3-6)

PART OF GOD'S MISSION NOW

The pertinent question for us now is, 'Where are we in this story? Where are we who as the church of Jesus Christ are responsible for the continuance of his "mission" in today's world?' There are four identifications for us to make. First, the deaf man came to Jesus only because some people brought him. He came to Jesus as a result of their love and concern and care. Part of our mission is to be a caring community. In our caring itself we can bring people to Jesus.

Next, the church is the body of Christ. We are his action in the world. We are therefore called to work as Jesus worked. This involves being prepared to go out to the margins, beyond the safe limits: that is where Jesus is found with this deaf man. It also means learning to speak appropriate language, language which connects, not remaining content with the predictable, tired, religious language which is manifestly failing to make connections today. It means using a language which encourages folk to open out and stay open, as a sign of their wholeness. Perhaps here there is a tangential warning of the hidden danger of a 'big' church, where too many confident and articulate people may inhibit rather than enable the stammerer's tongue. In a big church it can be too easy to become like the deaf man in the crowd; people remain closed up rather than receiving the invitation and encouragement to 'be open'. How do we become aware of those who need extra help and how do we ensure that they get it ?

As the church, we can also identify readily with the deaf man, since we too need help as we hope and wait for change. We know that we are not whole; we constantly need to be open to hear Jesus' word, to be receiving his touch, to be aware of his sacramental power.

Out of an awareness of our deafness, our continuing prayer is to be open to receive his word, his truth, his life. Elsewhere in the gospels it is clear that Jesus' hardest words were spoken to those who used their religion to keep them deaf to the demands of God and their neighbour. If there is anything in us and in our understanding of our faith which encourages us to judge and condemn, we need to ask if in our hearts and minds we are truly open to the Human One we claim to serve and follow.

In this story we can also identify with the crowd, who marvelled and were amazed. They saw what Jesus did and praised him as the chosen one of God. Today we are the ones who see, recognise and celebrate his continuing creativity in the world, and thus proclaim the way he brings God's love and justice to birth among us. In this one story there is a rich web of insights into the work of mission today. The church is sent out to the frontiers, as a community of care, prepared to meet people where they are and to discern their true situation and their needs. To do that we need to work and pray to be ever open to the word of life, in order to witness to that living word, alive in us and in our world now.

STUDY

BY YOURSELF
Read over the passage (Mark 7:24-37) several times. Which character are you more drawn to - the Syro-Phoenician woman or the deaf man? Imagine yourself in the situation. Now, imagine yourself in their situation. What do you notice? How do you feel? Imagine that you continue in conversation with Jesus beyond the brief incident recorded here. What do you want to say to Jesus? What does he say to you?

FOR GROUP WORK
This takes the form of an exercise in listening. In both these incidents, Jesus listens. Listening carefully is fundamental to good communication and taking other people seriously.
- Ask each person in the group individually to identify an issue he/she feels strongly about. It does not need to be particularly 'serious', but must be firmly held. Then, working in pairs , present to the partner the issue each has chosen.
- Each person makes the presentation twice. In the first instance, the listener should be thoroughly difficult; appear bored, try to interrupt or persuade of a different viewpoint as much as possible. The second time the listener should listen as carefully as possible, without interruption, asking for clarification if necessary and reflecting back what has been said.
- Although this is an artificial situation, now share how the speaker felt in each instance?
- How does your experience of being listened to/not listened to relate to your experience of evangelism as you have known it?
- What might evangelism that listens be like?

chapter 18

Feeding More People

MARK 8:1-10

Jesus feeds four thousand People

(Matt 15:32 -39)

Not long afterwards another large crowd came together. When the people had nothing left to eat, Jesus called the disciples to him and said, 'I feel sorry for these people, because they have been with me for three days and now have nothing to eat. If I send them home without feeding them, they will faint as they go, because some of them have come a long way.'

His disciples asked him, 'Where in this desert can anyone find enough food to feed all these people?'

'How much bread have you got?' Jesus asked.

'Seven loaves,' they answered.

He ordered the crowd to sit down on the ground. Then he took the seven loaves, gave thanks to God, broke them, and gave them to his disciples to distribute to the crowd; and the disciples did so. They also had a few small fish. Jesus gave thanks for these and told the disciples to distribute them too. Everybody ate and had enough - there were about four thousand people. Then the disciples took up seven baskets full of pieces left over. Jesus sent the people away and at once got into a boat with his disciples and went to the district of Dalmanutha.

THE GENTILE FEEDING

Once again, geography is of central importance to this story. Here we come to the second of the two desert feedings. We have discussed what this feeding of the four thousand has in common with the feeding of the five thousand earlier, in Chapter 14. Now we look briefly at what is distinct, its location.

The feeding of the five thousand took place within the borders of Israel, among Jesus' own people. The feeding of the four thousand sees Jesus moving out beyond the confines of his own people. This feeding takes place among the Gentiles, the foreigners. Their need is just as great, and the promise is that they too will have a place at the Messianic feast. Once again the door opens wider. The message is reinforced. The gospel breaks down all those old tribal barriers and boundaries of kith and kin. At the frontiers, beyond the pale, there also all who come will have their despair and hunger overcome as they eat the bread of abundance, freely distributed.

STUDY

BY YOURSELF
A Prayer
Loving God, take our hands,
take our lives,
ordinary as wheat or oatmeal,
daily as bread-
our stumbling generosity,
our simple actions,
and find them good enough
to help prepare the feast
for all your people.
(Christian Aid)

The scale of world problems is overwhelming. Is there any reassurance in this prayer from Christian Aid? Are you prompted to any action?

chapter 19

Through a Glass Darkly, Beginning to See

MARK 8:11-9:1

The Pharisees ask for a Miracle
(Matt 12:38-42, 16:1-4)

Some Pharisees came to Jesus and started to argue with him. They wanted to trap him, so they asked him to perform a miracle to show that God approved of him. But Jesus gave a deep groan and said, 'Why do the people of this day ask for a miracle? No, I tell you! No such proof will be given to these people!'

He left them, got back into the boat, and started across to the other side of the lake.

The Yeast of the Pharisees and of Herod
(Matt 16:5-12)

The disciples had forgotten to bring enough bread and had only one loaf with them in the boat. 'Take care,' said Jesus, 'and be on your guard against the yeast of the Pharisees and the yeast of Herod.'

They started discussing among themselves: 'He says this because we haven't any bread.'

Jesus knew what they were saying, so he asked them, 'Why are you discussing about not having any bread? Don't you know or understand yet? Are your minds so dull? You have eyes - can't you see? You have ears - can't you hear? Don't you remember when I broke the five loaves for the five thousand people? How many baskets full of leftover pieces did you take up?'

'Twelve,' they answered.

'And when I broke the seven loaves for the four thousand people,' asked Jesus, 'how many baskets full of leftover pieces did you take up?'

'Seven,' they answered.

'And you still don't understand?' he asked them.

Jesus heals a Blind Man at Bethsaida
(8:22-26)

They came to Bethsaida, where some people brought a blind man to Jesus and begged him to touch him. Jesus took the blind man by the hand and led him out of the village. After spitting on the man's eyes, Jesus placed his hands on him and asked him, 'Can you see anything?'

The man looked up and said, 'Yes, I can see people, but they look like trees walking about.'

Jesus again placed his hands on the man's eyes. This time the man looked intently, his eyesight returned, and he saw everything clearly. Jesus then sent him home with the order, 'Don't go back into the village.'

Peter's Declaration about Jesus
(Matt 16:13-20; Lk 9:8-21)

Then Jesus and his disciples went away to the villages near Caesarea Philippi. On the way he asked them, 'Tell me, who do people say I am?'

'Some say that you are John the Baptist,' they answered, 'others say that you are Elijah, while others say that you are one of the prophets.'

'What about you?' he asked them. 'Who do you say I am?'

Peter answered, 'You are the Messiah.'

Then Jesus ordered them, 'Do not tell anyone about me.'

Jesus speaks about his Suffering and Death
(Matt 16. 21 -28; Lk 9. 22 -27)

Then Jesus began to teach his disciples: 'The Son of Man must suffer much and be rejected by the elders, the chief priests, and the teachers of the Law. He will be put to death, but three days later he will rise to life.' He made this very clear to them. So Peter took him aside and began to rebuke him. But Jesus turned round, looked at his disciples, and rebuked Peter. 'Get away from me, Satan,' he said. 'Your thoughts don't come from God, but from human nature!'

Then Jesus called the crowd and his disciples to him. 'If anyone wants to come with me,' he told them, 'he must forget self, carry his cross, and follow me. For whoever wants to save his own life will lose it; but whoever loses his life for me and for the gospel will save it. Do people gain anything if they win the whole world but loses their life? Of course not! There is nothing they can give to regain their life. If a person is ashamed of me and of my teaching in this godless and wicked day, then the Son of Man will be ashamed of him when he comes in the glory of his Father with the holy angels.'

And he went on to say, 'I tell you, there are some here who will not die until they have seen the Kingdom of God come with power.'

THREE STORIES OF BLINDNESS

From the theme of deafness, we move to that of blindness. Through these themes Mark presents Jesus as the one who lets the deaf hear and opens the eyes of the blind. Promises that this would happen with the coming of the Messiah had been given in the Old Testament (Isaiah 35). The themes are also interpreted symbolically as well as physically. The connection between blindness and sight and their relation to faith runs like a binding thread through this part of the gospel and beyond.

Verses 11 to 26 tell three stories of blindness, but it is only in the last story that sight is actually given. First, the Pharisees come looking for a sign, a wonder, 'Jesus, do us a miracle and show us God approves of you'. Jesus groans. 'Show us your bag of tricks, Jesus, be the magician' ... surely they are not asking for that again? (8:11-13) Unlike other gospel writers, Mark deflects attention from Jesus the wonder worker. He says that you either believe by what you already see, or you come to believe through what you will see - in the ultimate sign and wonder which is the cross. That is *the* sign from heaven, other signs are sought only by unbelievers, however pious their outward appearance.

It is no great surprise to find that the Pharisees, Jesus' chief opponents, are blind to who he is. However, the crisis deepens as Mark turns our attention to the blindness of the disciples. Here they are, on their final boat journey across the lake, and again, the theme of their conversation is bread. Jesus bids them beware of the leaven of the Pharisees and the followers of Herod, that unlikely coalition of opposites who have been reported (much earlier in the gospel) as plotting to kill Jesus (3:6). He then turns on the disciples' complaints that they have not enough bread.

Remember where they have come from. They have just witnessed a second amazing feeding and they are on the last of many journeys across the lake, in the course of which they have been led to make connections between Jew and Gentile. All their recent experience has been of being with Jesus, learning and discovering the fullness of his mission. They have seen Jesus building a new community which brings insider and outsider together, with room for the poor, the sick, the hungry, the unclean, the alien. Still they do not understand.

'Are your minds so dull; why don't you use your ears, why don't you use your eyes?' (8:17-21) Minds, ears and eyes; a deliberate echo of Moses' words to the children of Israel in the wilderness after their deliverance from Egypt. Moses complains about their inability to see what God has done in rescuing them from Pharoah and in walking with them and providing for them in the desert (Exodus 16,17). The disciples' most recent and vivid experience has been of receiving bread, food in the wilderness, as part of their continuing pilgrimage with Jesus, who complains, 'Have you forgotten so quickly, are you so blind?'

Jesus is saying to them. 'Are you so blind to the meaning of this abundance of bread, sign of the Messiah's coming? Are your minds closed to the symbolic meaning of the five loaves and the twelve baskets, representing the community of Israel, and the seven loaves and the seven baskets, standing for the world of the Gentiles? Do you not understand that now one loaf is all that you need since, through the dangers of your journeys outwards, through the cycle of the healings, through the attack on exclusiveness you now know that two communities formerly estranged have been reconciled and called together into one indivisible humanity? Are you so blind? There is enough food for the journey, but there is only one loaf.' We leave off here, troubled by the disciples' blindness...

THE HEALING OF THE BLIND MAN

... And we turn to the healing of the blind man. As with the deaf and dumb man in the previous story, Jesus takes this man apart. Again he uses spittle as a visceral and sacramental sign to enable healing. It is significant that in this story the blind man's healing moves in stages. Initially, he sees people as fuzzy shapes, 'like trees walking' (8:24), before he comes to full clarity of sight. A commonly held view is that all Jesus' healings were instant events; not so, here clear sight comes only with the passage of time. The description of the healing is so natural and true to life that we can easily miss its deeper purpose in relation to what comes next. Mark tells this story of a blind man coming little by little to fullness of sight. He then places immediately following it the story of how Peter sees, or half sees, who Jesus is. We are alerted for what is to come.

The story has meaning for today, as wars and rumours of wars continue to make news. During the Gulf War of 1991, a Vigil for Peace was held in St Mary's Episcopal Cathedral in Glasgow and I vividly remember a prayer focused on this story: 'O Lord, spit on the eyes of Saddam Hussein, spit on the eyes of George Bush, spit on the eyes of John Major, spit on our eyes, take away our blindness, give to us vision and sight, and a knowledge of the truth, a deeper knowledge, a saving knowledge, lest we perish.'

THE TURNING POINT

With the story of the conversation at Caesarea Philippi and its aftermath, we have come now to the crux of Mark's gospel. As we approach it, let's keep in mind the road we have travelled so far and remember particularly the contrast between blindness and sight. The writer has laid down a marker - the journey from blindness to sight is often a process, not merely in physical terms, but also of coming to see with the eye of faith. Here is a story of Peter beginning to see, but not yet having sight in all its fullness.

Jesus takes his disciples away from the heat of ministry, out to the frontiers again. They go to the villages near Caesarea Philippi (8:27). It is time to assess the mission. He sits them down. 'Now,' he says, 'tell me who people are saying that I am?' He asks them his question about the central Marcan motif for discipleship, soon to be sharpened into the way of the cross. '*Who am I?*' Again there is an echo, this time of the great name of God revealed to Moses before the burning bush in Exodus 3, '*I am that I am.*' The disciples answer in words reported earlier in Chapter 6:14-15 when Herod asked about Jesus' reputation. 'Some folk are saying you are Elijah, or one of the prophets, some are saying you are John the Baptist come back to life' (8:28).

WHO DO *YOU* SAY I AM?

'Now,' says Jesus, 'Who am I? What do you say?' (8:29) Peter gives his momentous answer, '*You are the Messiah, the Christ.*' (8:29) This is the first time a disciple has made such a statement, such a confession. It is also the first time we have encountered these words since the very first words of the gospel (1:1). Here is the moment of truth, the first great faith confession. Peter sees! Or does he? Jesus immediately *orders* the disciples, using the same strong word he has employed to silence demons and still the waves, to keep silence (8:30). Perhaps Peter's sight is not all it seems...

CHRIST'S CROSS ...

What happens next? As soon as Peter says, 'Christ', Jesus says, 'Cross'. There is more to be revealed; Peter must see more and so must we, the readers. 'The Son of Man, the Human

One *must* suffer.' (8:31) This is an essential part of his destiny. As the story unfolds it becomes clear it is also in the very nature of the calling of the disciples' community. Notice the way Jesus puts aside the title, 'Messiah' or 'Christ' and uses instead, 'Son of Man,' 'Human One'. Mark's Jewish readers would well understand the title 'Son of Man' from the book of Daniel and especially Chapter 7. The 'Son of Man' was the one whom God would send to judge the nations, establish justice and free people from brutality and oppression when the end time comes, when God calls all before the court of his Judgement. Notice also the way Jesus enumerates the coalition of powers - 'elders, chief priests, teachers of the Law' - who will be ranged against him (8:31).

This new revelation is all too much for Peter. As soon as Jesus says 'suffer', Peter buckles. His 'seeing' does not stretch quite that far. He protests, vehemently. 'That's not the way! Everybody's waiting to see you riding in triumph, especially us, we've invested everything in you and now you're going to throw it all away!' (It is very interesting how Peter hears so clearly Jesus' word about death that it prevents him hearing the following word about life at all. Human nature's penchant for the negative has a long history.) Just as Jesus has stunned Peter with his predictions, now Peter rounds on Jesus with raging protests. Jesus has the last word, strongly recalling for us the story of his own initial temptation (1:12). 'Peter,' he says, 'you're like Satan to me. Don't tempt me, you think like human beings, not like God. Don't try to stop me.' (8:33) Strong words! The language of the devil has entered the inner core of the disciples' community.

... OUR CROSS

Elsewhere in the gospels Jesus says, 'Blessed are those who do not find me a cause of offence' (Matt 11:6, Lk 7: 23). Here we begin to see the supreme scandal of Jesus' claim. What kind of Christ do we seek and follow? Are we, like Peter, looking for the invincible one who will carry us on his back and make short work of our enemies, or are we willing to hear the word from Jesus and see the lowly, suffering one who makes peace and brings victory by another way and still follow? Have we also not known Peter's temptation to construct Jesus the Superman rather than follow the real Jesus Christ?

The story gets worse. After having 'words' with Peter, Jesus turns and reaches out to the crowd. Having predicted his own death, he goes on to speak of *our* cross (8:34). The trouble about the cross is that it has been such an all-pervasive Christian symbol that we are thoroughly used to it. How can we begin to sense the original force of Jesus' introduction of the stark reality of the cross into the disciples' lives and into the consciousness of his less immediate followers? Hengel points out that:

> Crucifixion was and remained a political and military punishment... Among the Romans it was inflicted above all on the lower classes, i.e. slaves, violent criminals, and the unruly elements in the rebellious provinces, not least Judea,... These were primarily people who had no rights,... by the public display of a naked victim at a

prominent place... at a crossroads, in the theatre, on high ground, at the place of his crime... crucifixion represented uttermost humiliation.
(Hengel 1978, p.86-7)

It is a pretty brutal picture of the meaning of self-denial. Reading between the lines, it seems clear that, when Mark wrote his gospel, he was writing for those who might be called to put their own lives on the line. Faith for them would not simply be inner spirituality, but a choice in court between saying 'Yes' to Jesus and 'No' to this life, or 'No' to Jesus for the sake of saving their own skin. Remember the words of Albert Camus, that insightful non-believer. He called on Christians to take a stand in the face of the horrors of our times. If they do not, he said, 'Christians may live, but Christianity will die'. Jesus utters a clear call for self-denial, but not in any mere inward sense, rather publicly, in the face of those who hold the power of life and death. In Bonhoeffer's phrase, he issues the call to 'the cross in the midst of life'.

Peter says 'Christ'. Jesus says 'Cross'. He says 'Cross,' not once but twice. He speaks of his cross and ours. Here is the crux, the place of transformation. Our lives and the world's life are turned upside-down. Invoking Daniel, Jesus brings to mind a picture of two contrasting courtrooms. In the first we find Jesus and his followers accused of perverting this world's peace, threatening its order, ranged against the powers-that-be. They will be humiliated and condemned and are prepared and willing to accept this. In the second court, the accused becomes the accuser, the judged becomes the judge as the shame of the cross is overturned and life is reborn. The first is an all too earthly courtroom, the second is the court of heaven. Disciples are called to put their trust in the Judgement of God rather than human judgement. They are asked to take the way of God rather than a human way. To take the new, divine way which Jesus unfolds is not an act of self justification or self glorification. It is neither to seek a martyr's crown nor to book our seats in heaven. The new way beckons because Jesus says and shows that this is the way. Being prepared to lose, to deny ourselves, to accept many 'dyings', great or small, across the breadth of every area of life, is the way to a deeper and a more profound engagement with life in its fullness. It is the way to life reborn, to life resurrected.

The last words of this passage are, 'I tell you, there are some here who will not die until they have seen the Kingdom of God come with power.' Scholars agonise about when the kingdom comes with power. What did Jesus mean? We could agree with the opinion that these words look no further forward than that Friday we call Good - and rightly so, for Mark's message is that on the cross the Messiah will be revealed, the disciples will see Christ unveiled and we will know of the Kingdom's coming in the way of love that is endless.

As the hinge of the gospel swings, the cross which is our life stands stark before us. At the beginning by the lakeside Peter heard the first call from Jesus to leave what he was doing, rise up and follow. Now the call intensifies to Peter and to all who hear. It is the second call, 'If anyone would come after me, let them deny themselves, take up their cross and follow me.' (8:34)

CROSSROADS

The beginning of Mark's gospel was likened to an invitation to embark on a an extended trip on a roller-coaster. From this turning point in Jesus' confrontation with Peter and the linking of 'Christ' and 'Cross', the gospel story intensifies. The invitation is extended to concentrate on the cross which lies increasingly clearly across both the path of Jesus and the way of any would-be disciple.

There are many significant parallels between the start of the gospel and the beginning of the second part of the story. In both there is an announcement that Jesus is the Messiah, the Christ. In both there is a call to Peter and, through him, to all disciples. The first call by the lakeside is to leave the nets and follow and we have just heard the call intensified, 'If anyone would follow me, let them forget themselves, take up their cross and follow me' (8:34). At the start of each part there is also an 'eschatological' moment, a moment when the voice of heaven breaks in, when Jesus is given divine authority and legitimation. At the start there is the moment of the baptism when the voice says, 'This is my son, the beloved' (1:11). In the passage we are about to meet, the story of the transfiguration, the voice repeats the message, 'This is my son, the beloved, listen to him' (9:7).

One other significant parallel is that the second half of the gospel, like the first, involves us on a path of momentous ups and downs, surprising twists and turns. It is no less a roller-coaster ride than the first.

STUDY

BY YOURSELF

Across the breadth of every area of life, being prepared to lose, to deny ourselves, to accept many "dyings", great or little, is the way to a deeper and more profound engagement in life in all its fullness, the way to life reborn, to life resurrected.
Take time to think about each phrase in this long sentence. What crossroads do you stand at today? This week? At this point in your life? What does it mean to choose to follow Jesus in each case?

FOR GROUP WORK

• The story of the blind man coming slowly to sight is a comment on the whole of the second half of the gospel, where it will take till resurrection morning for Peter and the disciples fully to 'see' who Jesus is.
Share with one another any experience you have had of truth slowly 'dawning', of times when you saw something you hadn't seen before, of times when a new truth made you change your mind or attitude towards a person or an issue.

• Peter says 'Christ', Jesus says 'cross'. Spend some time reflecting on this sentence. What do you think Jesus is saying here about himself? What does 'cross' mean for you? Share your thoughts with one another.

chapter 20

Disclosure: the Second Moment of Glory

MARK 9:2-12

The Transfiguration

(Matt 17:1-13; Lk 9:28-36)

Six days later Jesus took with him Peter, James and John, and led them up a high mountain, where they were alone. As they looked on, a change came over Jesus, and his clothes became shining white - whiter than anyone in the world could wash them. Then the three disciples saw Elijah and Moses talking with Jesus. Peter spoke up and said to Jesus, 'Teacher, how good it is that we are here! We will make three tents, one for you, one for Moses, and one for Elijah.' He and the others were so frightened that he did not know what to say.

Then a cloud appeared and covered them with its shadow, and a voice came from the cloud, 'This is my own dear Son - listen to him!' They took a quick look round but did not see anyone else; only Jesus was with them.

As they came down the mountain, Jesus ordered them, 'Don't tell anyone what you have seen, until the Son of Man has risen from death.'

They obeyed his order, but among themselves they started discussing the matter, 'What does this "rising from death" mean?' And they asked Jesus, 'Why do the teachers of the Law say that Elijah has to come first?'

His answer was, 'Elijah is indeed coming first in order to get everything ready. Yet why do the Scriptures say that the Son of Man will suffer much and be rejected? I tell you, however, that Elijah has already come and that people treated him just as they pleased, as the Scriptures say about him.'

To the mountain top

After the confrontation between Jesus and Peter at Caesarea Philippi, the way of discipleship is resumed and literally takes the high ground. After the depth of the call to take up our own cross, to lose ourselves for the sake of the gospel, Jesus takes the inner group of the disciples, Peter, James and John, up the mountain where, alone and in stillness, he is transfigured before them. This precious moment of glory is unveiled and they can see with undimmed clarity of vision, Who He Is. Remember two things. He has just been asking them, 'Who Am I?' (8:29), and 'I Am' is the great name of the God of Israel (Exodus 3:14). In this moment of luminous intensity, they can see and know the one we are all called to follow.

The contemporary question - which power dazzles?

Children of the atomic age can never forget that it was on the day of the Feast of the Transfiguration, 6 August 1945, that the first atomic bomb was dropped on Hiroshima. Eyewitnesses spoke of a flash 'brighter than a thousand suns'. There could be no sharper posing of the question, 'Which power do we in reality worship and follow?' Is it that power which harnesses the forces of God's world for blind and indiscriminate destruction, in which human beings are 'wasted', reduced to shadows on the pavement, or is it the power of the one who shines on the mountain top, the One whom our Celtic ancestors called 'the Sun behind all suns', in whom our humanity is glorified?

The significance of Moses and Elijah

The disciples meet a dazzling whiteness and also are aware of the presence of Moses and Elijah. In the stories of Moses and Elijah, both met with God on the mountain top. Moses had to turn his face aside since to see the brightness of God was to be annihilated. When he returned from the mountain, it seemed to the people that his own face shone with reflected glory (Exodus 34:30). At Elijah's famous meeting, after the passing of storm, earthquake and fire (all ways through which God had previously made himself known), God disclosed himself in the still small voice (1 Kings 19). Another factor links these three mountain top revelations; none occurs under auspicious circumstances. Both Moses and

Elijah met with God in the midst of discouragement. Moses had just seen his message rejected in the building of the Golden Calf. Elijah was fleeing for his life as King Ahab uttered murderous threats against him. Jesus climbs the hill with his disciples who have just been shown to be blind with misunderstanding and incomprehension after his announcement of the cross.

Moses and Elijah signify the way God has previously shown himself to and been with his people. Moses and Elijah, as symbol and sum of the Law and the Prophets, have been implicitly 'with' Jesus from the beginning, Moses in Jesus' question, 'Who Am I?', Elijah through the figure of John the Baptist. Moses and Elijah stand for the Law and the Prophets, the way which God has shown in times past. What of Jesus? Certainly he confirms what has been, he is revealed as their colleague and inheritor. What does he add, what is the revelation he brings? Jesus and the disciples have come to the mountain immediately after the first disclosure of the cross. The cross is Jesus' significant addition. From now on it is through Law, Prophets and *Cross* that God makes himself known. Through Law, Prophets and Cross, God shares his life with his people.

THE DISCIPLES' RESPONSE

Before this moment of transfiguration, the disciples are amazed and terrified. Once again, from the best of motives, Peter displays his uncanny ability to put his foot in it. 'Master,' he says, 'let's build three booths (tents, GNB), one for you, one for Moses and one for Elijah' (9:5). Tents or booths were the places where Israel worshipped in the wilderness. Peter is saying, 'Let's stop and linger. Let's worship rather than follow. Let's build a cult of adulation round Jesus rather than follow the way of Jesus, particularly now that crosses have been mentioned.' Twice in two episodes poor Peter gets it grievously wrong. He *is* us, isn't he? He highlights so well the temptations and hang-ups we know on our way of discipleship.

'LISTEN TO HIM'

This time Peter's vacillations are not challenged by Jesus himself, they are interrupted by the voice from heaven which calls him to attention. Out of the holy ecstasy in which Peter lingers comes the voice, 'This is my Son, the Beloved, listen to him.' The command to 'listen' has already been heard and will soon be heard again. In the gospel it is a key word, here it is a word which heightens and then dissolves the vision as the disciples are called onward.

Down the hill they go. On the way, Jesus issues another injunction to silence. 'Don't tell anyone until the Son of Man, the Human One, is risen.' After the reality of the cross the disciples are now introduced to the mystery of resurrection. To anticipate, when we come to the end of Mark's gospel, we will find that the mystery is not solved but deepened.

What do we learn from the downhill journey? We are told that the disciples did obey and keep silence. We also learn that they discussed among themselves what rising from the dead meant, implying that they were unwilling to ask Jesus about this directly. They do ask him about the place of Elijah in the coming final judgement (9:11). This question may have been much in dispute in Jesus' time. Jesus' answer is worth careful attention. He directs them away from futile speculation about the end time, (good advice for today's millenarians), and brings them right back to the present. 'Yes,' he says, 'Elijah will come first. But at the centre is the suffering of the Human One - (the cross again!) - and, anyway, Elijah has come in the figure of John the Baptist and look what happened to him' (9:12-13). Everybody is down to earth with a vengeance.

In the dazzling whiteness of the mountain top, there is the presence of God. 'Yes,' says Jesus, 'in the rejected and beheaded prophet John, above all in the sufferings of the Human One, there is also the presence of God'. This moment of transfiguration, of divine disclosure, is precious. Yet it is not only in the illumination, it is also in the ambiguities of life, in Jesus' own strange suffering, in his way which we are invited to make our way; it is in and through all of these realities there is the presence of God.

STUDY

BY YOURSELF

This is yet another crucial story in the gospel's development.

- Read the Bible passage a few times until you are familiar with it. Shut the book and tell the story to yourself in your own words, trying to visualise the event as you do so. (You might use the questions in the 'By yourself' part of Chapter 12.) Open the book and read the passage again. Now that the story is in your memory, live with it for the next week, consciously bringing it to mind as you go about your daily life.
- Reflect at the end of the week on your experience.

  This method of reading the Bible, internalising its words and stories, is very valuable. It gets the gospel inside us. The method can be used for any of the gospel stories.

chapter 21

Back Down to Earth

MARK 9:13-29

Jesus heals a Boy with an Evil Spirit

(Matt 17:14 -21; Lk 9:37-43a)

When they joined the rest of the disciples, they saw a large crowd round them and some teachers of the Law arguing with them. When the people saw Jesus, they were greatly surprised, and ran to him and greeted him. Jesus asked his disciples, 'What are you arguing with them about?'

A man in the crowd answered, 'Teacher, I brought my son to you, because he has an evil spirit in him and cannot talk. Whenever the spirit attacks him, it throws him to the ground, and he foams at the mouth, grits his teeth, and becomes stiff all over. I asked your disciples to drive the spirit out, but they could not.'

Jesus said to them, 'How unbelieving you people are! How long must I stay with you? How long do I have to put up with you? Bring the boy to me!' They brought him to Jesus.

As soon as the spirit saw Jesus, it threw the boy into a fit, so that he fell on the ground and rolled round, foaming at the mouth. 'How long has he been like this?' Jesus asked the father.

'Ever since he was a child,' he replied. 'Many times the evil spirit has tried to kill him by throwing him in the fire and into water. Have pity on us and help us, if you possibly can!'

'Yes,' said Jesus, 'if you yourself can! Everything is possible for the person who has faith.'

The father at once cried out, 'I do have faith, but not enough. Help me to have more!'

Jesus noticed that the crowd was closing in on them, so he gave a command to the evil spirit, 'Deaf and dumb spirit,' he said, 'I order you to come out of the boy and never go into him again!'

The spirit screamed, threw the boy into a bad fit, and came out. The boy looked like a corpse, and everyone said, 'He is dead!' But Jesus took the boy by the hand and helped him to rise, and he stood up.

After Jesus had gone indoors, his disciples asked him privately, 'Why couldn't we drive the spirit out?'

'Only prayer can drive this kind out,' answered Jesus, 'nothing else can.'

EARTHED AGAIN

Jesus and the three disciples come down the hill to be confronted with a shambles. Having been told on the mountain top to 'Listen' (9:7), they find the other disciples, a large crowd and a group of Scribes, all arguing like fury in the face of the disciples' inability to do anything about a boy who, (surprise, surprise) is deaf, unable to hear, unable to listen. The boy's father tells of his son's disability and Jesus loudly laments the unbelief he sees all around him. His complaint is about the failure of all those assembled who have not heard and responded to the word of faith, present in their midst (9:19).

The boy has another convulsion (9:20) and then there is a very suggestive moment. Instead of dealing authoritatively, miraculously and instantly with the situation, Jesus turns aside and asks the father, 'How long has your boy been like this?' (9:21) It sounds very like good clinical practice in the consulting room. 'Take your time. Tell me the whole story, give me all his history.' There is no instant cure, no momentary transfiguration. Rowan Williams comments in his book, *The Truce of God*:

> Dramatically speaking, here is Jesus, grimly fascinated, almost obsessed by the detail of what he sees; needing to see closely and without any softening. It's only when the full suicidal destructiveness of the boy's condition is clear, and the honest hopelessness of the father is out in the open at last, that Jesus acts.
>
> Jesus transfigured. Jesus, fresh from the glory of the timeless kingdom, stands still to watch a single small incident of pain, mental and physical. The transforming clarity of the mountain top is here as well, picking out each detail with a new light. At the centre, Jesus stands still, in both landscapes, with Moses and Elijah, and with the epileptic youth. Where he stands is not a middle ground, but a space where worlds

overlap. In his life and person, he defines what it is for glory and misery to come together and interpret each other. The kingdom conquers, but not by abolishing the memory of the world of human failure and distress; only by taking it into its life. (Williams 1983, p.74-75)

It is ordinary human life, ground level, painful human life, that becomes the continuing arena for transfiguration. This story acts as a foil and corollary to the events on the mountain top. It is also interesting to look at how this healing story contains echoes of earlier healing stories in Mark. However, the central theme of this story is about the struggle between faith and unbelief. On the mountain top we learn that faith grows from hearing the word of the Son, from listening to him. Down to earth again, the disciples who have already 'heard' the word and been given the power to cast out demons are powerless. So soon has faith melted in the heat of real need. Jesus castigates the crowd and disciples alike for their unbelief. At the same time Jesus is responding to the despairing father's cry, 'If you can do anything, help us and have compassion on us.' Jesus replies, 'If I can? All is possible for the one who believes.' 'I believe, help me in my unbelief,' cries out the father. That cry is enough, the boy can hear. (9:20-27)

THE STRUGGLE FOR FAITH

Certainly the story dramatises the boy's father's struggle for faith. It also reassures us when the father's desperate cry is shown to be enough. At a deeper level this story is about the faith of the disciples. They are the ones called to 'listen' and 'hear'; their failure to listen adequately has rendered them dumb, unable to command the departure of this troubling spirit. Remember, they have just been discussing resurrection. At the crux of the story, the boy lies on the ground as if dead, and Jesus raises him up; resurrection is here. What does this 'rising from death' mean? The disciples asked themselves this question on the way down the mountain (9:10). The meaning is demonstrated here in Jesus' action, setting father and son free from disabling unbelief so that the boy is raised to new life. 'Faith' is the key to 'resurrection' throughout the journey of discipleship.

....THROUGH PRAYER

After the action comes the reflection. With the boy restored to health, Jesus and the disciples retreat indoors. 'Why were we so helpless, useless?' ask the disciples. 'Why could we not drive out this demon?' Underneath the physical symptoms and actions, this story is about casting out the deadly demon of unbelief. Jesus says, 'It will only be cast out by prayer.' And what is prayer? Ched Myers writes:

When Jesus next returns to the subject (11:23), he will explicitly connect prayer with the 'power to believe'. To pray is to learn to believe in a transformation of self and world which seems, empirically, impossible - like moving mountains. What is unbelief but the despair, dictated by the dominant powers, that nothing can really change, a despair that renders revolutionary vision and practice impotent. The disciples are instructed to battle this impotence, this temptation to resignation, through prayer. 'Keep awake and pray, that you do not fall into temptation' (14:38), Jesus will urge them later. The strength (or inability) to cast out demons is deeply connected with the 'strength to stay awake' (14:37); tragically, the disciples will sleep while Jesus sweats in prayer in Gethsemane, and they will flee while he turns to face the powers. (Myers 1988, pp. 255-6)

So true prayer is about change, within ourselves and in the world. Not everyone would agree with such a statement. Listen to a bitter letter to the *Guardian* newspaper from an American professor during the Gulf War (1991):

Prayers for peace didn't do any good in 1914, nor in 1939, nor have they done any good in 1991. They never have and they never will. If you really want peace (and there are plenty that don't), you'll have to convince the Archbishop of Canterbury, the Pope, Mr Bush, Mr Major et al that they have to do a hell of a lot more than pray. Praying is so easy, isn't it? - and so utterly futile. The only possible function it can serve is to balm the consciences of those responsible for war, and/or those like His Grace who tells us it is a "Just War".

The professor speaks for many in our world with his dismissal of prayer. Sometimes we have only ourselves to blame when people see our prayers as wish fulfilment, a pious device to keep us firmly where we are. But that is far from the full story of prayer. Dietrich Bonhoeffer, in a dark and troubled world, linked 'prayer and righteous action', as the twin necessities for Christians living in a dark time. Here Jesus' talk of prayer with the disciples is already overshadowed by the cross. Myers' linking of this prayer with Jesus' own prayer in Gethsemane is surely right, for Jesus' prayer before the cross gives a moment of profound illumination into true prayer. The prayer of faith is often the prayer of intercession for others and for our world. It is always linked with the prayer for the strength to choose the cross-way, in the midst of life, and still keep going. The promise is that on the way we will find through death and dying, through our surrender and following, the possibilities of transfiguration, rising into life. And we will find the truth of the promise even at the cross itself, the most awful place of cynicism, abuse of power, abandonment, pain and death. The summons is to remain steadfast in prayer, in commitment to following, in determination to believe and in the quest and struggle for right.

Study

- Two separate themes in this section are in tension with one another; the negative one of unbelief, and the positive one of finding signs of transformation and healing in our daily lives. Reflect on them in turn.
- 'I believe, help my unbelief.' When have you used this prayer? What were your feelings and experience at the time?
- Think about 'evidences of transformation' you have seen or experienced in everyday life.

For group work

- There is a close connection between prayer and faith, but not a simple one. This story raises the issue of the importance of prayer for others (intercession), in the face of the apparent failure of intercession (the disciples fail to heal the boy). Jesus then speaks of the importance of persevering in face of that seeming failure. It is about not giving in to the 'dominant powers', to the world as it is.
- Brainstorm together under the heading 'Prayer is ...'
- Prayer is not about changing the mind of God, it is about changing our minds and attitudes and changing the lives of individuals, families and communities.
- Dietrich Bonhoeffer said that in hard times the two essentials for Christians are prayer and righteous action (doing right). What on your list needs action? What kind of action?
- Now prepare a gracious response to the professor who says that prayer is just useless conscience salving. It isn't!

chapter 22

First and Last

MARK 9:30-50

Jesus speaks again about his Death
(Matt 17:22-23; Lk 9:43b-45)

Jesus and his disciples left that place and went on through Galilee. Jesus did not want anyone to know where he was, because he was teaching his disciples: 'The Son of Man will be handed over to those who will kill him. Three days later, however, he will rise to life.'

But they did not understand what this teaching meant, and they were afraid to ask him.

Who is the Greatest?
(Matt 18:1-5; Lk 9:46 -48)

They came to Capernaum, and after going indoors Jesus asked his disciples, 'What were you arguing about on the road?'

But they would not answer him, because on the road they had been arguing among themselves about who was the greatest. Jesus sat down, called the twelve disciples, and said to them, 'Whoever wants to be first must place himself last of all and be the servant of all.' Then he took a child and made him stand in front of them. He put his arms round him and said to them, 'Whoever welcomes in my name one of these children, welcomes me; and whoever welcomes me, welcomes not only me but also the one who sent me.'

Whoever is not against us is for us
(Lk 9:49-50)

John said to him, 'Teacher, we saw a man who was driving out demons in your name, and we told him to stop, because he doesn't belong to our group.'

'Do not try to stop him,' Jesus told them, 'because no one who performs a miracle in my name will be able soon afterwards to say evil things about me. For whoever is not against us is for us. I assure you that anyone who gives you a drink of water because you belong to me will certainly receive his reward.'

Temptations to sin
(Matt 18:6-9; Lk 17:1-2)

'If anyone should cause one of these little ones to lose his faith in me, it would be better for that person to have a large millstone tied round his neck and be thrown into the sea. So if your hand makes you lose your faith, cut it off! It is better for you to enter into life without a hand than to keep both hands and go off to hell, to the fire that never goes out. And if your foot makes you lose your faith, cut it off! It is better for you to enter life without a foot than to keep both feet and be thrown into hell. And if your eye makes you lose your faith, take it out! It is better for you to enter the Kingdom of God with only one eye than to keep both eyes and be thrown into hell. There "the worms that eat them never die, and the fire that burns them is never put out."

Everyone will be purified by fire as a sacrifice is purified by salt.

Salt is good; but if it loses its saltiness, how can you make it salty again?

Have the salt of friendship among yourselves, and live at peace with one another.'

'Have the salt of friendship among yourselves, and live in peace with one another.' This passage (from verse 42 onwards) ends with the terrifying words about cutting off hands and feet and plucking out eyes. They illustrate vividly one tension which runs through the ministry of Jesus, that between words of deep comfort, generous invitation and words of terrible demand. There's not much of the spirit of 'Come to me all you who labour and are heavy laden, and I will give you rest' (Matt 11:28) in these words.

How are they to be interpreted? First, we remember their context, the giving of a stern warning against words or actions that would cause the 'little ones' to stumble. The 'little ones' refers to the children in verse 35ff; children were indeed the least of the least, easily dismissed and disregarded. Again Jesus is saying, 'In this new community of mine, there needs to be a special place for the weak, the vulnerable, the sinner, the struggler, the disregarded. The greatest of sins is to do anything which would weaken or threaten them.' The new community is built around the needs of the least rather the wishes of the strong. How far is that true of our churches?

In the wider context, Mark offers these words of Jesus to his own audience, his 'church'. The faith of this church was under attack and the Christian community was constantly fighting apostasy and desertion. There was always the possibility that those who had come to faith would lose their hold in the bitter and hostile climate in which they had to live and bear witness. The enemy within was real: voices who might entice the frail company of faith into false compromise, backsliding or idolatry. Reading between the lines, here is a picture of a young church under trial where strenuous efforts had to be made to affirm and confirm faith under fire.

When all has been said, the choice offered in these verses remains brutal - amputation or the fire. It is interesting that the word which the GNB translates as 'hell' in 9:43 is literally 'Gehenna'. Gehenna was the name of the constantly smouldering, putrefying rubbish dump at the outskirts of Jerusalem, an ever-visible, aromatic reminder of smoke, fire and worms. Jesus does not spare us hard choices. Certainly, exaggeration was part of the Jewish preacher's stock and trade; verse 25 of Chapter 10 gives a richly ridiculous picture of the camel struggling with the needle's eye. However, in the search for a comfortable interpretation of this passage, there are no easy answers.

The final two verses (9:49,50) are linked by the metaphor of salt and introduce an element of healing. Salt and fire (cauterising) were the traditional remedies applied to an amputee to encourage healing and prevent infection. Jesus moves on to speak of the salt of friendship and the importance of community life lived in the framework of peace. These hard words should therefore be interpreted within some general injunctions to peace and friendship.

A disciple's arrogance

Continuing to work backwards, we move from problems within the community to a perceived problem in the community of faith's relationship with those outside it. After two blunders by Peter (8:32, 9:5), it is now John's turn to get things wrong. It seems that a man was practising exorcism in Jesus' name and John was anxious to stop this 'because he did not belong to our group' (9:38); the age-old, recurring problem of exclusiveness. The arrogance in John's objection lies in his attempt to erect boundaries around the exercise of compassionate ministry 'in Jesus' name'. Myers describes this as, 'He equates exorcism with the accrual of power and status, and wishes to maintain a monopoly of it.' (1988, p. 261). What makes John's position ironic is that the disciples have just failed miserably in their attempts to exorcise the deaf and dumb spirit in the boy.

Jesus has been talking of receiving and releasing. About the exorcist, he says simply, 'Don't stop him.' (9:39) In practical terms he is saying that those who use his name will not speak evil of him; he is also pointing out to the disciples that they are to 'see' or 'regard' those who are not against them as for them. They are being discouraged from drawing rigid lines round their community and encouraged to look out on the world with unsuspicious eyes. Jesus then offers this beguiling word; 'Those who offer a drink of cold water to you because you belong to me have their reward in the kingdom.' (9:41) The disciples, those who belong to the faith community, have no monopoly of acts of healing, service and caring. Beware against drawing rigid lines and barriers. These words have many applications to today's church. For example, at the centre of our faith and worship, they raise a question for eucharistic practice. The Lord's Table belongs to the Lord, not to his followers; by this stage in the gospel it should be very clear that Jesus' invitation to sit down and sup with him is wide open.

The last ... first

We come to the beginning of this passage last because it is another key text, a vital stage on the way to the cross and the revealing of the true Messiah. The disciples are on the move again and are learning discipleship as they go. After the debacle of Caesarea Philippi and Peter's great misunderstanding, Jesus speaks for a second time about his death and rising; he attempts once more to teach the disciples of the reality of the cross and the event of Easter. The disciples are no further on in their understanding, they remain blind and deaf, still afraid to ask questions. (9:32)

They have plenty to say to one another, however, perhaps to cover up their fear, uncertainty and confusion. When they arrive at Capernaum it is Jesus who does the questioning, 'What was all that talk about back there?' Now they are afraid to answer, for the truth is they have been arguing about power and status, about who is the greatest among them. They could hardly pick a more graphic way of displaying their failure to understand than by arguing about such a topic. Sadly, just a few verses on (10:35-45), they'll do it all over again.

Mark describes very deliberately what happens next. 'Jesus sat down, called the twelve disciples, and said to them ...' (9:35) It is like a board meeting or a council of war. Pointedly Jesus says, 'Right, we stop here and we thrash things out and we get this straight. In this new community (which we call church), 'the first shall be last and servant of all. (9:35) And, just to make sure you understand, here's a picture you will never forget.' He took a child, set him in the midst of all those grown men, put his arm round him and said, 'Whoever welcomes in my name one of the children, welcomes me, and whoever welcomes me welcomes also the one who sent me.' (9:37) It is hard to feel the full force and shock of Jesus' word and action. In the society of his time, the child was the last and the least, indeed 'the least of the least'. Children had no status in society. By law and custom they were literally non-entities.

What does Jesus do? He does more than receive and pay attention to the child, which would have been disturbing enough; he thrusts the child centre stage, and says, 'Look and learn'. He makes the child a key element in his new call to faith. And not only here (9:34-37), very soon he will do it again to underline the message. 'Receive this child,' he says (10:15). He makes it quite clear that the manner of receiving is no mild, paternalistic, non-threatening of existing power relationships. It is about receiving *and learning* from the discarded, the discounted, the disregarded. The child, 'the least of the least', becomes a model for discipleship, for the way of the kingdom.

Try to picture this scene. The disciples are all arguing over their relative importance; 'I've been with him longest' ... 'But I'm really much more intelligent' ...'I am a much more spiritual person' ... 'I'm the one who sticks by him when things get rough' ... 'I'm the one he trusts with the money.' Jesus hears it all. He's trying to prepare them for a cross; he must be angry and dismayed. He gets this scruffy urchin, a willing accomplice, puts his arm round him and shoves him right into the middle of them all and says, *'LOOK! Will you LOOK!'*

'The first shall be last and the last first. (10:31) That's the way it will be in the kingdom I have come to bring. That's the way it is in the upside-down kingdom. That's the way it is in this new reversal of the world's values.'

'The first shall be last and the last first.' This is one of a great litany of sayings of Jesus which lie at the very core of the gospel, sayings which multiply on the way to the cross. Here is the list.

> 'The first shall be last and the last first.' (10:31)
> 'Whoever loves his life will lose it, whoever loses his life for my sake will find it.' (8:35)
> 'Unless you receive the kingdom of God like a child, you will never enter it.' (10:15)
> 'It is easier for a camel to go through a needle's eye than for a rich man to enter the kingdom of God.' (10:25)
> 'If anyone of you would be great among you, they must be servant of all; whoever would be first, must be slave of all.' (10:43-44)
> 'For the Son of Man did not come to be served, but to serve ...and to give, to give his life to redeem many people.' (10:45)

The logic and the imagery of the gospel are relentless. The new call to the way of discipleship piles up images in our minds. Come like a child, stripped of all adult pretensions to power and ready to learn. Come and receive, and the new community of Christ will take form within us and around us. Come and learn what the disciples have yet to learn, learn of death, not simply accepted and endured, but defeated and transformed. It is the way of the upside-down kingdom.

STUDY

BY YOURSELF

Reflect on this list, and how Jesus radically overturns our expectations. Focus on one item on the list each day of the week. As there are six, a Sabbath rest is given!

chapter 23

Women and Children FIRST!

MARK 10:1-14

Jesus teaches about Divorce
(Matt 19:1-12; Lk 16:18)

Then Jesus left that place, went to the province of Judea, and crossed the River Jordan. Crowds came flocking to him again, and he taught them, as he always did.

Some Pharisees came to him and tried to trap him. 'Tell us,' they asked, 'does our Law allow a man to divorce his wife?'

Jesus answered with a question, 'What law did Moses give you?'

Their answer was, 'Moses gave permission for a man to write a divorce notice and send his wife away.'

Jesus said to them, 'Moses wrote this law for you because you are so hard to teach. But in the beginning, at the time of creation, "God made them male and female," as the scripture says. "And for this reason a man will leave his father and mother and unite with his wife, and the two will become one." So they are no longer two, but one. No human being then must separate what God has joined together.'

When they went back into the house, the disciples asked Jesus about this matter. He said to them, 'A man who divorces his wife and marries another woman commits adultery against his wife. In the same way, a woman who divorces her husband and marries another man commits adultery.'

Jesus blesses Little Children
(Matt 19:13-15; Lk 18:15-17)

Some people brought children to Jesus for him to place his hands on them, but the disciples scolded the people. When Jesus noticed this, he was angry and said to his disciples, 'Let the children come to me, and do not stop them, because the Kingdom of God belongs to such as these. I assure you that whoever does not receive the Kingdom of God like a child will never enter it.' Then he took the children in his arms, placed his hands on each of them, and blessed them.

HEADING INTO TROUBLE - TOWARDS JERUSALEM

It's to the road again! Now Jesus and the disciples cross the Jordan and move into Judea. Jerusalem looms ahead as the final destination. They travel to meet the earthly powers in the place of metropolitan authority. With deliberation they go forward to the enemies' camp.

THE EQUALITY OF MAN AND WOMAN

First there is teaching about divorce through the familiar form of a confrontation between Jesus and the Pharisees. It is important to remember that at this time, the status of women was very little better than that of children. Within marriage women had no rights, they were regarded as their husband's possession. Debate on divorce within the community of the Pharisees was confined to what were and were not sufficient grounds for a man to dismiss his wife. There were no reciprocal rights.

The question the Pharisees bring is, 'Can a man dismiss his wife?' (10:2) Jesus will not give a simple answer to a complex question. Typically, he turns the question back on his Pharisaic interrogators and asks, 'What does Moses teach you?' (10:3) The reply is that Moses did give permission for husbands to write a bill of divorce in certain circumstances. Jesus' response is very interesting. He refers his inquirers away from the law of Moses back to the creation story in Genesis. He sets scripture against scripture in a way that would have been unheard of among the rabbis. In his reply he moves the focus of the debate away from the narrower issue of male rights within a patriarchy to the original status of men and women in the Genesis creation ordinance. He refuses to be drawn into the debate simply in terms of existing legal casuistry. He affirms that man and woman were created together and belong together.

Jesus refuses the nit-picking of legal debate. Instead, he points out how exclusive male rights have skewed and distorted the original purpose of the creation of male and female for each other. He argues that it is for no one to drive a wedge into that God-willed unity and equality. He does not actually forbid divorce, he forbids interference in the marriage covenant, and he reasserts God's original intention in the making of male and female.

When Jesus returns privately to discuss the matter with the disciples, he allows divorce but prohibits remarriage (10:11). Once more, he asserts that what is significant is the principle of equality. He speaks both of a man putting away his wife, and a woman putting away her husband. In both instances Jesus moves beyond Jewish law. In stating that a man could be guilty of committing adultery against his wife he is giving the woman rights previously denied her. The law also forbade the possibility of a wife's leaving her husband.

THE CHILDREN, 'DO NOT STOP THEM'

After discussing the male/female relationship the scene moves back to the child. This story is very familiar. The disciples are abruptly dismissive of some children who are brought to Jesus. Their attitude, not unknown in adults today, kindles Jesus' indignation. 'Let them come to me,' he says, 'the kingdom belongs to them'. (10:14) He goes on, 'Who does not receive the Kingdom of God like a little child, will not enter!' (10:15) Here are strong words to stop us short. What does it mean to receive the Kingdom as a child? The gifts children bring are vulnerability, openness, dependence. Again Jesus strips away our adult notions of power, status and knowledge. Nothing in our hands we bring, yet with hands open, we will receive.

'He took the children in his arms, placed his hands upon each of them, and blessed them.' (10:16) The same generous, warm, enfolding embrace he offers freely to those who are not too proud and self-encumbered to receive it.

THE UPSIDE-DOWN KINGDOM, BUILDING UP THE PICTURE

This passage offers two stories, one about male/female relationships, the other about the place of children. We know enough now about Mark's gospel to see Jesus as the bringer of the upside-down Kingdom, in which the old relationships of status and hierarchy, which disempower and exclude, are challenged and dethroned by a revolution from below. A new community is being built which finds a welcoming place for the excluded and a security for the poor and the powerless. Jesus and the early church were much concerned with building this new community, founded on a different set of social relationships, rooted in an ethos of genuine mutuality and sharing.

The re-ordering of family relationships was crucial to the forging of this new community. They would present the greatest difficulties in the struggle to discard the built-in privileges of sex and age. Old and male were at the top of the heap, young and female at the bottom. It is hardly surprising that in teaching about the family, Jesus shows a male/female relationship built on a recognition of mutuality rather than the domination/dependence pattern, and gives children an important place in sharp contrast to their previous neglect.

We inhabit a very different world from that of the first century. Many changes are occurring in patterns of family life, in child/adult and female/male relationships. Within the context of church, however, there are still questions to be asked about the place of women and children. Do we respect and honour the fundamental equality of the sexes which Jesus discovers in the creation stories? Do we see children with the eyes of Jesus, as those from whom we can learn, as well as teach?

Having children as teachers by giving young people a significant part in leading worship and sharing the life of the local church has been liberating for myself and many others. In wider society, where some children bear a too heavy weight of fulfilling parental expectations while others are neglected and abused, it is good to listen closely to Jesus' words. He invites us to treat children as persons in their own right, with their own integrity and with the same needs for love and freedom as we have.

> 'Whoever receives the child receives me. (9:37)
> Whoever receives me, receives the one who sent me. (9:37)
> Whoever does not receive the Kingdom of God as a little child, cannot enter.' (10:15)

STUDY

BY YOURSELF

In the Jesus' world, women and children were without rights, voiceless, marginalised and disempowered. Through the coming week, think about those in our society who are discriminated against, looked down upon, the butts of prejudice, and hold them all before God in prayer.

FOR GROUP WORK

Two stories about children follow in quick succession.

• As children in the gospel represent those without power and rights, share with one another your personal list of those who are victims and victimised today. Ask what needs to be done to bring 'good news' to them.

• Jesus not only holds up the child as having a claim on our welcome, love and justice, he offers us a picture of the child as teacher. Share with one another one thing that each person has learnt from a child, then talk together about what you think children teach us about faith and living the Christian life.

chapter 24

Of Camels and Needles

MARK 10:15-31

The Rich Man

(Matt 19:16-30; Lk 18:18-30)

As Jesus was starting on his way again, a man ran up, knelt before him, and asked him, 'Good Teacher, what must I do to receive eternal life?'

'Why do you call me good?' Jesus asked him. 'No one is good except God alone. You know the commandments: "Do not commit murder; do not commit adultery; do not steal; do not accuse anyone falsely; do not cheat; respect your father and your mother".'

'Teacher,' the man said, 'ever since I was young, I have obeyed all these commandments.'

Jesus looked straight at him with love and said, 'You need only one thing. Go and sell all you have and give the money to the poor, and you will have riches in heaven; then come and follow me.' When the man heard this, gloom spread over his face, and he went away sad, because he was very rich.

Jesus looked round at his disciples and said to them, 'How hard it will be for rich people to enter the Kingdom of God!'

The disciples were shocked at these words, but Jesus went on to say, 'My children, how hard it is to enter the Kingdom of

God! It is much harder for a rich person to enter the Kingdom of God than for a camel to go through the eye of a needle.'

At this the disciples were completely amazed and asked one another, 'Who, then, can be saved?'

Jesus looked straight at them and answered, 'This is impossible for human beings, but not for God; everything is possible for God.'

Then Peter spoke up, 'Look, we have left everything and followed you.'

'Yes,' Jesus said to them, 'and I tell you that anyone who leaves home or brothers or sisters or mother or father or children or fields for me and for the gospel will receive much more in this present age. He will receive a hundred times more houses, brothers, sisters, mothers, children and fields - and persecutions as well; and in the age to come he will receive eternal life. But many who are now first will be last, and the last will be first.'

AN INTERRUPTION - ENTER A RICH MAN

Jesus and the disciples are about to get on the move again when suddenly, they are halted. A man runs up to Jesus and exaggeratedly abases himself. He then addresses him as 'good teacher', a title of the greatest respect. (10:17). Maybe, in return for this compliment he expects an equally fulsome reply. What he gets is an abrupt and dusty riposte, 'Why call me good? Only God is good.' (10:18) The man has asked what he needs to do to inherit eternal life. Jesus refers him to the Ten Commandments, adding 'Do not cheat/defraud'. 'Don't cheat' very often referred to depriving the poor of their due wages (10:19).

'FOLLOW ME, COME ON!'

The stranger, as Mark calls him, can honestly answer 'Yes'. He has kept the commandments. There follows the sentence which brings this encounter electrifyingly to life. 'Jesus looked straight at him with love ... and said ... "There's one thing more, ... If you really want to live, if you want to know life in God's fullness, then ... sell what you have, sell all you have, give it to the poor and come on, follow me."' (10:21) The stranger slowly deflates like a bursting balloon, 'he went away sad, because he was very rich.' (10:22)

'IT CAN'T BE DONE.'

Jesus warms to this earnest young man, he wants him in his company, but not at any cost. So he says, 'OK, you sound serious, if you're really serious, let's talk about wealth redistribution.' For the rich man it's all too much. He could not shake himself loose from his wealth. What he thought was his security was in truth his prison. His treasure on earth prevented his following the treasure from heaven. This is quite the starkest refusal of the offer of discipleship in the gospel; it is no accident that the refuser is a rich man.

Jesus goes on. 'How hard it will be for rich people to enter the Kingdom of God.' (10:23) The disciples are shocked. It gets worse, he then gives them his famous picture of the camel struggling with the needle's eye, in a flash of good rough peasant humour, meanwhile looking them right in the eye. We might say it's as hard as for Richard Branson to get into the sleeve of one of his own CDs or Anne Gloag to get into the ticket machine on a Stagecoach bus.

Jesus gives a clear challenge to the prevailing view which regarded wealth as a blessing from God. That challenge throws the disciples. 'You mean all those worthy pillars of society with their fine big houses and their sleek transport aren't going to make it?' 'That's right,' says Jesus. 'Only if they rid themselves of their baggage, only if they redistribute their wealth will the doors of the kingdom begin to swing open.'

The history of the interpretation of this passage is littered with examples of attempts to water down this radical statement. Let us not try. Remember the gospel challenge to 'listen'.

'IT CAN!'

This passage ends on a different note. It speaks of those who have surrendered all for the sake of the gospel - they will in their lives see fulfilled the promise of the parable of the sower, bearing fruit one hundred-fold, though not without trouble. Another picture is painted of the new, growing community, rooted and grounded in the new values of the Kingdom.

> 'The first will be last, and the last first.' (10:31)

Again the summons comes to enter the upside-down Kingdom. Put the picture of the child and the picture of the camel side by side and ask, what are the values we live by? To enter the Kingdom is to receive it as a child, knowing and acknowledging dependence and vulnerability, living in openness to God and his world. All adult defences and pretensions will be stripped away. What we think we need is actually holding us back.

We can become like the unburdened camel. As we lay aside the baggage and share it, we discover we have entered into the world of God's new possibilities. Going through the eye of the needle means new eyes for seeing, vision no longer blinkered or skewed by the distorting lens of privilege. Jesus throws out this radical challenge to our established certainties and securities and to our society's values. The mystery is, as the encounter with the stranger shows, that this is much more than a challenge, it is a loving, open, life-giving invitation. Jesus says, 'Come on, come with me.'

> 'The first will be last, and the last first.' (10:31)

Study

- We often think of laughter and tears as opposites, yet they can be closely connected. At the very least, Jesus must have been disappointed at the rich man's refusal of his offer. Is he shrugging off his hurt when he draws the funny picture of the laden camel struggling with the needle's eye? Very often we use humour to prick pomposity and 'bring down the mighty from their seats'. (Luke 1: 52)
- The gospel story is moving to its climax around the serious and painful story of the cross. Before moving into the depths, take time out this week to look at the pretensions of the rich and powerful with a humorous eye.

chapter 25

True Greatness

MARK 10:32-45

Jesus speaks a third time about his Death
(Matt 20:17-19; Lk 18:31-34)

Jesus and his disciples were now on the road going up to Jerusalem. Jesus was going ahead of the disciples, who were filled with alarm; the people who followed behind were afraid. Once again Jesus took the twelve disciples aside and spoke of the things that were going to happen to him. 'Listen,' he told them, 'we are going up to Jerusalem where the Son of Man will be handed over to the chief priests and the teachers of the Law. They will condemn him to death and then hand him over to the Gentiles, who will mock him, spit on him, whip him, and kill him; but three days later he will rise to life.'

The Request of James and John
(Matt 20. 20 -28)

Then James and John, the sons of Zebedee, came to Jesus. 'Teacher,' they said, 'there is something we want you to do for us.'

'What is it?' Jesus asked them.

They answered, 'When you sit on your throne in your glorious Kingdom, we want you to let us sit with you, one at your right and the other at your left.'

Jesus said to them, 'You don't know what you are asking for. Can you drink the cup of suffering that I must drink? Can you be baptised in the same way I must be baptised?'

'We can,' they answered.

Jesus said to them, 'You will indeed drink the cup I must drink and be baptised in the way I must be baptised. But I do not have the right to choose who will sit at my right and my left. It is God who will give these places to those for whom he has prepared them.'

When the other ten disciples heard about it, they became angry with James and John. So Jesus called them all together to him and said, 'You know that those who are considered rulers of the heathen have power over them, and the leaders have complete authority. This, however, is not the way it is among you. If one of you wants to be great, he must be the servant of the rest; and if one of you wants to be first, he must be the slave of all. For even the Son of Man did not come to be served; he came to serve and to give his life to redeem many people.'

JESUS SPEAKS OF HIS DEATH FOR THE THIRD TIME

Repetition is a great aid to learning. Mark and Jesus follow this teaching device well. For the third time within three chapters, Jesus attempts to speak of his death to the disciples. Again they are on the road together. This time journey's end is clearly in view; they are about to enter Jerusalem. The picture Mark gives is striking. Jesus is going on ahead, firm of purpose, resolute, eyes fixed on what lies ahead while the disciples are trailing behind, filled with alarm. The crowd lags even further back, full of foreboding. Remember that conjunction; Jesus going ahead, the disciples fearful. It will recur at the gospel's end and climax, at faith's new beginning in face of the resurrection (16:8).

Jesus turns to the disciples, 'Listen' (that word again), he says. 'Hear, open your ears. We are going to Jerusalem where the Human One will be handed over to the chief priests and the teachers of the Law. They will condemn him to death and then hand him over to the Gentiles, who will mock him, spit on him, whip him, and kill him; but three days later he will rise to life.' (10:33-34)

DEAF DISCIPLES

Do the disciples listen, do they understand? After this third time of telling are their ears and eyes opened? Not a whit! Immediately after Jesus had foretold his death, the disciples argued about who was the greatest among them. This time he is confronted with an even greater lack of understanding. James and John come up to him - the sons of Zebedee, nicknamed 'Sons of Thunder' ('the great talkers'). 'Teacher,' they say, 'Would it be possible for us to get the best seats, the seats of honour, in your glorious kingdom?'(10:37) Once again the request is crass and blind. Always, reading this story, I see the contrasting picture of Jesus hoisted high on a cross, with the criminals hanging to his left and right. That is what lies on the road ahead, not James' and John's rosy and presumptuous picture of sitting to right and left of King Jesus at the throne of glory.

Perhaps James and John are showing a common psychological reaction in the face of confusion, emptiness and fear - they chatter inanely. However, their request is specific. They obviously have a picture of Jesus reigning in Messianic glory as the restored Son of David. The request to sit at the right and left hand echoes Psalm 110, one of the psalms connected with the ceremony of Royal Enthronement. Jesus refuses the request, deflecting it by helping them to see that they can share his sufferings without earning any special privileges at the time of his triumph. Readers are alerted again to the reality that the disciples' popular view of Jesus as the conquering Messiah is being called into question.

DEALING WITH DISSENSION

The request is gently refused. Naturally, when the other disciples come to hear what has been going on, they are very angry. There is dissension in the ranks. It is easy to imagine what would be said. 'Who do that pair of upstarts think they are? What a cheek!' Look closely at the way Jesus deals with this dispute.

What is the first thing Jesus does? He recognises that there is a problem. Next, he deals with the problem right away. Often the human response to trouble is denial, evasion or pro-crastination. Jesus shows no such indecision, he tackles the issue there and then.

Jesus' first reported action is to call all the disciples together. He deliberately chooses not to deal with the two parties separately. He does not take the rest of the disciples away and say, 'Isn't it terrible the kind of things James and John are asking; you've got to make allowances for them, they have a very ambitious mother.' (Matt 20:20-21) He says, 'We'll sit down and talk this through as a community, face to face.' Yet when they do, Jesus immediately takes the spotlight off James and John. There is no big showdown, such as 'James and John, I'm the leader of this community and I want you to know that the others here have had enough of your big-headedness'. On the contrary, Jesus moves from the particular (and the contentious) to the general.

BEGINNING WHERE WE ARE

Jesus' first words are key words for any good teacher. '*You know,*' he says - he begins from where they are and builds on what they do know. He affirms their experience. This passage ends with a very deep statement of Jesus' own purpose but he begins on more familiar ground. 'You know that the men who are considered rulers of the heathen have power over them, and the leaders have complete authority.' (10:42) He reminds them how the world works. He brings them face to face with the day-to-day reality under which they sweat. He speaks of this reality twice, in slightly different terms, to underline his point. He makes them confront and acknowledge the world as it is, without pretence or illusion.

Jesus also does something in this sentence which will be no surprise to those who have followed the Marcan journey so far. He is not willing to attribute to the rulers the power with which they invest themselves. The adjective the GNB uses to qualify the 'rulers of the heathen' is 'considered'. Other translations speak more pungently of the rulers as 'so-called'. Jesus calls their power and authority into question. You can learn from the way the world works, he says, but that does not mean you have to accept it, or bow down before its powers.

Jesus has now established a familiar situation in the disciples' minds. They have been focused away from the original dispute, which was trivial, and united in a common sense and experience of oppression.

Now comes the challenge. 'This, however, is not the way it *is* among you.' The key word is *is*. Jesus does not say, 'must be,' 'should be,' 'shall be,' 'ought to be.' He says, *is*. The tense is present - it is a statement of fact. The new community to which they belong *is* different. 'You know that also,' says Jesus, 'you've been living in it'. Again his appeal is to lived, shared experience. Therefore, 'If anyone of you wants to be great ...' Here is the next significant stage. Jesus doesn't deny the quest for greatness, it is simply that 'greatness' is being radically redefined. This new community, where things are different, neither denies or belittles greatness, it transforms it. 'If anyone of you wants to be great, he must be the servant of the rest.' (10:43) Not in domination but in mutual, caring service is the new greatness found.

The saying is reinforced. 'If anyone wants to be great, he must be the servant of the rest, if anyone wants to be first, he must be the slave of all.' 'Servant' appears only twice in this gospel, once here and once earlier when Jesus put the child in their midst (9:35). Servants had no esteem and a good case can be made that most servants were women. It is true that from the instance of Peter's wife's mother at the start of the gospel (1:31) right through to the women at the tomb at its close (16:1), women in Mark are shown as properly fulfilling the vocation of *diakonia*, 'service'. We have come through a section of the gospel where the male disciples have been shown increasingly to be a blind, deaf and feckless lot, and it will get worse. It is also interesting that most of the women in the gospel appear without husbands and are therefore at the bottom of their society's heap. Reading between the lines, it may well be that women had key roles of leadership and service in the church of Mark's time, roles where leadership and service went genuinely hand in hand and the new community made an end of the old patterns of male domination and hierarchical structures.

Jesus invites the disciples to be not only 'servants' but 'slaves'. Slaves had no rights and were at the beck and call of everyone in the household, male and female. There is no doubting the centrality and significance of the call to humble service as a key mark of the faith community.

'To serve and give'

The passage moves to a climax. The old ways are called into question, root and branch, as in Jesus' punch-line all is made plain. 'The Son of Man did not come to be served; he came to serve and to give his life to redeem many people.' (10:45) 'Many' in this usage is almost a synonym for 'all'. This section began with the cross, it ends with the cross. The cross is not only about the ransoming of many, it determines the future shape of the new community. The love of God in Jesus, the Human One, which stoops down low to meet us here, now determines and informs all our relationships with one another. The crossway becomes the paradigm for all our attitudes towards and relationships with one another.

The end of the third quarter of the gospel is almost in sight. From Caesarea Philippi and Peter's simultaneous confession of the Christ and repudiation of the cross there has been a movement of gathering intensity. Three times the cross has been raised. Three times the disciples have shrunk from knowledge of it, preferring the old ways and the old powers to the new way and the new power in their midst. More than three times Jesus has tried to get his message home. He has come to bring a whole new set and ordering of relationships stretching from family to all of society.

* 'The first will be last, and the last first.' (10:31) * 'To love your life is to lose it, to lose it is to find it.' (8:35) * 'Whoever would be great must be a servant.' * 'Whoever must be first must be a slave.' (10:43-44) * 'Whoever does not receive... like a child, will not enter.' (10:15)

The teaching, the challenge, the invitation is clear and plain. 'Whoever has ears to hear, let them hear.' (4:9)

Study

By yourself

- Do you know anyone whose greatness is matched by their humility? Spend some time considering what makes him/her great, and what keeps him/her humble.
- Think about any situations you are part of where the balance of power seems to be more of the world than of the Kingdom. Remember: 'This is not the way it is among you.'
- Now, as appropriate, offer your thoughts to God as prayers of thanksgiving or repentance or intercession...

For group work

- Discuss Jesus' approach to difference and dispute as demonstrated in this incident. What are the strengths of this approach? What are the difficulties? In what ways are 'Kingdom values' to be seen in Jesus' approach?
- Perhaps share stories from your own experience of when dissension has been resolved successfully, or been mishandled. What attributes does a leader need in these circumstances?
- What does this story say to us about leadership within the church today?

chapter 26

A Voice from the Edge

MARK 10:46-52

Jesus heals Blind Bartimaeus

(Matt 20:29-34; Lk 18:35-43)

They came to Jericho, and as Jesus was leaving with his disciples and a large crowd, a blind beggar named Bartimaeus son of Timaeus was sitting by the road. When he heard that it was Jesus of Nazareth, he began to shout, 'Jesus, son of David! Take pity on me!'

Many of the people scolded him and told him to be quiet. But he shouted even more loudly, 'Son of David, take pity on me!'

Jesus stopped and said, 'Call him.'

So they called the blind man. 'Cheer up!' they said. 'Get up, he is calling you.'

He threw off his cloak, jumped up, and came to Jesus.

'What do you want me to do for you?' Jesus asked him.

'Teacher,' the blind man answered, 'I want to see again.'

'Go,' Jesus told him, 'your faith has made you well.'

At once he was able to see and followed Jesus on the road.

Sight to the blind

Now the group around Jesus has come to the very outskirts of Jerusalem. The end is almost in sight. There is one final healing story to complete the cycle, the story of blind Bartimaeus. It involves two contrasts. There is the obvious clash between the appearance of this poor beggar who comes with only his need, receives sight and immediately follows Jesus, and the blind disciples who have just been portrayed as fearful and lagging far behind. There is also the disparity between this man who comes with nothing and Jesus' last encounter with the rich man who had everything, and whose 'everything' prevented him from taking the way of Jesus. He could not give up his 'abundance'. The poor man, in his eagerness to follow Jesus, throws off the cloak he spread out every day to catch the coins he begged, his only means of livelihood. Bartimaeus' action in discarding his cloak is powerful. The cloak is his protection, his working clothes, his fashion statement, his bank, yet he throws it away eagerly. He knows he needs something else, therefore what he has he casts aside to receive it. Exit the security blanket!

In the story we see the crowd, full of the uncaring and heedless attitudes of an unreformed world, 'Keep this nobody out the way!' 'Tell that beggar to shut up!' (10:48) Watch the way the portrayal of the crowd changes as the cross looms. This crowd is no longer merely hungry and needy, it has become mean and malevolent. Listen to the beggar with his insistent cries for help, quite deliberately naming Jesus with a Messianic title, 'Jesus, Son of David.' Watch Jesus himself, preoccupied as he is with all that lies before him, taking time to stop and turn aside to attend to this man. By his attention, he shows in actions more powerful than any words that, in the eyes of God, no one is nobody; everyone has a name, a place and a value.

If we had only the disciples' progress in faith and insight to look to, by this stage in the gospel drama we would be near despair. What can Jesus do in the face of their seemingly immovable blindness? Here the story of blind Bartimaeus reminds us that Jesus does indeed bring sight to the blind, even in the most unlikely, unexpected circumstances. There is yet hope for all that lies ahead. In a strange way Bartimaeus, a man with nothing who rises up and follows Jesus, fulfils the recently spoken words: '... many who are now first will be last, and many who are now last will be first.' (10:31)

Here is Myers' comment on this story.

> Mark draws a devastating contrast between the beggar's initiative and the aspirations of the disciples. Upon their approach, Jesus had asked James and John, 'What do you want me to do for you? (10:36). To the beggar's petition, Jesus responds with exactly the same words. But how different the requests! The disciples want status and privilege; the beggar simply asks for his 'vision'. It is Bartimaeus who is told to take courage, as the disciples have been told earlier during their dangerous crossing of the sea. (6:50) And it is the beggar who follows. The narrative discourse of hope is now clear in this last discipleship/healing episode. Only if the

disciples (or the readers) struggle against the internal demons that render us deaf and mute, only if we renounce our thirst for power - in a word, only if we recognise our blindness and seek true vision - only then can the discipleship adventure carry on. (Myers 1988, p.282)

STUDY

BY YOURSELF

Meditation
- Picture yourself sitting by the roadside. Hear the harsh comments of the crowd; feel the hostile atmosphere. Jesus of Nazareth is to pass by. What do you want from him?
- As Jesus stops to speak, feel the cloak of your past around your shoulders. What do you need to leave behind here in order to see clearly and follow Jesus?

PAUSE

ON ENTERING JERUSALEM

We have arrived at Jerusalem, place of the final drama of the gospel. Chapter 11 sees the beginning of the penultimate section of the gospel, which runs to the end of Chapter 13. Before we plunge into the narrative, let's take our bearings in the gospel as a whole. We have just come through a section which began at the gospel's turning point in Chapter 8 when Jesus announced his cross immediately after Peter's confession of 'the Christ'. Throughout that section, from mid-Chapter 8 through Chapters 9 and 10, Mark shows Jesus trying to get the disciples to face up to who he truly is, to 'see' him, and also to 'see' what it means to follow him, to belong to the new community he creates. In a way, Chapters 8 to 10 correspond to the first chapter of the gospel whose themes are also Jesus revealed, the Kingdom announced, the call to follow issued. All these themes are taken up and intensified at the start of the second half of the story.

Think back to Chapters 2 and 3. They chart Jesus' confrontation with the Scribes and the Pharisees. Chapters 11 to 13 parallel this. Here is the second major confrontation, this time with the power of the Temple State itself, at the centre of the metropolitan heartland in Jerusalem. Jesus makes three consecutive visits to the Temple: the first to find out the lie of the land; the second to take decisive action; the third to engage in long debate, providing the structure of Chapters 11 and 12. Another extended reflection on what has gone before and what is yet to come forms the substance of Chapter 13, a parallel to the Sower Sermon in Chapter 4. We then move into the final section, the gospel's culmination around the trial, cross and resurrection in Chapters 14-16.

chapter 27

Crowd Trouble

MARK 11:1-11

The Triumphal Entry into Jerusalem

(Matt 21:1-11; Lk 19:28-40; Jn 12:12-19)

As they approached Jerusalem, near the towns of Bethphage and Bethany, they came to the Mount of Olives. Jesus sent two of his disciples on ahead with these instructions: 'Go to the village there ahead of you. As soon as you get there, you will find a colt tied up that has never been ridden. Untie it and bring it here. And if someone asks you why you are doing that, tell them that the Master needs it and will send it back at once.'

So they went and found a colt out in the street, tied to the door of a house. As they were untying it, some of the bystanders asked them, 'What are you doing, untying that colt?'

They answered just as Jesus had told them, and the bystanders let them go. They brought the colt to Jesus, threw their cloaks over the animal, and Jesus got on. Many people spread their cloaks on the road, while others cut branches in the fields and spread them on the road. The people who were in front and those who followed behind began to shout, 'Praise God! God bless him who comes in the name of the Lord! God bless the coming kingdom of King David, our father! Praise God!'

Jesus entered Jerusalem, went into the Temple, and looked round at everything. But since it was already late in the day, he went out to Bethany with the twelve disciples.

INTO THE CITY

Jesus has arrived at Jerusalem. Preceding verses have prepared the reader for this moment: 'They were going up to Jerusalem.' (10:32) 'They came to Jericho.' (10:46) 'They came to Bethany and Bethphage, near Jerusalem.' (11:1) With each step they take, Jesus and his followers draw nearer. The tension mounts as the arrival is imminent. Jesus' entry into Jerusalem on what we call Palm Sunday is another of those gospel stories we often approach through the simplistic understanding of childhood songs and memories. 'Hosanna, loud Hosanna, the little children sang.' There are no children here in Mark's story. We should guard against regarding this as a simple festive occasion by recalling that the only disciple shown as following Jesus into Jerusalem with enthusiasm is Bartimaeus, blind until recently (10:52). There is a close and reinforcing connection between the poor blind disciple and the unlikely, lowly king. This is no simple story of the entry of King Jesus. Irony and paradox fill the air - Jesus' deliberate intention, as is made clear by his actions.

THE QUESTION RAISED, WHAT KIND OF KING?

The story is often called 'Jesus' triumphal entry into Jerusalem'. Closer scrutiny reveals the occasion is less than triumphal and not much of an entry. The 'entry' comes only in the last verse which states very tersely, 'Jesus entered Jerusalem, went to the temple, had a look round, but, since it was late, he left.' (11:11) Myers' commentary on this story is called, 'Liberator on an ass? Political street theatre' (Myers 1988 p. 294). Note the question mark. 'Political street theatre' is a very good description for the happenings here. From the opening verses with their detailed instructions to the two disciples to collect the ass it is clear that Jesus planned this whole affair with care. He deliberately arranges a demonstration to encourage people to ask questions about who he is and what he is about. 'Find the ass,' he says, 'and bring it to me at the Mount of Olives.' (11:2)

The Mount of Olives had a number of associations with triumphant victories. In Zechariah 14 is written:

I will gather all the nations against Jerusalem to battle, and the city shall be taken and the house plundered ... Then will Yahweh, the Lord go forth and fight against the nations as when he fights on a day of battle. On that day his feet shall stand on the Mount of Olives.

(Zechariah 14:2-4; tr. Myers 1988, p.294)

Zechariah's words probably refer to the military entry of Simon Maccabeus at the time of the Maccabean revolt in the second century BCE. There may be a more contemporary reference in the time of Mark's writing, that of the entry of the Sicarian leader Menahem in the summer of 66CE, during the revolt against Roman power before the destruction of the Jerusalem Temple.

THINK AGAIN!

Jesus is inviting people to ask the question, 'Do you see me as *this* kind of Messiah, the political warrior, the one who by force will restore the kingdom of David? If you do, think again'. Think again, for there are some very obvious conflicting signals. There is the ass itself, calling to mind another strand of the Zechariah tradition, the Messiah who comes not as the warlord but in peace, 'meek, riding upon an ass'. (Zech 9:9) That text is also about the liberation of Jerusalem, but is expressly anti-military in its tone. Jesus is not coming to fight for Jerusalem as leader of the nation, but to invoke a third strand in Zechariah (13:3), that is, to call the nation to judgement.

In the light of 'before' and 'after', the procession into Jerusalem seems a like an ironic interlude. There is something off-key about this exuberant procession so close to the cross itself. The scene recalls a device used by tragedians (particularly in classical Greek tragedy by Sophocles), that of placing a joyful scene, full of confidence and happiness and often including a dance or procession, immediately before the play's central tragedy. Here, Mark challenges his readers to look deeper, not to be like the crowd who see Jesus only in terms of the restoration of the great King David. We are about to witness a battle for Jerusalem, a power struggle over the place and meaning of the Temple, which is ultimately about the place of God in his world. It will be a different type of battle, fought with very different weapons and with an unexpected outcome.

Mark and Jesus heighten the tension so that we see the point of conflict and understand what the battle is about. This is no simple story - think about the cry of the crowd, 'Hosanna'. In its origin, 'Hosanna' means 'God save'. May God save the one who comes, the one who all through his recent journey towards this point has been insistently announcing his death. Look at the final verse, 11:11. After the excitement with the crowd on his entry into Jerusalem, what happens when Jesus finally arrives? 'He entered the city, went to the temple, looked round, but since it was late, he left.' (11:11) We are left wondering - what next?

STUDY

A prayer

As you enter Jerusalem, Lord Jesus, and as you enter into the awesome intensity of the last week of your earthly life, the final, crucial stages of your journey, help me to wait, and watch and pray with you. Open my eyes in new ways to love's cost and love's glory. *Amen*

FOR GROUP WORK

Karl Barth said we should pray with our Bibles in one hand and the daily newspaper in the other. We could say that in Jesus' carefully prepared entry into Jerusalem he was making the news. In today's world, the influence of the media is all-pervasive, and we are increasingly aware of the media's role in making news as well as reporting it. The group leader could assemble a collection of recent daily newspapers and then get the group members to read through them to see how much of the 'news' in them is 'staged', i.e. comes from press conferences, releases, leaks, etc.

The discussion can focus on two questions:
- How do we discern the truth in today's media jungle?
- How can the church be more 'media wise' in communicating its message?

chapter 28

Temple Trouble

MARK 11:12-26

Jesus curses the Fig Tree
(Matt 21:18-19)

The next day, as they were coming back from Bethany, Jesus was hungry. He saw in the distance a fig tree covered with leaves, so he went to see if he could find any figs on it. But when he came to it, he found only leaves, because it was not the right time for figs. Jesus said to the fig tree, 'No one shall ever eat figs from you again!'

And his disciples heard him.

Jesus goes to the Temple
(Matt 21. 12 -17; Lk 19. 45 -48; Jn 2. 13 -22)

When they arrived in Jerusalem, Jesus went to the Temple and began to drive out all those who were buying and selling. He overturned the tables of the money-changers and the stools of those who sold pigeons, and he would not let anyone carry anything through the temple courtyards. He then taught the people: 'It is written in the Scriptures that God said, "My

Temple will be called a house of prayer for the people of all nations." But you have turned it into a hideout for thieves!'

The chief priests and the teachers of the Law heard of this, so they began looking for some way to kill Jesus. They were afraid of him, because the whole crowd was amazed at his teaching.

When evening came, Jesus and his disciples left the city.

The lesson from the Fig Tree
(Matt 21. 20 -22)

Early next morning, as they walked along the road, they saw the fig tree. It was dead all the way down to its roots. Peter remembered what had happened and said to Jesus, 'Look, Teacher, the fig tree you cursed has died!'

Jesus answered them, 'Have faith in God. I assure you that whoever tells this hill to get up and throw itself into the sea and does not doubt in his own heart, but believes that what he says will happen, it will be done for him. For this reason I tell you: when you pray and ask for something, believe that you have received it, and you will be given whatever you ask for. And when you stand and pray, forgive anything you may have against anyone, so that your Father in heaven will forgive the wrongs you have done.'

THE SYMBOL OF THE FIG TREE

Two botanical specimens in the Bible bring out a great deal of sympathy. One is the poor fig tree here in Mark, the other is that extraordinary plant in the story of Jonah which grew and withered in a day over the head of the disgruntled prophet (Jonah 4). The plant in the Jonah story, which is worthy of a place in a comedy sketch, should give a clue to interpreting the story of the fig tree. It is very obviously symbolic and surreal. Plants do not grow and wither in a day.

Something similar is going on here. Beneath the realistic narrative there is a much deeper symbolism. It is often difficult to understand the gospels unless we know something of the Old Testament. As soon as the fig tree was mentioned, Jesus' Jewish audience would recognise this commonly used metaphor for the Temple-based nation of Israel and its religious practices. The symbol of the fig tree occurs in Isaiah, Jeremiah, Hosea, Micah and Joel.

Listen to William Telford's words from his essay, 'The barren temple and the withered tree':

The fig tree was an emblem of peace, security and prosperity and is prominent when descriptions of the Golden Ages of Israel's history, past, present and future are given - the Garden of Eden, the Exodus, the Wilderness, the Promised Land, the reigns of Solomon and Simon Maccabeus, and the Coming Messianic Age. It figures predominantly in the prophetic books, and very often in passages with an *eschatological* import ... [*i.e. passages which deal with the end of history and God's judgement*]

The blossoming of the fig tree and its *giving of its fruits* is a descriptive element in passages which depict Yahweh's visiting of his people with *blessing*, while the *withering of the fig tree*, the destruction or withholding of its fruit, figures in imagery describing *Yahweh's judgement* upon his people or their enemies. The theme of judgement is especially pronounced in the prophetic books. Very often the reason given... *a corrupt Temple cultus and sacrificial system.* In some cases, indeed, the fig or the fig tree can be used expressly as a symbol for *the nation itself...* Who could doubt, then, the extraordinary impact that Jesus' cursing of the fig tree would have produced upon the reader of Mark, schooled to recognise symbolism where it occurred.
(Telford 1980, p.161ff)

This symbolism from the scriptures is reinforced by later Jewish teaching. Indeed, the teachers of the first and second centuries (CE) taught that the fruits of the fig tree had lost their savour since the Temple was destroyed.

ATTACK ON THE TEMPLE

Jesus is pointing here to nothing less than the fall of the Temple and its entire power structure, religious, economic, cultural and ideological. In the context of prophesied destruction, the story of the Temple's cleansing follows. It forms the centrepiece of Mark's attack on the Temple's political economy, an attack based on the way Temple economics exploited the poor. We follow Jesus' actions with some care. First he drives out the buyers and sellers. There are echoes here of Hosea's judgement on the ruling class in Israel. 'I will drive them out of my house,...all their rulers are disobedient.' (Hos 9:15, paraphrase) Remember how at the gospel's beginning, there was an exorcism in the synagogue at Capernaum (1:23-27). In driving out the buyers and sellers, the Temple itself is now being exorcised. Is there here another cross-reference to the parable of the strong man's house and the casting out of Satan? (3:23-27)

It is important to recognise that the point at issue was not the buying and selling itself, as much as the treatment of the place of prayer. (There's no need to dismantle your local church's Traidcraft stall.) Every temple of the Ancient World had its associated commercial activity, like many of our cathedrals today. What Jesus objected to was monopoly masquerading as public service. Jeremias says that many of the commercial interests were concentrated within the High Priestly family. Josephus claimed that the Temple was going to rack and ruin because of avarice and mutual hatred.

After dealing with the buyers and sellers in general, Jesus moves in on two specific targets. He overturns the tables of the money changers and the pigeon sellers. The money changers exchanged the foreign currency brought by the Jews of the *Diaspora*, the pilgrims from beyond Israel. The changers rigged the exchange rate so that the pilgrims had to buy the authorised coin to buy animals for sacrifice at an inflated price. The banking system was corrupt. Today it is the international banking system which is under scrutiny. Echoing the action of Jesus, the churches were prominent in the Jubilee 2000 coalition with its campaign to end the harmful effects of Third World debt on the poorest of the world's poorest countries.

The pigeon sellers' trade was aimed at the poor. Pigeons were all that poor people could afford to sacrifice. They were specified as offerings for the purification of women and the cleansing of lepers, and their cost lay heavily on the poor. The scales of trade were unbalanced. Today, following the Debt Cancellation campaign, Christian Aid has a new campaign on Trade Justice. It invites us to discover how world trade rules discriminate against the world's poor, and to make intelligent and persistent protest against this. This campaign is also rooted in the action of Jesus in the Temple.

Jesus objects not only to the monopoly, but also to the exploitation of strangers and the despoiling of the poor. He doesn't ask for reform, for lower, fairer prices. His actions call for the whole cultic system to be overturned. We can recall his earlier full frontal attacks on the Purity and Debt Codes, cornerstones of the system, and we remember the reasons for his challenge, that the system itself is biased against the weak, the poor and the sinner.

The third step in Jesus' action against the Temple is to forbid any carrying in or out of goods. He suspends Temple trading for a day, a deeply symbolic action. We are reminded again of the parable of the strong man bound, 'No one can go into a strong man's house to plunder his goods ...' (3:27) After the action, bold, provocative, radical, outrageous, comes the reason for it. Jesus teaches the people why. He uses two texts: the first is from Isaiah, 'My temple will be called a house of prayer for the people of all nations.' The words occur towards the end of Isaiah (56:7), where the prophet sets out a great vision of the inclusion of all peoples in the worship and service of God - *all* people, including eunuchs and foreigners.

The second text comes from Jeremiah 7, a chapter notable for these strong words: 'Do not trust in these deceptive words, "This is the Temple of the lord, the Temple of the lord, the Temple of the lord."' (Jer 7:4 *NRSV*). Jeremiah 7 insists that the Temple must not be seen as a magic charm which will protect God's people regardless of how they treat one another. The prophet is quite definite, the rules of the covenant between God and his people mean that the Temple will be preserved only if there is justice towards the alien, the fatherless, the widow, the innocent. Without such right dealings the Temple and its people will suffer the same fate - destruction - that befell the shrine at Shiloh. The specific reference is to Jeremiah 7:11; 'Do you think my Temple is a hiding place for robbers?'

Jesus lays it on the line. The days of the great Temple are numbered. Those for whom the

Temple represented their bread and butter, the Chief Priests and the Scribes, heard what was being said all too clearly (11:18). The plot to kill Jesus now gathers momentum, as they search for a scheme to do away with him.

'A house for thieves - a robbers' den.' (11:17) How has the Temple sunk from its calling to be a house of prayer for all. Here is the third reference to the strong man parable (3:27). 'A house divided' is the Temple itself, its vocation betrayed by exploitation and greed.

WHERE IS GOD?

Jesus and his disciples now leave the city. The second half of the fig tree story is told as the disciples pass the withered and blasted bush. At the end of the conversation about the fate of the bush, Jesus tells the disciples to have faith, sorely needed at this point in the story, 'I assure you that whoever tells this hill to get up and throw itself into the sea, and does not doubt in his heart, but believes that what he says will happen, it will be done for him.' (11:23) The context here is important. Jesus has just predicted the destruction of the Temple and all its power. In the Middle Eastern world of Jesus' day, all gods were closely identified with their temples. If the Temple is destroyed, the critical question immediately arises, 'Where is God? How do we find faith in a God whose temple lies in ruins?' Jesus explicitly challenges the connection between God and his Temple. He claims that we can see God's continuing activity in his world through the eyes of faith, even if Zion's hill with its Temple is in the middle of the Mediterranean Sea!

In Jewish circles, mountain-uprooting images were common. The Temple mount was also *the* mountain. By the time of the first readers of Mark's gospel, the mountain has indeed moved - the Temple has become a heap of charred rubble. Mark's readers were having to find faith without the reassuring grandeur of the Jerusalem Temple. Jesus and Mark combine to say, 'You must find faith in the God-who-is-not-in-the-Temple, the God who will overthrow the Temple as the mountain ends in the sea. And you find faith by a new political imagination, a new way of looking at the world not dominated by these old powers of exclusive religion, economics and military might.' (Myers 1988 p. 305.) The new way of seeing comes through prayer and needs prayer, the profound prayer of faith, the prayer of profound faith. Remember parallel words in John's account of Jesus' conversation with the Samaritan woman at the well; 'believe me, the time is coming when you will worship the Father neither on this mountain nor in Jerusalem....God is spirit, and those who worship him must worship in spirit and in truth.' (John 4:23-4, *NRSV*)

WHERE GOD IS

In verse 25 we see the new place where God is to be found, within the reconciled and reconciling, forgiven and forgiving community. 'When you stand and pray, forgive anything you may have against anyone, so that your Father in heaven will forgive the wrongs you have done.' (11:25) These words are in the tradition of the Lord's Prayer, with its concern for forgiveness as basic to all true prayer and all true belief. Jesus is saying that the home of faith, the new house of prayer, has moved from the stone Temple into the living temple of the community of faith, the community that lives by forgiveness, reconciliation and mutual service, which we call church.

STUDY

BY YOURSELF

As Christians, we often have trouble with anger and even more trouble over the suggestion that we should be involved in political protest or action. At the temple Jesus is involved in both.

• Reflect on your experience of anger. We tend to divide emotions into 'good' or 'bad'. They aren't. It's what we do with them that matters. What should I be less angry about? What should I be more angry about? And what should I be, if not angry, at least indignant about?

• *Everything is politics but politics is not everything* is the title of a recent book of theology. Reflect on that statement.

• Look at this ancient Celtic symbol. It has no beginning or end. It tells us that life is a continuum, reality is seamless. Jesus came to help us stop dividing life up into separate, watertight compartments and to show us life as whole. Look at your life in the light of Jesus' teaching and action. See it whole.

chapter 29

Of Land and Money

MARK 11:27-12:17

The question about Jesus' Authority
(Matt 21:23-27; Lk 20:1-8)

They arrived once again in Jerusalem. As Jesus was walking in the Temple, the chief priests, the teachers of the Law, and the elders came to him and asked him, 'What right have you to do these things? Who gave you this right?'

Jesus answered them, 'I will ask you just one question, and if you give me an answer, I will tell you what right I have to do these things. Tell me, where did John's right to baptise come from: was it from God or from human beings?'

They started to argue among themselves: 'What shall we say? If we answer, "From God," he will say, "Why, then, did you not believe John?" But if we say, "From human beings ..."' (They were afraid of the people, because everyone was convinced that John had been a prophet.) So their answer to Jesus was, 'We don't know.'

Jesus said to them, 'Neither will I tell you, then, by what right I do these things.'

The Parable of the Tenants in the Vineyard
(Matt 21:33-46; Lk 20:9-19)

Then Jesus spoke to them in parables: 'Once there was a man who planted a vineyard, put a fence round it, dug a hole for the winepress, and built a watch-tower. Then he let out the vineyard to tenants and left home on a journey. When the time came to gather the grapes, he sent a slave to the tenants to receive from them his share of the harvest. The tenants seized the slave, beat him, and sent him back without a thing. Then the owner sent another slave; the tenants beat him over the head and treated him shamefully. The owner sent another slave, and they killed him; and they treated many others the same way, beating some and killing others. The only one left to send was the man's own dear son. Last of all, then, he sent his son to the tenants. "I am sure they will respect my son," he said. But these tenants said to one another, "This is the owner's son. Come on, let's kill him, and his property will be ours!" So they seized the son and killed him and threw his body out of the vineyard.

'What, then, will the owner of the vineyard do?' asked Jesus. 'He will come and kill those tenants and hand the vineyard over to others. Surely you have read this scripture:

"The stone which the builders rejected as worthless

turned out to be the most important of all.

This was done by the Lord;

what a wonderful sight it is!"'

The Jewish leaders tried to arrest Jesus, because they knew that he had told this parable against them. But they were afraid of the crowd, so they left him and went away.

The Question about paying Taxes
(Matt 22:15-22; Lk 20:20-26)

Some Pharisees and some members of Herod's party were sent to Jesus to trap him with questions. They came to him and said, 'Teacher, we know that you tell the truth, without worrying about what people think. You pay no attention to anyone's status, but teach the truth about God's will for people. Tell us, is it against our Law to pay taxes to the Roman Emperor? Should we pay them or not?'

But Jesus saw through their trick and answered, 'Why are you trying to trap me? Bring a silver coin, and let me see it.'

They brought him one, and he asked, 'Whose face and name are these?'

'The Emperor's,' they answered.

So Jesus said, 'Well, then, pay the Emperor what belongs to the Emperor, and pay God what belongs to God.'

And they were amazed at Jesus.

A QUESTION AND A KIND OF ANSWER

Jesus quickly returns to Jerusalem. He is to be found again in and around the Temple. The noise of clattering tables, clinking coins and cooing doves is replaced by sharp and serious cross-questioning. Understandably, the authorities were more than a little put out by yesterday's upset. The Chief Priests, the Teachers of the Law and the Elders, the three groupings who together made up the temple's ruling body, the Sanhedrin, confront Jesus and ask this rural upstart just who he thinks he is. More precisely, they ask him twice in the way that people do when they are outraged. 'What right have you to do these things? Who gave you this right?' (11:28)

In typical response to their questions, Jesus offers no direct answer, rather he poses them another question, whose relevance is not immediately obvious. 'Tell me, gentlemen, did John's right to baptise come from God, or was it merely a human authorisation?' (11:30) The question is not simple. John the Baptist ended up minus his head at the hands of human earthly authority, therefore Jesus is suggesting that since John's undoubted authority was denied by earthly powers, it must have had its origin in heaven. Jesus himself is an inheritor of the tradition and authority of John the Baptist. In opposition to him stands the Sanhedrin, principal Jewish rulers of the time and exercisers of considerable economic, religious and legal power. It was their claim that legitimation of their earthly power came from heaven, that they were exercising their authority on behalf of God.

If the authority of John (and Jesus) is from heaven, then big questions are raised about the Sanhedrin's legitimacy. They are not able to answer Jesus' question. The power of John, the dead prophet, and Jesus, inheritor of his role and authority, is too much for them. The rulers of the great house on the Temple mount are divided, the strong man silenced (3:27). They can only offer a feeble, 'I don't know.'

'Well,' says Jesus, 'if you don't know, I'm not going to tell you.' (11:33) A community under threat needs to be careful and economical with its words, walking the tightrope between jeopardising its principles and endangering its fragile freedom. As leader of such a community, Jesus successfully alludes to his authority while offering no hostages to fortune.

THE STONE WHICH THE BUILDERS REJECTED

The parable which follows is full of plain speaking. Remember, parables are well suited to conveying truths which cannot be stated openly. Fresh from the recent symbolic use of the fig tree and its fruits to represent the people of Israel, we meet the vineyard, fenced around and protected by the law, another persistent and potent symbol.

The identity of the storyteller matters. It is Jesus the Galilean, the man from the rural North country. Anyone who is aware of Scotland's history will understand one of the problems of the rural poor in Galilee. Galilee suffered greatly from absentee landlords. The absentee landlords whose stewardship alienated and oppressed the poor of the North were from the class of the rulers of the Sanhedrin, Jerusalem's upper crust.

Look what Jesus does! He stands the situation on its head. In the parable the landlords are represented as tenants, as the true Lord of the Land comes into view, Yahweh, God himself. 'The earth is the Lord's in all its fullness, this whole world and every living creature.' (Psalm 24:1) The ruling class entrusted with the stewardship of the land from and under God are depicted as callous and greedy, giving short shrift to the messengers of the creator-owner of the vineyard, ignoring the prophets and dismissing the rights of God. In the end, near despair, the Lord of the Land sends his own son. The allusion is clear, the son is Jesus himself. Treated with no more respect, he is summarily killed. Nothing will stop the tenants in their greed to own what they steward, to keep for themselves what belongs to God for the people (12:1-11).

THE QUESTION OF LAND TODAY

This central parable has many applications. In the church world, gifts which are given to be shared openly for the good of all are clung to fiercely for the sake of status and power. The parable itself centres round the question of land. Urban dwellers can be blind to the vital importance of the land question in so many parts of the world. For millions of people today, land issues involve more than identity and belonging, they are matters of life and death. So often land ownership is vested in the hands of a few while the many of the community are impoverished and disempowered. Inequalities may be even more marked elsewhere, 'Who owns Scotland and what account can the owners offer of their stewardship?' remains a fair, legitimate and relevant question for Christians to pursue in the company of all who seek justice. Land Tenure and Reform formed one of the main reports of the Church and Nation Committee to the Church of Scotland General Assembly of 1998.

God's own complaint is voiced in the Old Testament reference to the vineyard in Isaiah 5; the words still stand, a living reproach:

> For the vineyard of the Lord of hosts is the house of Israel,
> and the people of Judah are his pleasant planting;
> he expected justice, but saw bloodshed;

righteousness, but heard a cry!
(Isaiah 5:7 *NRSV*)

This prayer is from Christian Aid's *Bread of Tomorrow, Praying with the World's Poor.*

> God of creation, the earth is yours
> with all its beauty and goodness,
> its rich and overflowing provision.

> But we have claimed it for our own,
> plundered its beauty for profit,
> grabbed its resources for ourselves.

> God of creation, forgive us.
> May we no longer abuse your trust,
> but care gently and with justice for your earth. *Amen.*
> (Jan Berry 1992, p. 174)

At the end of the parable, Jesus turns again to scripture and quotes from Psalm 118, 'The stone which the builders rejected has become head of the corner. This is the Lord's doing, it is marvellous in our eyes.' (Ps 118:22-23 *RSV*) Jesus is the cornerstone, the living foundation of the new temple. Jesus, like David before him in the Psalm, will be rejected before he is restored; it will be a very different kind of restoration. The powers-that-be get the point of the parable without any difficulty. 'The Jewish leaders tried to arrest him because they knew that he had told this parable against them.'(12:12)

THE QUESTION ABOUT TAXATION

Time for another question, this time about taxes. This question is about the other power in the land - Roman colonial rule. If the parable of the vineyard evoked memories of the Highland Clearances, the question about taxes has more contemporary reference. The tax at issue in this encounter is 'the popularly despised poll tax'. (Myers 1988, p. 311)

Jesus is confronted again by the unholy alliance of Pharisees and Herodians; the Pharisees, self-righteous middle class anti-Romans, the Herodians, smooth, urbane upper class people who knew and played the system well. The Herodians were adept (and unrepentant) at managing the ambiguities and compromises involved in sharing power with Rome. Look at the way they approach Jesus. 'Teacher, we know that you tell the truth fearlessly, without worrying about other folk's opinions. *You* don't pay any attention to status, you tell God's truth as it is.' (12:14) With sickening unctuousness, these unscrupulous opponents are already plotting doom. Obviously, the question contains a trap. Yet Jesus is not found in the ranks of the unwary.

HEADS OR TAILS?

The question is, 'Is it against our law to pay taxes to the Roman Emperor? Should we pay them or not?' (12:14) The double-bind works like this. If Jesus says 'pay', he shows himself up as a collaborator; if he says 'don't pay', he opens himself to the charge of lawlessness.

To pay or not to pay, shall we pay or not? In the 1980s, the thud of our own poll tax bills through the letterbox concentrated our minds and demanded real choices. Is Jesus involved, is he part of the *'we'* or not? After the question, picture a pause while Jesus appears to ponder. He then asks a not-so-innocent question. 'That's a truly difficult question. Let me think hard. Excuse me, has anyone got a coin? Could you bring me a coin, please?' In asking for a coin, the obvious implication is that he hasn't got one himself. If he has no coin, then he won't be paying, though he never actually says so. His question forces his opponents to produce a coin, and he invites them to tell him and all around what is on the coin. 'Whose face and name are these?' (12:16)

The face is that of the Roman Emperor, the inscription underneath is 'Son of the Divine'. On the coin produced by Jesus' opponents is an image and a title which, taken together, would be considered by any devout Jew to be blasphemous and idolatrous. One ancient source speaks of patriotic and devout Jews who would 'never touch a coin on the ground that one should never carry, nor look upon, nor make an image'.

So the claims of Caesar, depicted on his money, were more than politically unwelcome and oppressive, they were blasphemous and idolatrous. By calling for the coin, Jesus springs the trap set for him; by not having a coin himself he distances himself from standing under Caesar's allegiance; by making his opponents produce the coin he implicates them in a collaboration which would be anathema to many fellow Jews.

ONLY ONE HEAD

At the last, there is Jesus' famous aphorism, 'Render to Caesar the things which are Caesar's and to God the things which are God's' (12:17). This is probably one of the most misconstrued texts in the whole Bible. Its abuses are well known. The text has been used to justify a rigid separation of faith and politics, church and state; to assert that God and money have nothing to do with one another, that the things of God belong to a realm called 'spiritual', while the concerns of Caesar belong to worldly reality from which faith must keep its distance. No Jew in Jesus' audience would divide reality between the rule of God and the sway of Caesar. On the contrary, many believed that Caesar had usurped God's place and must be driven out by armed revolt. Even those who had some sympathy with Caesar's ways were clear that he was only a human ruler. His power was but the trusteeship of a steward, given for a time to any earthly ruler by the only Lord of heaven and earth, the Lord of Hosts.

The misinterpretation is based on a misapprehension that in some way God and Caesar are to be considered as equals. In the mind of Jesus and his audience this is not so. God the

Creator is the supreme authority who alone has the power to give and sustain life. Remember the famous graffiti: 'God is dead. Nietzsche'; 'Nietzsche is dead. God'. At the very least, Caesar is totally subordinate to God, if not seen in direct opposition.

Hebrew speech and writings often used parallel statements or 'doublets', where the second statement either reinforced the meaning of the first (a figure of speech called 'synthetic parallelism'), or negated the first (called 'antithetical parallelism'). 'The first shall be last and the last first' (10:31) is a classic antithetical parallelism. 'Whoever would be great among you must be a servant, whoever would be first must be a slave' (10:43-4) is a synthetic parallelism. 'Render to Caesar the things that are Caesar's and to God the things that are God's' (12:17) is a parallelism, but of which kind? Often it has been interpreted as synthetic, with the inference that God and Caesar belong to equal spheres of influence. However, it is not synthetic, it is antithetical; the two injunctions stand in opposition to one another because God and Caesar are not equal. The claims of God over-ride the pretensions of Caesar, the things of God include all that belongs to the Emperor. One simple and direct restatement of the passage is 'Repay the one you owe.' God is the one to whom we owe everything.

The church and Christians sometimes get things wrong in that, while they see the point in dethroning and relativising Caesar, they set themselves up in authority in Caesar's place. The church no less than Caesar stands under the judgement of God, and has life only through his word and grace. We too have to guard against the temptations of imperial hubris.

Mark depicts here a very subtle position where Jesus accepts neither the authority of the Sanhedrin nor that of Rome, yet does not sanction open - and certainly not armed - revolt. The revolution will come, the day of the old powers is done; their authority is shown as bankrupt and bereft of legitimacy. However, revolution will come in a new way, it will come only through Jesus' own sacrifice, whose time is imminent.

STUDY

BY YOURSELF

- The unequal division of land remains one of the main causes of poverty and powerlessness in our world. Do some research and find out more about contemporary questions of land and justice. The resources of Christian Aid provide a good starting place.
- To begin reflection on what money means to you, make a list of your fears associated with money and also any joys you experience with money. Make as long a list as you like, but three of each would do.

FOR GROUP WORK

'The world belongs to God, the earth and all its inhabitants.' (Psalm 24:1, author's paraphrase)
- Discuss together ways in which your faith community can witness to the truth that this world is God's world, in its care for creation and its attitude to money.

chapter 30

More or less about Money

MARK 12:18-13:3

The Question about Rising from Death
(Matt 22:23-33; Lk 20:27-40)

Then some Sadducees, who say that people will not rise from death, came to Jesus and said, 'Teacher, Moses wrote this law for us: "If a man dies and leaves a wife but no children, that man's brother must marry the widow so that they can have children who will be considered the dead man's children." Once there were seven brothers; the eldest got married and died without having children. Then the second one married the woman, and he also died without having children. The same thing happened to the third brother, and then to the rest: all seven brothers married the woman and died without having children. Last of all, the woman died. Now, when all the dead rise to life on the day of resurrection, whose wife will she be? All seven of them had married her.'

Jesus answered them, 'How wrong you are! And do you know why? It is because you don't know the Scriptures or God's power. For when the dead rise to life, they will be like the angels in heaven, and will not marry. Now, as for the dead being raised; haven't you ever read in the Book of Moses the passage about the burning bush? There it is written that God said to Moses, "I am the God of Abraham, the God of Isaac, and the God of Jacob." He is the God of the living, not of the dead. You are completely wrong!'

The Great Commandment
(Matt 22:34-40; Lk 10:25-28)

A teacher of the Law was there who heard the discussion. He saw that Jesus had given the Sadducees a good answer, so he came to him with a question: 'Which commandment is the most important of all?'

Jesus replied, 'The most important one is this, "Listen, Israel! The Lord our God is the only Lord. Love the Lord your God with all your heart, with all your soul, with all your mind, and with all your strength." The second most important commandment is this: "Love your neighbour as you love yourself." There is no other commandment more important than these two.'

The teacher of the Law said to Jesus, 'Well done, Teacher! It is true, as you say, that only the Lord is God and that there is no other god but he. And to love God with all your heart and with all your mind and with all your strength; and to love your neighbour as yourself, is more important than to offer animals and other sacrifices to God.'

Jesus noticed how wise his answer was, and so he told him, 'You are not far from the Kingdom of God.'

After this nobody dared to ask Jesus any more questions.

The Question about the Messiah
(Matt 22:41-46; Lk 20:41-44)

As Jesus was teaching in the Temple, he asked the question, 'How can the teachers of the Law say that the Messiah will be the descendant of David? The Holy Spirit inspired David to say:

"The Lord said to my Lord:

Sit here on my right

until I put your enemies under your feet."

David himself called him "Lord"; so how can the Messiah be David's descendant?'

Jesus warns against the Teachers of the Law
(Matt 23:1-36; Lk 20:45-47)

A large crowd was listening to Jesus gladly. As he taught them, he said, 'Watch out for the teachers of the Law, who like to walk around in their long robes and be greeted with respect in the market-place, who choose the reserved seats in the synagogues and the best places at feasts. They take advantage of widows and rob them of their homes, and then make a show of saying long prayers. Their punishment will be all the worse!'

The Widow's Offering
(Lk 21:1-4)

As Jesus sat near the temple treasury, he watched the people as they dropped in their money. Many rich men dropped in a lot of money; then a poor widow came along and dropped in two little copper coins, worth about a penny. He called his disciples together and said to them, 'I tell you that this poor widow put more in the offering box than all the others. For the others put in what they had to spare of their riches; but she, poor as she is, put in all she had - she gave all she had to live on.'

Jesus speaks of the Destruction of the Temple
(Matt 24:1-2; Lk 21:5-6)

As Jesus was leaving the Temple, one of his disciples said, 'Look, Teacher! What wonderful stones and buildings!'

Jesus answered, 'You see these great buildings? Not a single stone here will be left in its place; every one of them will be thrown down.'

A LESS THAN HONEST QUESTION

George MacLeod often told a story of wrestling with that most demanding of audiences, a group of teenagers. He was in the middle of a question-and-answer session with questions raining on him. One bright spark thought he had the ultimate in unanswerable questions. He asked, 'What was God doing before he made the world?' With a glint in his eye George replied, 'Making hell for people who ask questions like that!'

Not all questions are necessarily as serious as they sound. Underneath the apparently serious may lurk the deeply frivolous. This happens here in Jesus' encounter with the Sadducees (12:18-27). The Sadducees were a rich, land-owning class, deeply conservative in all their ways. As landowners they had a vested interest in the laws of inheritance. As religious conservatives they took their stand on the Law of Moses, the Torah. There is a certain cynicism here - the Sadducees who, as the text tells, did not believe in the resurrection, ask a question about resurrection. Behind the question is the more mundane question of property. Concerning the story of the woman who marries seven brothers in turn who each predecease her, leaving her in that most shameful of states, childless, the real question they are asking is, 'To whom will she finally belong: whose "property" will she be?'

Jesus' replies that the question is built on false assumptions. Inheritance is irrelevant since in heaven, the domain of God, patriarchal marriage rights will be no more. So the marriage part of the question falls. As to the resurrection - 'You work out your interpretation of the law by reducing it to the level of a dead letter, which you then use to create structures of dominance and dependence. God, however, is not the God of the dead, but of the living.' (12:27) God gave to Moses a life-giving word of promise.

THE GREATEST COMMANDMENT

After the Sadducee comes the Scribe. This is the last of the questions put to Jesus. It is the only conversation in this series which is not hostile. The question lies at the heart of the people's faith, 'What is the greatest commandment?' Jesus offers not one but two commandments. He quotes the great commandment from the *Shema*, 'Hear, O Israel, the Lord your God is the only God. Love the Lord your God with all your heart, all your soul, all your mind, all your strength.' (Deuteronomy 6:4, author's paraphrase) He then adds words from Leviticus 19:18, '"Love your neighbour as yourself," there is no other commandment greater than these two.' Jesus makes clear that the love of God and the love of our neighbour go together. They are inextricably linked. Love of our neighbour arises out of love for God and love for God is expressed in the love of our neighbours.

The quotation from Leviticus is particularly interesting. Its context links love of neighbour with a number of commands against the oppression and exploitation of the weak, the vulnerable and the poor (Leviticus 19:9-17). These laws are specifically designed to protect such groups. Mark has already shown that these were the groups that Scribal law discriminated against. Once again we are aware of our perverse human ability to take what God offers us for good and to turn it to our own self-interest.

'NOT FAR FROM THE KINGDOM OF GOD'

Returning to the encounter, the Scribe, perhaps surprisingly, agrees with Jesus. Jesus in turn is warm in his reply, 'You are not far from the Kingdom of God'. Not far - but not quite there. A gap remains since right thinking, orthodoxy, by itself is never enough. Coupled with right thinking must go right action. It is also relevant that while the Scribe personally may draw very near to Jesus' way and Jesus' Kingdom, it is the system which he stands for and benefits from which so greatly impedes the Kingdom's coming.

CONCERNING THE MESSIAH

'After this, nobody dared to ask Jesus any more questions.' (12:34) In the heart of the strong man's territory, at the gates of his house in the Temple court itself, the opposition is reduced to silence. In the war of words, Jesus wins. The talk is not yet over, however. Now Jesus goes on the offensive. How can the Scribes say that the Messiah will be a descendant of King David? If the Messiah is a descendant of David, his purposes will be limited to the restoration of the rule of David, the renewal of the Davidic state, and that is the whole point at issue: Jesus simply is not such a Messiah (12:35-37).

Jesus quotes from another of the great Messianic Psalms, Psalm 110: 'The Lord said to my Lord, "Sit here on my right until I put your enemies under my feet".' The argument is that if David calls the Messiah 'Lord', then the Messiah must exist before him. Jesus is here refusing to be identified simply with the title 'Son of David'. Instead of submitting to the tradition of David, that tradition must allow itself to be reinterpreted by him. Those who cheered his entry into the city with the words, 'Blessed be the coming kingdom of our father David' (11:10) had better think again!

RICH SCRIBES AND POOR WIDOWS

The teaching continues and the next two episodes belong together. They are about rich Scribes and poor widows. 'Watch out for them,' says Jesus, 'in their long fine robes, strutting about the place with everybody bowing and scraping before them. Look at them getting the best seats in the synagogue and the best places at the dinner table.' (12:38 -40) And all the time the discipleship litany is ticking away in our heads, 'The first shall be last and the last first.'(10:31) 'The Son of man came not to be served but to serve and to give his life.'(10:45) Jesus goes on to complain that Scribal piety is a cloak for the oppression of widows and the powerless of the land. The point of his complaint is that it was the special duty of the Scribes as the keepers of the law to be the protectors of widows and orphans.

There are two possible reasons for Jesus' attack. Very likely, because of the Scribes' outwardly pious posture, widows were willing to entrust to them the administration of their affairs. The image of the respectable family solicitor has a long history. If they were so entrusted, the Scribes then became entitled to a percentage of the widow's estate for services rendered. This practice was open to embezzlement and abuse. Underneath the pious exterior could lurk a very greedy type of legal vulture.

It is also possible that Jesus is here redoubling his attack on the Temple system and repeating his charge that the house of prayer has become the house of robbery. 'The site of Scribal piety is the temple, and the costs of this Temple devour the resources of the poor.' (Myers 1988, p. 320) Scribal piety is being attacked and debunked as a thin veil for economic opportunism and exploitation. The fat cats of the Temple system are scathingly exposed. Every time the Christian church tends towards a clerical monopoly it should keep Mark's gospel firmly in view.

THE WIDOW AND HER ALL

Now the attack on the Temple moves to its climax. First, there's the poignant juxtaposition of the poor widow and the rich, self-important Scribes. Watch with Jesus as the widow puts into the magnificence of the Temple treasury all that she has, her two small coins. The operation of the treasury was open to view, donors came forward and stated the amount of their gift and its purpose to the priest in charge - all highly visible and audible. Onlookers were invited to think, 'Isn't it wonderful to see and hear how much good X has contributed?' In the face of such munificence, Widow Y's two farthings are hardly worth a mention. Jesus says, 'Look again. Look at how the rich Scribes' system robs this exemplary poor widow of her very livelihood as it takes from her all that she has.' The contrast of widow and Scribe could hardly be greater. The Scribes stand doubly condemned. Looking back in the gospel, what a contrast there is between this poor widow, giving her all, and the rich young man who turns away and gives nothing (10:17-22).

The story of the widow also points to Jesus himself, whose end lies immediately before him in the cross which is the giving of his all. Again, a woman is given a place of prominence - this poor woman has a place of honour. Her act of giving at the Temple treasury prefigures the act of Jesus himself in the Garden of Gethsemane and the hill of Golgotha.

WHERE DOES GOD LIVE?

Jesus now leaves the Temple for the last time. The voices of the disciples, strangely silent for the last few chapters, are heard again. Once more, their comment on leaving the Temple is totally inappropriate. They manage to sound like many Christian pilgrims to the Holy Land in recent years who have eyes only for holy sites and history and shut out the reality of present struggle and suffering. As they leave, one of the disciples says to Jesus, 'Look, what a wonderful place this is. Isn't the building impressive?' (13:1) It *was* an awe-inspiring building, but Jesus has just been spending his time making it clear that, behind the majestic facade, there was a doomed house of the dead, a temple whose time was past. The Temple stood under God's judgement for dealing out alienation and disfavour to those it should have been affirming and empowering.

I remember the comments of a friend when he returned from serving as a priest in a country in the Asian sub-continent. He was always stopped short by finding magnificent places of worship in situations where people were living in grinding poverty. Moving into a different culture, he saw in a new way how the splendour of religious buildings can hold sway over the minds and lives of the poor and the despised. 'It wasn't till I got there,' he said, 'I really saw what the prophets were on about with their condemnation of religion in the name of faith and justice.' The prophetic heritage is common to the three great Abrahamic faiths, Judaism, Christianity and Islam. Jesus inherits the message of the prophets. In his insistent linking of the love of God and neighbour lies condemnation of a religious system which lacked a vital and life-giving dimension. In the words of the prophet Amos:

> Come to Bethel - and infringe my law!
> Come to Gilgal - and infringe it yet more!
> Bring your sacrifices for the morning,
> your tithes within three days.
> Burn your thank-offering without leaven;
> announce publicly your freewill-offerings;
> for this is what you Israelites love to do!'
> (Amos 4:4-5, REB)

'It may satisfy you, it doesn't satisfy me,' says God. Can there be anything worse than a corrupt religion which uses the name of God to prevent the outpouring and the outworking of his love and justice? It has been done and is being done in all kinds of ways, some blatant, some subtly cynical and covert. This is why the Temple and all that it stands for is doomed. It also leads us to the question what is happening in our own houses today.

In Scotland today we wrestle with the crumbling legacy of Victorian zeal in building churches - too many churches, by-products of our Presbyterian tendencies to schism. Now these churches are often in the wrong place, housing dwindling congregations in urgent need of 'hearing' Jesus' liberating teaching about the home of the true temple.

There's a wider question, too, about buildings. In William McIlvanney's novel, *Strange Loyalties,* Davy, a disillusioned and sometimes drunken architect, speaks in the tradition of the prophets:

> 'Theatre,' Davy said. 'That's what houses are, you know. Just theatre. All buildings are. Charades of permanence. They're fantasies. Fictions we make about ourselves. Right?... Well, most houses are lies, anyway. If we just built them as shelters, that would be fair enough. If we say, look, we're a pretty feeble species and it's cold out there and we need all the help we can get to survive, that makes sense. Let's make wee shelters and hide in them. That's honest. A tent's honest. But as soon as we go past function, we're at it. Big houses aren't an expression of ourselves. They're a denial of ourselves. We're not saying, see how feeble we are, but look at how important we are. Right? We're saying we could be here forever. We're a permanent

fixture. Houses are one of the main ways that we tell lies about ourselves. They're public statements of security and stability that deny the private truth. They're masks. They're where we play out roles that aren't us. Just theatre. Look at houses carefully. (McIlvanney 1991, pp. 238-9)

'Look at these great buildings.' (13:1) The disciples have been blinded by the trappings of religion so that they cannot see the new temple in their midst. Jesus says, 'Look more carefully.' He leaves them in no doubt as to whom the future belongs. 'You see these great buildings? Not a single stone here will be left in its place; every one of them will be thrown down!' (13:2) The future doesn't belong to the massive temple of a sclerotic religion built on division, oppression and alienation. It belongs to a frail temple of flesh and blood whose own final trial lies close at hand. It is through Jesus himself that our own flesh and blood can become living temples, homes and places where the living God, the God of Love and Justice and Peace, can live (1 Peter 2:4-10).

STUDY

BY YOURSELF

Two related themes emerge from this section: living without pretension and true giving.
• Reflect on the contrast between the finery of the Scribes and the poor clothes of the widow, and between the magnificence of the temple and the broken body of Jesus.
• Reflect also on your experiences of generosity.

FOR GROUP WORK

'The question is; am I ready to shift my security base from Mammon to God?' (Ministry of Money, Church of the Saviour, Washington DC).
• In the light of your personal reflections and your discussion in the previous section, construct a programme of actions for a generous church, living in today's divided world.

chapter 31

ApOcalypse then and nOw

MARK 13:3-37

Troubles and Persecutions
(Matt 24:3-14; Lk 21:7-19)

Jesus was sitting on the Mount of Olives, across from the Temple, when Peter, James, John, and Andrew came to him in private. 'Tell us when this will be,' they said, 'and tell us what will happen to show that the time has come for all these things to take place.'

Jesus said to them, 'Be on guard, and don't let anyone deceive you. Many men, claiming to speak for me, will come and say, "I am he!" and they will deceive many people. And don't be troubled when you hear the noise of battles close by and news of battles far away. Such things must happen, but they do not mean that the end has come. Countries will fight each other; kingdoms will attack one another. There will be earthquakes everywhere, and there will be famines. These things are like the first pangs of childbirth.

'You yourselves must be on guard. You will be arrested and taken to court. You will be beaten in the synagogues; you will stand before rulers and kings for my sake to tell them the

Good News. But before the end comes, the gospel must be preached to all peoples. And when you are arrested and taken to court, do not worry beforehand about what you are going to say; when the time comes, say whatever is then given to you. For the words you speak will not be yours; they will come from the Holy Spirit. Men will hand over their own brothers to be put to death, and fathers will do the same to their children. Children will turn against their parents and have them put to death. Everyone will hate you because of me. But whoever holds out to the end will be saved.

The Awful Horror
(Matt 24:15-28; Lk 21:20-24)

'You will see 'The Awful Horror' standing in the place where he should not be. (Note to the reader: be sure to understand what this means!) Then those who are in Judea must run away to the hills. Someone who is on the roof of his house must not lose time by going down into the house to get anything to take with him. Someone who is in the field must not go back to the go back to the house for his cloak. How terrible it will be in those days for women who are pregnant and for mothers with little babies! Pray to God that these things will not happen in the winter! For the trouble of those days will be far worse than any the world has ever known form the very beginning when God created the world until the present time. Nor will there ever be anything like it again. But the Lord has reduced the number of those days; if he had not, nobody would survive. For the sake of his chosen people, however, he has reduced those days.

'Then, if anyone says to you, 'Look, here is the Messiah!' or 'Look, there he is!' - do not believe him. For false Messiahs and false prophets will appear. They will perform miracles and wonders in order to deceive even God's chosen people, if possible. Be on your guard! I have told you everything before the time comes.

The coming of the Son of Man
(Matt 24:29-31; Lk 21:25-28)

'In the days after that time of trouble the sun will grow dark, the moon will no longer shine, the stars will fall from heaven, and the powers in space will be driven from their courses. Then the Son of Man will appear, coming in the clouds with great power and glory. He will send the angels out to the four corners of the earth to gather God's chosen people from one end of the world to the other.

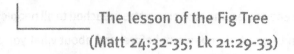
'Let the fig tree teach you a lesson. When its branches become green and tender and it starts putting out leaves, you know that summer is near. In the same way, when you see these things happening, you will know that the time is near, ready to begin. Remember that all these things will happen before the people now living have all died. Heaven and earth will pass away, but my words will never pass away.

No one knows the Day or Hour
(Matt 24:36-44)

'No one knows, however, when that day or hour will come - neither the angels in heaven, nor the Son; only the Father knows. Be on watch, be alert, for you do not know when the time will come. It will be like a man who goes away from home on a journey and leaves his servants in charge, after giving to each one his own work to do and after telling the doorkeeper to keep watch. Be on guard, then, because you do not know when the master of the house is coming - it might be in the evening or at midnight or before dawn or at sunrise. If he comes suddenly, he must not find you asleep. What I say to you, then, I say to all: 'Watch!'

STAY AWAKE!

Let the last word be the first word. The final word of this passage is Jesus' injunction to 'Stay awake!'. Wakefulness is essential, for interpreting the thirteenth chapter of Mark is not easy. Professor William Barclay called it the most difficult chapter in the New Testament. It will demand considerable vigilance.

SPEAKING OF THE END-TIME; DESCRIBING THE INDESCRIBABLE

'Apocalypse' refers to the Ultimate End: it seeks to describe the events of the End-time, when God would return to enact judgement and establish justice. Apocalyptic writing is therefore an attempt to describe the indescribable and foresee the unforeseeable.

Let's take a moment to recall the context of this passage. We have noted that there is considerable parallelism between the first and second halves of Mark's gospel, pivoting round the fulcrum of the 'Christ/cross' sequence with Jesus, Peter and the disciples in Chapter 8. However unlikely it may seem, Mark 13 in many ways parallels Jesus' parable of the sower in Chapter 4. Both offer an extended reflection on the action around them, before and after. Taking up the parallel, Ched Myers calls Chapter 13, 'The Second Sermon on Revolutionary Patience'. Hold on to the words 'revolutionary' and 'patience' throughout the passage.

The form of the discourse is significant. Jesus' way of speaking here is full of apocalyptic metaphors. Apocalyptic writing had become a substantial genre in Hebrew literature, largely in the inter-Testamental period from the third to the first centuries BCE. Such writing is found in the discourses of the Book of Daniel; in other late prophetic books and in the books of the Apocrypha. Apocalyptic writing pushes language to its descriptive limits - it is highly figurative, symbolic and metaphorical. As the literature developed, certain forms and metaphors became characteristic. In Mark 13, verses 24-27, the sections describing portents in the sky, dramatic meteorological events, and the coming of the Son of Man on the clouds of heaven, use classic apocalyptic imagery. (See Daniel 7, a key passage, expanded on later.)

Apocalypse has to do with God's future intervention. By its very nature, this is superhuman, beyond ordinary history; we could say 'other-worldly'. The symbolic language used to talk about it becomes intelligible through long usage in a people's history and tradition. Like speaking in parables, such symbolism makes the speech or writing very powerful. In a situation of oppression it can give voice to things that cannot be uttered directly. It is also used to place what is happening in people's own experience against the backdrop of a cosmic struggle between good and evil. The classic New Testament example is the Book of Revelation, the Apocalypse of St John the Divine. In Revelation the symbol of the great beast may be taken to refer to some general spiritual power of evil but it is also likely to be an allegorical reference to the malign power of the Roman Emperor. Such contemporary referencing was quite common. Scholars have discovered apocalypses where the same general form is used with specific references, distinct because they refer to different historical situations. The use of apocalypse here announces that the event of Jesus and his cross represents a fundamental turning point, not just in the history of the Temple, but of the cosmos.

A word about Mark's style is necessary here. It was an accepted literary convention of the time to put speeches into the mouths of the principal characters. This was not 'word for word' accurate reportage but intended to convey the characters' meaning and their specific situation. (No reporters' notebooks, digital cameras or recorders!) Greek historians including Thucydides bear witness to this practice. It does not belittle the Bible's status as inspired word to understand that Mark 13, indeed the whole gospel as we have it, is the product of Mark the editor as well as Jesus the speaker.

CONTEXT: JESUS' LIFE

It is important here to be aware here of the 'bifocal' nature of Mark's gospel. It has two immediate contexts: Jesus' own situation and the situations of Mark and his readers.

Apocalyptic writing was born out of a state of political and religious turmoil, and Jesus himself lived in a time of great political and religious unrest. He lived as a subject person in a land where the influence of the Roman Emperor disrupted his life from cradle to grave. We have also seen him repeatedly at loggerheads with the religious establishment of his own Jewish nation, who were extremely powerful figures. This chapter begins with Jesus predicting the Temple's doom, the collapse of the social and religious ideology and the power structure of his own society.

CONTEXT: MARK'S LIFE

The second context, the specific situation of Mark and his readers, is equally important. If we assume that Mark was writing for a mixed community of Jews and Gentiles around the borders of Galilee and consider a date of writing of around 70CE, we can appreciate that the situation is fraught. The years 66-70CE were times of great unrest in Palestine. Ched Myers gives a brief outline of the significant events:

> The [Jewish] revolt [against Rome] was launched in Jerusalem in June of 66, and quickly spread to the nearby provinces of Idumea, Perea and Galilee. In November of 66, Cestus Gallus, Roman legate of Syria, marched on Jerusalem in order to put down the insurrection. He occupied the northern part of the city, but was turned back in his siege of the temple mount. Stunned, he retreated in disarray, and sustained severe losses as Jewish guerrillas pursued him to the coast. Gallus sent an emergency message to Rome, and there was euphoria in Jerusalem: Palestine was liberated! Against all odds, outnumbered and outarmoured, the rebels had turned away the oppressors.
>
>   But the provisional government in Jerusalem was mired in internal power struggles, bordering on civil war. Indeed, the liberation was short-lived; Vespasian, probably the greatest general of his time and soon to become emperor, was dispatched to pacify Palestine. He gathered legions from Egypt and Syria, and with six thousand heavily armed troops, began a march down through Galilee toward Jerusalem. Despite heroic resistance by scattered guerrilla forces, within a short time Galilee, Perea and Western Judea were retaken by Vespasian. By June of 68, he was ready to begin his siege of Jerusalem. Once again, however, the unexpected occurred: the anticipated siege was aborted. Slowly word filtered back to the Zealot coalition now in power in Jerusalem that Rome was locked in a fierce civil war; Nero was dead, four candidates were vying to succeed him as emperor, and Vespasian had been urgently summoned back to Rome. The Jewish resistance would get a reprieve of almost a year and a half to prepare for the inevitable confrontation. Only Yahweh could have worked not one but two miracles to save the holy city!
> (Myers 1988 pp. 328-99)

There was, however, no happy ending. In the year 70CE, Vespasian won the power struggle in Rome and sent back Titus to sort out Palestine. In April he began the siege of Jerusalem; after five months of fierce fighting the city fell. It was looted and the holy of holies, the Temple, was burnt to the ground. Obviously in these years 66 to 70 one question dominated every person and every household in Galilee and Judea, *'Should we join the uprising or not? Do we join in the fight for the Temple and all that it means? Is this our moment of freedom?'*

JESUS AND RESISTANCE

The question of Jesus' relationship to those who fought to overthrow the Roman occupiers was a live one in his own lifetime. We know that Judas Iscariot and Simon the Zealot, two of the original twelve disciples, had connections with the armed struggle. Jesus has just completed his attack on the Temple; he has said that it is part of God's purpose that the entire political, religious and social power structure of the Temple State should be overthrown. People would be talking, 'There's this new prophet from Galilee, he's been having a go at the Scribes, the Pharisees and the High Priestly crowd. Good for him. What will he say to Rome? Will he join the rebels? About time too if he does - that lot occupy our country, desecrate our religion and bleed us dry with their taxes. Surely he'll fight for us and our God? Surely that's part of what being the Messiah means, if that's what he, or at any rate his friends, claim he is?'

In Mark's gospel Jesus says, 'No, this is not what I'm about: this is neither my way, your way, nor God's way. I am not that kind of king and I did not come to bring a kingdom built on force of arms, however well-intentioned. My followers are called to a revolution, but to a revolution made not with arms, but with patience.'

If we take these questions - 'Should we join the uprising or not? Do we join the fight for the Temple and all that means? Is this our moment of freedom?' - in the context in which they were first written, then Jesus' words become relevant again when the whole question of armed revolt recurs for the young church in the seething, urgent immediacy of Palestine in the years 66 to 70. Imagine the kind of pressure that the young church is under. 'Come on, this is our chance,' voices are saying. 'This may be the only opportunity we have. Call yourself a Hebrew, a patriot? Then support the rebellion. Call yourself a believer? Look how the hand of Rome has been stayed, not once, but twice; it's a sign, a miracle, God's hand must be in this.'

Mark says, in the words of our passage, 'This is not the way of Jesus. It was not the way of Jesus at the beginning and it is not the way of Jesus now. What Jesus brings is a deeper revolution, which comes neither by the sword nor by replacing one power structure with another. It therefore does not suffer the fate of most of this world's revolutions in ending by devouring its own children. Your calling as Christians is to be faithful to the Jesus way in the public place. Being faithful in the midst of this tumultuous and awful situation, is to endure, stand firm and be ever watchful.'

Now to the text itself. The chief disciples come to Jesus after he has predicted the Temple's destruction and ask him to explain when this will be and what signs they should look for. Jesus says, 'Be on your guard... many will claim to speak for me... many will say confidently, "I am the one from God."' (13:5-7) These words also sum up the situation in Jerusalem from 66 to 70CE, when it was desperately confused by a plethora of different leaders and prophets, all advancing their own unique and 'divine' claims.

'Don't be troubled by news of battles near and far.' (13:7) Again these words fit the 66 to 70 situation, with warfare close at hand and trouble in Rome. Mark says these troubles should not deceive the faithful. It does not mean that the end has come. Wait. Don't jump in. There is much more yet to be.

'You yourself must be on your guard... whoever holds out to the end will be saved.' (13:9-13) These verses set out the disciples' costly lot in this confused situation of insurrection. 'You'll be nobody's friend because it is your place to stay unaligned, to be critical of all the powers, yet from a position of defencelessness, not bearing arms. You'll be hauled to court. You'll be slandered and vilified. Families will split and divide, that's what always happens in this kind of situation. Just because you are disciples doesn't mean that you are under any kind of special physical protection and safety, indeed it means that you are doubly exposed. Just endure.'

Reference to 'the Awful Horror', 'the Abomination of Desolation', begins the section from Mark 13:14-20. 'You will see "The Awful Horror" standing in the place where he should not be.' (13:14) We readers are told to be sure to understand what this means! The phrase was first used during the attempted desecration of the temple by Antiochus Epiphanes IV in 168BCE (see Daniel 11:31, 12:11 and 1 Maccabees 1:54). It may well be that Mark is here using 'the Awful Horror' as an indirect reference to the current Roman attempt to take the Temple. In that case 'the Awful Horror' is the Roman army. The advice on how to respond to this threat to the heart of Israel is most significant. The disciples are exhorted not to stay and fight in a lost cause, but rather to flee from the city into the country (13:15). Such advice may reflect Mark's view, coming from a northern rural community and having a highly ambivalent attitude to metropolitan Jerusalem. At any rate, the central thrust is clear, the Temple is not to be defended, its survival is not what the substance of the struggle is all about.

The warning against being deceived by false prophets and Messiahs - the whole ragbag of visionaries and charlatans who were much in evidence at this time of Israel's crisis and who have diverted and perplexed Christian witness down to the tele-evangelists of our present day - is repeated in stronger terms in 13:21-23. For the third time the warning is, 'Be on your guard, don't be deceived, be watchful, endure.' (13:23)

The decisive moment

The 'sermon' comes to a climax around the coming of the Son of Man, the Human One (13:24-27). 'In the days after this time of trouble the sun will grow dark...' This scene is pure apocalypse with its reference to cosmic signs in the heavens, the falling of the powers of the heavenly world, the diversion of the highest powers over history. How will this be? Mark answers, 'With the coming of the Son of Man, the one decisive moment of heavenly intervention.' (13:26) When will this be? People argue and speculate endlessly yet the whole logic of the gospel is that the time of the coming is about to be; the moment and the event are contained in the story itself. All will be revealed in what happens next, in the events of the cross itself and its aftermath. Here heaven acts and intervenes in one decisive moment, for all. And then... 'will be gathered up from the four winds, God's own,' (13:27) those who have endured suffering, those who have resisted the powers, as the new world comes into being.

Remember the fig tree!

The chapter ends with two final pieces of advice. 'Remember the fig tree,' says Mark. (13:28-31) The parable of the fig tree, green of leaf but as yet barren of fruit, looking good but still to deliver, occurred at the point when Jesus was mounting his most explicit attack on the Jerusalem Temple, throwing out the money changers. The leafy fig tree which withered was a sign of the waning of the Temple, the eclipse of Israel. The Temple's destruction was a sign of the End-time, the final decisive moment when all will come to pass. The lesson of the fig tree is that now is the time for the old Temple to go and a new world to come to birth. Mark again concentrates our attention on what lies immediately ahead, 'It will happen in your own experience, very soon,' he says (13:30). Once again the focus is towards the cross. 'That is the decisive moment, concentrate on that.'

With patience, watch

The last word - 'No one knows, however, when that day or hour will come...' (13:32-37) is for the young church living after the cross in the troubled times around the Temple's destruction, and by extension, for any church living in troubled times. Don't look for signs of another decisive moment, for signs of the end of the world round every corner. It will come when it will come. The "when" God alone knows. Never mind looking in the teacups among the tea leaves, or in crystal balls, or examining sheep's entrails. Keep a critical distance from the spin-doctors, from all the political pundits, pollsters and predictors. Be careful you don't read too much into either earthly or heavenly portents. Just stay awake, be ever vigilant, ever watchful. The call is repeated for watchfulness, for endurance. 'Watch.' (13:37)

We began with an exchange between Jesus and the disciples. We end with the disciples. Very soon they will be found in anything but a state of vigilant watchfulness - fast asleep at the key moment in Gethsemane. They will fail, but their Lord will endure for them and for us. He will embrace the decisive moment and, in and through his surrender, he will prevail. As readers, we respond to the injunction to remain utterly watchful as the passion draws on, that we may be totally attentive to what is unfolded, the strange and mysterious wonder of the crucified God.

STUDY

BY YOURSELF

Much of our life is spent waiting, sometimes for trivial things like the traffic lights to change, sometimes for profound things like the results of hospital tests. Think about how good or bad you are at waiting. As a society we are always looking for a quick fix, a speedy solution. Much of Mark 13 is a warning about the allure and danger of the quick fix and about our temptation to 'wait for the wrong thing'. Pray for discernment, and active patience. Use this prayer.

> Wait for the Lord, his day is near.
> Wait for the Lord, be strong, take heart.

PAUSE

Before the cross, the final clash of powers, heaven and earth meet

On our journey through Mark's gospel, the pace has seldom been less than hectic. Ups and downs, comings and goings, strange conjunctions, familiar words confirmed, established ways challenged and subverted, predictions of disaster, hints of a promise beyond tragedy, community made, community expanded, community threatened; all are there. The last word we have heard from Jesus is the injunction to 'Stay awake!' The whole story has demanded a constant vigilance, now the final drama demands our concentrated attention. Let these contemporary words of Myers' set the scene for the final walk to the cross and beyond:

> There's a painting by a Guatemalan artist, living in exile, that depicts the Last Supper against the political landscape of Latin America. Swirling around Jesus in the smoke-filled room is a vivid tableau; woven in and around the disciples are military generals cavorting around with high-class prostitutes, wealthy landowners making payoffs, guerrillas whispering furtively, a peasant couple attending their malnourished children, a priest saying Mass, land reform organisers being attacked by vigilantes, several mutilated bodies under the table. There is no religious aura around Jesus; instead he seems hemmed in, caught in the middle of worldly passions, intrigues and the suffering of life as it really is.

Never have I seen a painting that more accurately captured the tenor of Mark's story of Jesus' last days. It is an intensely political drama, filled with conspiratorial back-room deals and covert action, judicial manipulation and prisoner exchanges, torture and summary execution. These themes we know well from today's world, but they rarely emerge in the standard interpretations of 'Holy Week'. Conditioned by centuries of liturgical and theological reproductions, we think of the 'Upper Room' as a lofty eucharistic moment, rather than the conflict-ridden final hours of a fugitive community in hiding, whose solidarity is crumbling in the face of state power. We envision Gethsemane as Jesus' obedient submission to the pre-ordained plan of salvation history, rather than the deep internal struggle of a leader coming to terms with the consequences of his own subversive practice.

Mark's 'Passion Play' is precisely such a political tableau, painted in hues of tragedy, realism and parody... We would do well not to forget that this very narrative of arrest, trial and torture is still lived out by so many in our world today.
(Myers 1988, pp. 354-55)

The contemplation of the cross makes us aware of two realities. We are summoned away from the security of our private lives and the temptation to inturned piety in our spiritual lives to look open-eyed at the reality of the pain and evil of our world. Mark draws us into a worldly drama played out in the live theatre of Jewish and Roman courts, jails and gallows. But there's another reality operating here, the reality of the beyond, of heaven's intervention in the earthy human story. We may miss the full force of this reality since, to describe it, Mark uses Jewish apocalyptic allusions, familiar to his first readers but more obscure to us.

The story of the cross is like a courtroom drama in which Jesus is tried, condemned and executed by thoroughly earthly powers. 'He was handed over to sinful men.' (Lk 24:7) Yet we discover at the trial a second court operating, the high court of heaven. To appreciate the heavenly court proceedings, Mark mentions three key Old Testament passages: Isaiah 53, Psalm 22 and Daniel 7. At the court of heaven it is the victim who is vindicated. Jesus, the one who is being judged, becomes the judge (8:33).

Mark's use of Daniel implies that in the long run it is Jesus' judges who will be judged; they, who today are scandalised by him and his words, will be condemned by him when they see him coming with the clouds at the *eschaton* [the last time].
(Marcus 1992, p.167)

Alerted to the significance of the Old Testament references and the activity of the higher court, we can now go forward to the final battle.

chapter 32

Holy Waste

MARK 14:1-11

The Plot against Jesus
(Matt 26:1-5; Lk 22:1-2; Jn 11:45-53)

It was now two days before the Festival of Passover and
Unleavened Bread. The chief priests and the teachers of the
Law were looking for a way to arrest Jesus secretly and put him
to death. 'We must not do it during the festival,' they said, 'or
the people might riot.'

Jesus is anointed at Bethany
(Matt 26:6-13, Jn 12:1-8)

Jesus was in Bethany at the house of Simon, a man who had
suffered from a dreaded skin-disease. While Jesus was eating,
a woman came in with an alabaster jar full of a very expensive
perfume made of pure nard. She broke the jar and poured the
perfume on Jesus' head. Some of the people there became
angry and said to one another, 'What was the use of wasting
the perfume? It could have been sold for more than three
hundred silver coins and the money given to the poor!' And

they criticised her harshly.

But Jesus said, 'Leave her alone! Why are you bothering her? She has done a fine and beautiful thing for me. You will always have poor people with you, and any time you want to, you can help them. But you will not always have me. She did what she could; she poured perfume on my body to prepare it ahead of time for burial. Now, I assure you that wherever the gospel is preached all over the world, what she has done will be told in memory of her.'

Judas agrees to betray Jesus
(Matt 26:6-13; Jn 12:1-8)

Then Judas Iscariot, one of the twelve disciples, went off to the chief priests in order to betray Jesus to them. They were pleased to hear what he had to say, and promised to give him money. So Judas started looking for a good chance to hand Jesus over to them.

THE TIME HAS COME

Now the crisis is at hand. 'It was now two days before the Festival of Passover and Unleavened Bread. The chief priests and the teachers of the Law were looking for a way to arrest Jesus secretly and put him to death. "We must not do it during the festival," they said, "or the people might riot."' (14:1-2)

A HOLY MOMENT

We start in an atmosphere of conspiracy and the threat of death. Jesus is safely at Bethany, lying low. Here is one last beautiful and portentous story of discipleship. This incident takes place in the house of Simon the leper, a reminder, on the edge of the end, that at the beginning of the gospel, Jesus brought healing to a leper (1:40-43). It is his compassionate ministry to all manner of 'untouchables' which has brought him to the point where he himself is, 'an untouchable'.

Before the moment of his 'shaming', Jesus is embraced and anointed. We recently heard the story of the poor widow who gave her all to the Temple treasury - her two meagre coins. Here is the tale of another woman who lavishes her abundance over the new temple, the body of Christ himself.

Picture this story. At a time of awful tension, Jesus and his disciples huddle together in their final house of retreat, while suspicion and uncertainty hang in the air. The group eats yet is not hungry. Suddenly, this woman takes her alabaster box with its expensive oil and anoints Jesus. The room is filled with its rich fragrance. It is a moment of profound peace and beauty among this tired and threatened household (14:3).

Not everyone thought like this. Whether it was nervousness or the result of uglier agendas, some of the group were angry. 'What a waste!' they said. 'We could have sold this perfume for a lot of money and given it to the poor.' They criticise the woman harshly: 'Woman, you got it wrong. Your lavish enthusiasm, your abundant affection, your expensive perfume are all out of place.' (14:4-5)

'Not so,' says Jesus. 'The needs of the poor you will have with you always.' Is Jesus saying here is that the needs and legitimate demands of the poor cannot be bought off by the simple doling out of charity? 'You won't always have me, she has done a fine and beautiful thing for me. She has prepared my body for burial.'(14:6-8)

A POTENT SIGN

Anointing... Burial... Waste. Take each of these three key words. Such an anointing would only be done to and for someone who was seen as precious - a king, or Messiah. The woman sees clearly who Jesus is. This act is her costly statement of faith concerning the one in whom she puts her trust. Freely she gives of herself and her substance in this moment of public display. She is a paradigm of committed, unselfconscious giving of wealth and affection to her Lord. The warmth and generosity of her action speaks - and convicts us. It is far from the cold, calculating, intellectual response that often passes for commitment.

The woman is also the first person in the gospel to see Jesus as a suffering Messiah. No wonder Jesus says of her, 'I assure you, that wherever the gospel is preached all over the world, what she has done will be told in memory of her.' (14:9) She is a crucial witness, the one person who sees what lies before Jesus and says, 'Yes, I see the cross, I see the death, a real death, I see the grave looming, and yet I will go with you as I begin to see the purpose.' Unlike the disciples who have been trying to deny and avoid the cross and are about to turn and run, this unnamed woman prepares. She will stand with her Lord, she has done what she could. She anoints him for burial, the main witness before the event. She belongs with the women who were eyewitnesses to the event of the cross (15:40, 41) and to the women who were the witnesses of the first Easter morning (16:1-8).

What a waste! (14:4) This is the comment of those who don't see, born out of the dismissive ignorance of blind disciples. It raises questions about the meaning of what happens next. Is the cross of Jesus Christ the ultimate example of waste in humanity's delusive search for a loving God who is not? In Jesus' embrace of the cross the same qualities are shown as in the action of the woman. It is also an act of generous, costly, committed giving. Here is the question at the gospel's heart. Is it all a savage, bitter, cruel waste, or is it the supreme, prodigal, abundant act of giving, which is the way - and no less than life itself? (John 14:6)

Betrayal begins

The story ends with brutal contrasts. After the woman's far-seeing act of love, Judas, one of the inner twelve (as we're reminded three times), goes to the High Priest to make his sordid act of betrayal. We are not told why. Disappointment, jealousy, hate, greed - there are plenty of theories of motivation. What is clear is that the way to the cross is prepared for at the heart of the discipleship community. It's an awful warning - anyone can let faith go sour. Yet somehow the fidelity of the woman's act of faith and love lingers longer than the bitterness of Judas' faith gone wrong; another hint of resurrection for those with eyes to see.

Study

By yourself

Reflect on the precious moment when Jesus receives this woman's love. Remember that at the very start of his ministry Jesus hears the voice from the heavens speaking the words of loving affirmation, 'You are my son, the beloved.' Hear these words as spoken to you now, through Jesus. 'You are my daughter... You are my son.'

For group work

This woman's lavish act of costly love 'will always be remembered'. It signals and anticipates Jesus' own act of costly love on the cross. The church exists to bear witness to this costly love.

- Talk together about ways in which your faith community can be more affirming of one another.
- Many acts of costly love are deeply personal. There is also a place for corporate witness and action. How do you and how can you, as a Christian community, mirror Jesus' love in word and practical action?

chapter 33

Broken Bread

MARK 14:12-26

Jesus eats the Passover meal with his Disciples
(Matt 26:17-25; Lk 22:7-14, 21-23; Jn 13:21-30)

On the first day of the Festival of Unleavened Bread, the day the lambs for the Passover meal were killed, Jesus' disciples asked him, 'Where do you want us to go and get the Passover meal ready for you?'

Then Jesus sent two of them with these instructions: 'Go into the city, and a man carrying a jar of water will meet you. Follow him to the house he enters, and say to the owner of the house: "The Teacher says, Where is the room where my disciples and I will eat the Passover meal?" Then he will show you a large upstairs room, prepared and furnished, where you will get everything ready for us.'

The disciples left, went to the city, and found everything just as Jesus had told them; and they prepared the Passover meal.

When it was evening, Jesus came with the twelve disciples. While they were at the table eating, Jesus said, 'I tell you that one of you will betray me - one who is eating with me.'

The disciples were upset and began to ask him, one after the other, 'Surely you don't mean me, do you?'

Jesus answered, 'It will be one of you twelve, one who dips his bread in the dish with me. The Son of Man will die as the Scriptures say he will; but how terrible for that man who betrays the Son of Man! It would have been better for that man if he had never been born!'

The Lord's Supper
(Matt 26:26-30; Lk 22:14-20; 1 Cor 11:23-25)

While they were eating, Jesus took a piece of bread, gave a prayer of thanks, broke it, and gave it to his disciples. 'Take it,' he said, 'this is my body.'

Then he took a cup, gave thanks to God, and handed it to them; and they all drank from it. Jesus said, 'This is my blood which is poured out for many, my blood which seals God's covenant. I tell you, I will never again drink this wine until the day when I drink the new wine in the Kingdom of God.'

Then they sang a hymn and went out to the Mount of Olives.

TENSIONS RISE

Two themes dominate this important passage. The announcement of Jesus' betrayal is followed by the transformation of the old feast of liberation, the Passover, into the new feast of liberation, the Communion.

It was the first day of the Festival. Jerusalem would be seething with the continual arrival of pilgrims. Rather than sharing with the pilgrims the heightened mood of holy celebration, the disciples are tense, expecting danger and crisis. This passage begins with a description of the cautious plans that Jesus makes for the disciples' keeping of the feast. The instructions he gives his friends, 'Look for the man with the jar of water, follow him, speak to the owner of the house he enters,' (14:13) sounds like the detail of a good thriller, a first-century John Le Carré. The arrangement is careful, clandestine. The disciples have gone underground, Jesus is painstakingly avoiding discovery.

MORE ABOUT BETRAYAL

When they sit down at the table in the evening, Jesus drops a bombshell. 'One of you is going to betray me.' (14:18). Mark does not introduce Judas by name into the scene at the table, what he does show is the dreadful darkness of a community disintegrating under mutual recrimination. In turn the disciples say, 'Surely it can't be me?' (14:19) Again Mark bluntly portrays the enemies of faith at the very heart of the faith community. Jesus knows what betrayal will mean; in the hands of the authorities, only death will beckon. For the betrayer also, the consequences are awful, 'it would be better for him that he had not been born' (14:21).The betrayer has to live with the knowledge that he has broken faith, fractured solidarity, trampled on love. Other gospels give Judas a leading role in the condemnation of the woman who anointed Jesus. Mark, while not mentioning Judas by name, places the first steps in Judas' act of betrayal immediately after that incident (14:10-11). Perhaps this was the final straw for Judas. Whatever the link between Judas and the woman there could scarcely be a greater contrast than in Jesus' comment on each, 'it would be better for him that he had not been born', 'wherever the gospel is preached, this will be told, in memory of her'.

LIGHT IN THE DARKNESS

Strangely and wonderfully, the darkness passes for a time. There is one lucid moment where community is affirmed and even transformed in spite of, or because of, all that lies ahead. Here are the words and actions of the feast in all their simplicity:

Jesus took the bread, broke it, gave it.

Jesus took the cup and passed it from hand to hand, from mouth to mouth.

Before each action, he gives thanks to God. With each action there is a word:

'This is my body.'

'This is my blood which is poured out for many, my blood which seals God's covenant.' (14:22-25)

For the disciples and for us, this is a time to remember all the other eatings and drinkings in the gospel story, with all sorts of folk. Unforgettably, there's the bread given to the crowds who were hungry (6:30-44, 8:1-10). Now the disciples are hungry not just for food, but for courage and reassurance. So it is that for those closest to him who, however falteringly and dimly, have shared his way, Jesus shares his life, symbolised in the sign of the bread, his body broken, which is for them... for you... for us.

The cup of the covenant from the old feast of Passover recalls the covenant of freedom begun in the Exodus. The blood, shed for many, echoes the words of Isaiah 53, and in particular,

Therefore I will allot him a portion with the great, and he shall share the spoil with the mighty, because he poured out his life to the death, and was reckoned with the transgressors, because he bore the sin of many, and interceded for the transgressors. (Isaiah 53:12, *NEB*)

For the Jewish people, blood was the home of the spirit, the source of life itself. In this feast Jesus invites disciples not only to share his brokenness within a broken world and his sufferings at the hands of a fallen world, but to share his life which endures.

'I'LL LIVE IN YOU IF YOU LIVE IN ME'

The old feast is transformed. There is no lamb on this table: Jesus is the Lamb. There is simply bread, elemental, basic bread, 'fruit of creation which human hands have made', yet also the bread of suffering of which all must partake. There is wine, the sign of blood, a totally forbidden drink, wine which becomes the sign and seal of the new covenant which can possess and transform us, body, mind and spirit. Here is the transformed and superseded Passover, the new feast of the indwelling presence of God, the promise of the abiding Christ, ever with his people no matter what lies before them.

It's interesting to note how formal the language of the institution of the Lord's Supper has become early in the gospel formation. Mark's words are closely paralleled in Matthew (Matt 26:26-28) and Luke (Lk 22:17-20) and also in Paul's first letter to the Corinthians (1 Cor 11:23-25). Reading between the lines, it is clear that it was very early in the life of the young church that this remembrance of Christ's death, the meal of Communion, became central. Communion gathers together so many different aspects of the life of discipleship, its gifts and challenges, material and spiritual, so it remains at the living heart of our life and worship.

The feast always points backwards and forwards simultaneously. It looks backwards to the remembrance of a death freely given for all, which is the ground and bedrock, source and measure of our whole faith, and forwards as Jesus himself points forwards, 'I tell you, I will never again drink this wine until the day when I drink it new in the Kingdom of God.'(14:25) The feast becomes a fast as Jesus pledges abstinence, yet there is the promise, 'I will drink it new in the Kingdom of God.' In the gathering gloom round the now imminent cross, there are still rare flashes of light, hints to those who would see and hear, that tomorrow will be other than the day of utter darkness.

The death which we remember every time we come to the Lord's Table contains in itself the seeds of a new future both for Jesus and for all who would follow him. Those who accept the invitation are bound together in the new community of love and justice he creates, through bread and wine, body and blood, love and giving. To return to an earlier metaphor, this new wine which bursts the old bottles never ages, decays or sours (2:22). The new wine, with the promise of the new life, is before us at every Table of the Lord where past and future combine in the living presence we meet in the living present moment.

'This,' he says, 'is all for you.'

> Hear us now, O Christ,
> And breathe your Spirit upon us
> And upon this bread and wine.
> May they become for us your body,
> Vibrant with your life,

Healing, renewing, making us whole.
And as the bread and wine which we now eat and drink
Are changed into us,
May we be changed again into you,
Bone of your bone,
Flesh of your flesh,
Loving and caring in the world.
(Iona Community Worship Book 1991, p. 67)

Study

Meditation

Taking, blessing, breaking, giving. These are the essential elements of Jesus' action.

He takes what is there, the ordinary stuff of life.

He blesses it, he gives thanks for it, he does not take it for granted.

He breaks the bread, makes it ready for sharing, and he gives it away.

• Reflect on the actions of taking, blessing, breaking and giving, signs of sacramental living - the way to live the sacrificial life of Jesus in our lives in the world today.

chapter 34

Betrayal and Binding

MARK 14:27-51

Jesus predicts Peter's Denial
(Matt 26:31-35; Lk 22:31-34; Jn 13:36-38)

Jesus said to them, 'All of you will run away and leave me, for the scripture says, "God will kill the shepherd, and the sheep will all be scattered." But after I am raised to life, I will go to Galilee ahead of you.'

Peter answered, 'I will never leave you, even though all the rest do!'

Jesus said to Peter, 'I tell you that before the cock crows twice tonight, you will say three times that you do not know me.'

Peter answered even more strongly, 'I will never say that, even if I have to die with you!'

And all the other disciples said the same thing.

Jesus prays in Gethsemane
(Matt 26:36-46; Lk 22:39-46)

They came to a place called Gethsemane, and Jesus said to his disciples, 'Sit here while I pray.' He took Peter, James and John with him. Distress and anguish came over him, and he said to them, 'The sorrow in my heart is so great that it almost crushes me. Stay here and keep watch.'

He went a little farther on, threw himself on the ground, and prayed that, if possible, he might not have to go through that time of suffering. 'Father,' he prayed, 'my Father! All things are possible for you. Take this cup of suffering away from me. Yet not what I want, but what you want.'

Then he returned and found the three disciples asleep. He said to Peter, 'Simon, are you asleep? Weren't you able to stay awake for one hour?' And he said to them, 'Keep watch, and pray that you will not fall into temptation. The spirit is willing, but the flesh is weak.'

He went away once more and prayed, saying the same words. Then he came back to the disciples and found them asleep; they could not keep their eyes open. And they did not know what to say to him.

When he came back the third time, he said to them, 'Are you still sleeping and resting? Enough! The hour has come! Look, the Son of Man is now being handed over to the power of sinners. Get up, let us go. Look, here is the man who is betraying me!'

The Arrest of Jesus
(Matt 26:47-56; Lk 22:47-53; Jn 18:3-12)

Jesus was still speaking when Judas, one of the twelve disciples, arrived. With him was a crowd armed with swords and clubs, and sent by the chief priests, the teachers of the Law, and the elders. The traitor had given the crowd a signal: 'The man I kiss is the one you want. Arrest him and take him away under guard.'

As soon as Judas arrived, he went up to Jesus and said, 'Teacher!' and kissed him. So they arrested Jesus and held him tight. But one of those standing there drew his sword and struck at the High Priest's slave, cutting off his ear. Then Jesus spoke up and said to them, 'Did you have to come with swords and clubs to capture me, as though I were an outlaw? Day after day I was with you teaching in the Temple, and you did not arrest me. But the Scriptures must come true.'

Then all the disciples left him and ran away.

A certain young man, dressed only in a linen cloth, was following Jesus. They tried to arrest him, but he ran away naked, leaving the cloth behind.

OUT INTO THE DARK

'They sang a hymn and went out to the Mount of Olives.' (14:26) The last moment of community togetherness is over. Jesus has pointed to the end which is very near and drawn the disciples round the new meal which points beyond the end. After the intensity and lucidity of the time of sharing the bread and wine, they all leave the warmth and light of the upper room - we can almost hear the finality of the door banging shut behind them - and go out exposed into the darkness of the night.

Here is the centre of the gospel's darkness, as we are brought to contemplate the emptiness of Jesus' experience of betrayal, desertion and denial at the hands of those closest to him, the community of disciples. We come face to face with the grimness of his experiences of trial and torture at the hands of both the Sanhedrin and the Roman powers and the final hell of the pain and weariness, the suffering and humiliation of death on the cross itself. It is a dark road that beckons, as Joe Nagle describes:

> At the outset we must say that as an act of powerlessness and self-immolation the Calvary event is something we do not like to contemplate. Good Friday is not one of our favourite days. We tend to pass quickly from the consolation of Thursday and the Supper of the Lord to Easter Sunday and the glory of the resurrection. But if we are to understand the central fact about Jesus - how evil is finally overcome - and understand something about our contemporary history, we have to look long and hard at Jesus' crucifixion.
> (Nagle 1991 p. 34)

DISINTEGRATING DISCIPLES

Jesus' first suffering comes around the disintegration of the disciples' community, an external disintegration mirroring the internal collapse of their faith under trial. The passage begins with Jesus' bleak prophecy, 'All of you will run away and leave me,' (14:27) and the specific word to Peter, 'before dawn three times you will say you did not know me.' (14:30) The disciples are under immense pressure. Why do they fall away? One reason they fail is because they have misunderstood Jesus. They have pinned their hopes on the wrong kind of Messiah, they are still looking for an all-powerful deliverer. They are unprepared for this final stage in the journey downward.

Mark makes it clear that we are not simply looking at a human story here. Three times, in verses 21, 27 and 49, Jesus quotes scripture to explain and justify what will happen to him. These scriptural references show that this story cannot be interpreted at a human level alone. There is another, greater agency at work, through whom we will see the purposes of God fulfilled. This journey downwards is not just the shipwreck of a movement, the end of a dream or a personal disaster. God is at work in it. He will bring to birth something quite new in our understanding of him, of ourselves and our world.

CHINKS OF LIGHT

There is some light in the gloom. In verse 28 Jesus says to his disciples, 'After I am raised to life, I will go to Galilee ahead of you.' There is also the curious story of the young man who witnesses Jesus' arrest and escapes the clutches of the soldiers only by leaving his robe behind and fleeing naked (14:52). It is such a strange appearance at a moment of high drama that it should alert us to be on the lookout for this young man again. Sure enough, he will appear, at the empty tomb.

Returning to the beginning of this passage, the site where Jesus predicts that the disciples will defect is significant - the Mount of Olives. The prophet Zechariah had spoken of the Mount of Olives as the site of messianic victory. The glory has departed! On the Mount, Jesus has already made his prediction of the fall of the Temple State. Now he speaks there of the collapse of his own community and of the rapidly approaching time when he will stand quite alone.

When Jesus speaks here of the smiting of the shepherd and the scattering of the sheep, there are two Old Testament references. One is to Zechariah 13:7-9 which speaks of God's purging and refining his people, the other is to a longer passage in Ezekiel 34 (11-16, 23ff). In it God speaks of his promise to gather the scattered, to care for the sick and the weak, to bring judgement and justice. Again comes a gleam of light for the future.

Right now, darkness prevails. While Peter's denial is singled out for notice, Mark stresses that in the community of disciples, there are no innocents - all are complicit and fail together. 'All we like sheep have gone astray;... and the Lord has laid on him the iniquity of us all.' (Isaiah 53:6 NRSV) These words echo poignantly.

'GETHSEMANE, CAN I FORGET?'

'They came to a place called Gethsemane.' Gethsemane was a garden or a field. For only the third time in the gospel, Jesus is shown alone at prayer. Roughly speaking, Mark shows Jesus' praying at the beginning, the middle and the end of the gospel. Always it is late or early, in a place of some isolation, around a time of crisis and endeavour. The words used to describe Jesus' demeanour in Gethsemane are strong indeed. He is shown as tormented with anguish (14:33,34). When Jesus speaks of his anguish to his disciples, he quotes from Psalm 42, which begins with the beautiful image, 'Like as the hart pants for the water brook, so my soul pants for the living God.' It is a psalm of urgent need and desire which ends with a question and an affirmation.

> Why am I so sad? Why am I so troubled?
> I will put my hope in God,
> And once again I will praise him,
> My saviour and my God.
> (Psalm 42:11)

When Jesus goes apart to pray, he addresses God as 'Father', using the familiar form 'Abba'. The word implies confidence, intimacy and nearness. Yet nothing could be further from sentimental, trivial, all-matey religion than this prayer. Jesus is seeking the strength to surrender his life, to bend his will to the will of the Father. No wonder he shudders as he struggles. In the end he prevails. 'Not what I want, but what you want.' (14:36) Prayer has been well called the act before the act, the deed before the deed. Here is the moment which makes the cross possible, the moment of complete and willing surrender from which our redemption springs.

Throughout the Gethsemane episode, the contrast could scarcely be greater between Jesus' active, watchful, anguished, prayerful obedience and the disciples' dull weariness as they fall asleep, blind to the hour ahead. There are two key references here. When Jesus prays, 'Let this cup pass from me,' (14:36) we recall the cup which he has just shared and the cup of suffering he has foretold in the encounter with James and John (10:38). At the end of the time in Gethsemane, Jesus' final words are. 'Enough, the hour has come.' The reference to the 'hour' recalls the 'hour' of the coming of the Son of Man in the second great sermon in Chapter 13.

'The coming of the kingdom has nothing to do with triumphalism; it comes from below, in solidarity with the human family in the dark night of its suffering. The world is Gethsemane, and we are called to "historical insomnia".' (Myers 1988, p. 353)

THE BETRAYING KISS

Enter Judas, with perfidious embrace. 'The heart is deceitful above all things, and desperately corrupt.' (Jer 17:9, AV) There are three stages in Jesus' final battle, first with himself in Gethsemane, then with friends turned fickle - Judas, Peter and the disciples - and last with the powers of Israel and Rome. The forces of evil ranged against him take many forms. The authorities bring the heavy team with them. The crowd, armed to the teeth, sneaking up on Jesus in the middle of the night, so typical of covert state action against dissidents. The authorities are taking no chances. Jesus is seized and secured. It seems that this is the end of Jesus as the strong one, that the forces of the other strong man, the evil one, have him in their grasp (14:43-46).

Jesus condemns the authorities' night attack on him. He asks, reasonably, why they treat him as a mere bandit with this clandestine arrest, when day after day he could have been found openly in the Temple, the most public place in the city (14:48). To have attempted to arrest him there would have been to run the risk of provoking a riot. Jesus again alludes to the scriptures, this time to no specific text, rather to the whole weight of their witness. The disciples flee; the sheep indeed are scattered. There is only the strange appearance of the young man. Watch for him later on (16:5).

STUDY

BY YOURSELF

• Reflect on the sentence, 'The world is Gethsemane'. In other words, the world is the place of our experience of darkness, the place to say 'Yes' to God in spite of ourselves and our wishes, the place where we are asked to remain awake. Reflect, remembering it is also the place where Jesus has been before us and still is.

FOR GROUP WORK

With Jesus in Gethsemane we learn to understand prayer as the place in our lives where we struggle to align ourselves with God's will. Such prayer involves listening to what God is saying: discernment, decision, assent and action.

• Spend time in the group listening to Jesus' words in Gethsemane. Let one group member read these words very slowly, with a significant silence between each sentence. As the words are read, each group member should mentally note her/his feelings, reactions, thoughts.

'Sit here while I pray.'

'The sorrow in my heart is so great that it almost crushes me. Stay here and keep watch.'

'Father, my Father! All things are possible for you. Take this cup of suffering away from me. Yet not what I want, but what you want.'

'Simon, are you asleep? Weren't you able to stay awake for one hour?'

'Keep watch, and pray that you will not fall into temptation. The spirit is willing, but the flesh is weak.'

'Are you still sleeping and resting? Enough! The hour has come! Look, the Son of Man is now being handed over to the power of sinners. Get up, let us go. Look, here is the man who is betraying me!'

• Take each sentence in turn and ask the group members for their reflection on each phrase.

• Finally, read Jesus' words slowly once more, with a short period of silence to end.

chapter 35

Judgement I

MARK 14:53-65

Jesus before the Council

(Matt 26:57-68; Lk 22:54-55, 63-71; Jn 18:13-14, 19-24)

Then Jesus was taken to the High Priest's house, where all the chief priests, the elders, and the teachers of the Law were gathering. Peter followed from a distance and went into the courtyard of the High Priest's house. There he sat down with the guards, keeping himself warm by the fire. The chief priests and the whole Council tried to find some evidence against Jesus in order to put him to death, but they could not find any. Many witnesses told lies against Jesus, but their stories did not agree.

Then some men stood up and told this lie against Jesus: 'We heard him say, "I will tear down this Temple which men have made, and after three days I will build one that is not made by men".' Not even they, however, could make their stories agree.

The High Priest stood up in front of them all and questioned Jesus, 'Have you no answer to the accusation they bring against you?'

But Jesus kept quiet and would not say a word. Again the High Priest questioned him, 'Are you the Messiah, the Son of the Blessed God?'

'I am,' answered Jesus, 'and you will all see the Son of Man seated on the right of the Almighty and coming with the clouds of heaven!'

The High Priest tore his robes and said, 'We don't need any more witnesses! You heard his blasphemy. What is your decision?'

They all voted against him: he was guilty and should be put to death.

Some of them began to spit on Jesus, and they blindfolded him and hit him. 'Guess who hit you!' they said. And the guards took him and slapped him.

TWO TRIALS, TWO COURTS

Now we come to the trial of Jesus. In Mark there are two trials, first before the Sanhedrin, the highest religious court of Jesus' own people, then before Pilate the Procurator, delegate of the supreme power of Rome. Scholars largely agree that Mark's account of the trials of Jesus comes from a genuine historical base; they disagree considerably as to how far Mark has edited the history for his own purposes. At one level the trials identify Jesus with the trials of political and religious prisoners through many ages and with victims of kangaroo courts. Rough hands in the middle of the night, disproportionate force, a hurried trial, rigged evidence, beatings and torture - the story is depressingly contemporary, as media reportage and the work of Amnesty make clear.

However, the account of Jesus' trials has another dimension. Mark reduces the story to the barest outlines, yet it is full of irony, vividly lampooning Jesus' opponents. The irony lies in Mark's imputation that there is another trial going on before the High Court of Heaven. There, the earthly accusers become the accused and the victim is the Judge. Again, we must 'listen' closely and imaginatively to 'hear' the word of God within the babble of human cynicism and brutality.

JESUS BEFORE THE HIGH PRIEST, CAIAPHAS

The first trial begins with the hurriedly convened court in the house of Caiaphas, the High Priest. It is still night. Under Rabbinic law, courts were forbidden from meeting during the hours of darkness. At the very outset of the so-called due process of law the guardians of the legal establishment resort to illegality. It is plain that the whole purpose of the trial is not justice but Jesus' death - a kangaroo court with a vengeance.

The charge against the accused is blasphemy, the critical question, 'Are you the Messiah?' The trial begins with a parade of false witnesses whose evidence is neither consistent nor adds up (14:56-59). The nature of their evidence is very interesting. It focuses on Jesus' prediction of doom on the Temple State and his foretelling of his own death and resurrection. It is hardly surprising that the people of Jerusalem felt acutely uncomfortable with Jesus' temple talk, as the whole economy of their city was geared to the service of the Temple. This outsider threatened their daily bread. There is an uncomfortable ring of truth in the words of the 'false' witnesses who fail to agree.

Now comes the critical question from the High Priest himself, 'Jesus, are you the Messiah?' (14:61) Up to this point, Jesus has kept resolutely silent, like the Suffering Servant of Isaiah 53 before his accusers 'he opened not his mouth.' (Isaiah 53:7 NRSV) At last Jesus speaks, 'I am, and you will all see the Son of Man seated on the right of the Almighty and coming with the clouds of heaven.' (14:42) Never before in the gospel has Jesus revealed who he is to any except the inner core of the disciples; rather, the gospel is full of injunctions from Jesus to silence. The weight of evidence from the gospel would suggest that the last thing Jesus would do would be to answer the High Priest's question. Yet he does, with 'I am', a simple 'Yes'. On the face of things, it does not tally.

Many scholars argue that Jesus does not give such an affirmative and open answer here. Their arguments run as follows. In the accounts of this episode in Matthew and Luke, Matthew gives Jesus' answer as, 'You say so,' (Matt 26:64) and Luke, 'You say that I am.' (Lk 22:70) There is textual evidence to support the view that the original in Mark may well have been, 'You say that I am', and it fits with the words in Matthew and Luke. Vincent Taylor translates here, 'The word is yours.' (14:42) The Greek original does not indicate a distinction between the indicative and the interrogative, so another possibility is that 'I am' could equally well be rendered as an ironic 'Am I?'

However, even if Jesus denies the formal title of 'Messiah,' he is quite prepared to claim for himself the title 'the Son of Man', 'the Human One', that is, the one who is chosen to bring God's judgement and justice, the messenger of end-time judgement. The argument against those who argue for Jesus' secret being preserved and his silence maintained here is this: on the day of the cross, there is no longer any reason for the secret. On the edge of the moment of truth, the denouement, this is the right time for Jesus to break silence and to put into words who he is; to articulate the meaning and promise of the events ahead.

Jesus' 'Yes' is quite enough for Caiaphas. 'Blasphemy,' he shouts, 'Guilty!' In an extravagant display of distress he tears his robes. 'Case proved!' Surprise, surprise, he gets his verdict, unanimously, as he desires. Jesus is led away and beaten up. He suffers his first attack of petty cruelty at the hands of the state's officials (14:63-65). We are left with the question, 'How can the one who speaks in the Name of God be found guilty of defaming that very Name?' If, as is clear, he cannot be so judged, then the accusers stand accused.

STUDY

BY YOURSELF

At his trial before Caiaphas, Jesus is charged and condemned on religious grounds. Two millennia after the death of Jesus, religion is still implicated in people's violent deaths.

Faith in Jesus, 'the Human One' should make us more human and humane. Reflect on your faith in the light of Jesus, 'the Human One' to whom Mark witnesses. Does it make you more human and humane?

chapter 36

Cock Crow

MARK 14:66-72

Peter denies Jesus

(Matt 26:69-75; Lk 22:56-62; Jn 18:15,18,25,27)

Peter was still down in the courtyard when one of the High Priest's servant women came by. When she saw Peter warming himself, she looked straight at him and said, 'You, too, were with Jesus of Nazareth.'

But he denied it. 'I don't know... I don't understand what you are talking about,' he answered, and went out into the passage. Just then a cock crowed.

The servant woman saw him there and began to repeat to the bystanders, 'He is one of them!' But Peter denied it again.

A little while later the bystanders accused Peter again, 'You can't deny that you are one of them, because you, too, are from Galilee.'

Then Peter said, 'I swear that I am telling the truth! May God punish me if I am not! I do not know the man you are talking about!'

Just then a cock crowed a second time, and Peter remembered how Jesus had said to him, 'Before the cock crows twice, you will say three times that you do not know me.' And he broke down and cried.

PETER'S DENIAL

Sandwiched between the story of the two trials is the significant incident of Peter's denial. In indicating the bitter end of the disciples' betrayal and desertion, it gives us much to reflect on. At the High Priest's palace where Jesus has been taken, Peter sneaks to the edge of the crowd. It is as far as his courage allows him to venture. It is also prudent (14:54). But he is recognised - perhaps his rough Galilean accent betrays his origins among the urbane city dwellers of Jerusalem (14:66-70). We are reminded again that Jesus' ministry was on the edge and to the outsider. Not only does Peter's accent betray him, his courage fails. As the servant girl and then the bystanders ask, 'Aren't you a friend of Jesus, one of his company?' with increasing vehemence he makes his denial, 'I don't know... I don't understand what you're talking about... I'm not one of them! I swear I'm telling the truth, by God, may he punish me if I'm not, I do not know this man.' (14:71)

'I DO NOT KNOW HIM'

'I do not know him.' How ironic these words are. It was Peter's 'knowing' who Jesus is in the council of war at Caesalem (8:29) which formed the hinge on which the gospel turned toward Jerusalem and the cross. Yet, from the time of the 'confession', all the way through the second half of the gospel, Peter and the disciples have been portrayed as not truly 'knowing' Jesus. Peter's impassioned denial speaks more truth than he knows. Indeed he does not know 'Who he is'. He is not alone. This is also a signal to us, the readers. We too, do not fully 'know'. The secret, however, is about to be made manifest.

And the cock crowed, a second time. For Peter, the commonplace sound and sign of a new day's dawning means the pit of guilt and despair. For us, it signals the day when at the last, all will be made known. In spite of appearances and circumstances, light will come. In and through the events of this day, begun with a meal round a table, (remember the Jewish day begins at sunset), all people of all time may learn 'Who he is'.

STUDY

BY YOURSELF
Meditation

'You were with that Jesus of Nazareth.'
A shrug, a frown, a puzzled, frightened look.
The cock crows...
'You're one of them, aren't you?'
A deeper fear gnawing, denial.
'Don't deny it, you too are from Galilee.'
A fierce shake of the head, a turning away, a curse, a furious denial.
Again the cock crows...

And then, the memory: 'Before the cock crows twice, you will deny me three times.' (14:30)

Realisation dawns, sight is restored, things are plainly understood - and tears fall. Although this must be one of Peter's lowest moments, the honesty of his tears and the depths of his regret form a turning point: are there echoes of Peter's experience in your own?

• Here is a simple prayer of confession for the depths and for everyday,
  'I confess to God that my life and the life of the world are broken by my sin.'

FOR GROUP WORK

• At the end of this passage there is the unforgettable picture of Peter, broken, acutely aware of his failure and his powerlessness. Experiencing the failure of our hopes, plans, dreams and actions is a real and profound part of being human. Share with one another as you feel comfortable, times when you have known failure and how you felt about it. (It is important to let people speak for themselves without jumping in either to help them out or correct them.)

• On the other side of Easter, it is the broken Peter who becomes the leading disciple of Jesus. In the life of faith and the community of faith, failure is not the end. Yet often in church we are very unforgiving and despairing of failure. If we are a genuine community of risk, we have to live with our failures and begin again. Share with one another ways in which as a Christian community we can be more positive about accepting and overcoming failure.

• At the end of your session, share this prayer of mutual confession and forgiveness.
  Leader: I confess to God and in the company of all God's people that my life and the life of the world are broken by my sin.
  ALL: May God forgive you, Christ renew you, and the Spirit enable you to grow in love.
  Leader: Amen.
  ALL: We confess to God and in the company of all God's people that our lives and the life of the world are broken by our sin.
  Leader: May God forgive you, Christ renew you, and the Spirit enable you to grow in love.
  ALL: Amen.
  (The Iona Community Worship Book, Revised Edition 1991, p.9)

chapter 37

Judgement 2

MARK 15:1-20

Jesus is brought before Pilate
(Matt 27:1-2, 11-14; Lk 23:1-5; Jn 18:28-38)

Early in the morning the chief priests met hurriedly with the elders, the teachers of the Law, and the whole Council, and made their plans. They put Jesus in chains, led him away, and handed him over to Pilate. Pilate questioned him, 'Are you the king of the Jews?'

Jesus answered, 'So you say.'

The chief priests were accusing Jesus of many things, so Pilate questioned him again, 'Aren't you going to answer? Listen to all their accusations!'

Again Jesus refused to say a word, and Pilate was amazed.

Jesus is sentenced to Death
(Matt 27:15-26; Lk 23:13-25; Jn 18:39-19:16)

At every Passover Festival Pilate was in the habit of setting free any one prisoner the people asked for. At that time a man named Barabbas was in prison with the rebels who had committed murder in the riot. When the crowd gathered and began to ask Pilate for the usual favour, he asked them, 'Do you want me to set free for you the king of the Jews?' He knew very well that the chief priests had handed Jesus over to him because they were jealous.

But the chief priests stirred up the crowd to ask, instead, for Pilate to set Barabbas free for them. Pilate spoke again to the crowd, 'What, then, do you want me to do with the one you call the king of the Jews?'

They shouted back, 'Crucify him!'

'But what crime has he committed?' Pilate asked.

They shouted all the louder, 'Crucify him!'

Pilate wanted to please the crowd, so he set Barabbas free for them. Then he had Jesus whipped and handed him over to be crucified.

The Soldiers mock Jesus
(Matt 27:27-31; Jn 19:2 -3)

The soldiers took Jesus inside to the courtyard of the governor's palace and called together the rest of the company. They put a purple robe on Jesus, made a crown out of thorny branches, and put it on his head. Then they began to salute him, 'Long live the King of the Jews!' They beat him over the head with a stick, spat on him, fell on their knees, and bowed down to him. When they had finished mocking him, they took off the purple robe and put his own clothes back on him. Then they led him out to crucify him.

JESUS AND PILATE

In the second trial before Pilate, the dialogue between Jesus and Pilate closely parallels the previous confrontation with Caiaphas. This time the question is different. Pilate asks Jesus, 'Are you the King?' (15:2) Pilate is not interested in religious matters, his concern is with political realities. His question is, 'Are you stirring up rebellion or not?' Again, Jesus does not answer; he will not defend himself and his silence astonishes Pilate. By refusing to answer, he is quietly denying Pilate's authority over him, and the authority of the imperial power he represents. And there is a deeper echo:

> He was oppressed, and he was afflicted,
> yet he opened not his mouth;
> like a lamb that is led to the slaughter,

and like a sheep that before the shearers is dumb,
so he opened not his mouth.
(Isaiah 53:7, *RSV*)

Now follows the curious exchange between Pilate and the Jerusalem crowd (15:6-15).
There is a problem here. What we know of Pilate from other non-Biblical sources tell us that
he was a decisive and tough ruler with a considerable contempt for all things Jewish. Why,
then, does Mark show us this farce of consultation with the crowd? Some argue that Mark
is concerned to whitewash the Roman authorities and play down their part in Jesus' death.
In this interpretation, it is the baying of the crowd that settles Jesus' fate and Pilate is too
weak to resist. However, there is another, more plausible explanation. Pilate is simply
playing the crowd along. It suits his purposes to have this troublemaker permanently out of
the way. In this instance, he will quite happily collude with the High Priest and the fickle
crowd for his own ends. 'Mark's picture of the trial before Pilate, including the Barabbas
deal, is quite intelligible as a portrait of procuratorial pragmatism at work.' (Myers 1988
p.374)

It is a classic example of political opportunism.

IN THE HANDS OF THE ENEMY

Leaving Barabbas for a moment, we follow Jesus into the hands of the Roman soldiers
(15:16-20). Jesus is stripped, dressed in a robe of imperial purple, given instead of a laurel
wreath, a crown of sharp thorns and savagely mocked. Jeering words of salute are followed
by contemptuous spitting. Then Jesus is stripped again, he is doubly shamed and
humiliated. Mark does not let Rome off lightly as he shows this ghastly moment of Jesus'
ridicule and torture at the hands of the soldiers of the Empire. Fernando Belo's comment on
the scene is telling:

> Throughout this scene (in which the body of Jesus is dressed and undressed at the
> whim of the soldiers, thus calling attention to its powerlessness in this space that is
> dominated by force of arms) we have a parody, a carnival...This scene shows people
> being unleashed who have been subjected to a constricting military discipline, and
> who now take advantage of a conquered adversary who might have forced them to
> fight and possibly even be killed. This sort of thing is often shown in the ferocity
> lower-rank police officials demonstrate when dealing with political prisoners.
> (Belo, in Myers 1988 p. 379)

We ask, 'How can people treat one another in such an inhuman way?' Part of the answer
is in labelling others, reducing them to less than human. Labels such as 'unbeliever', 'Jew',
'Communist', 'Fenian', 'Orange', 'Tory', 'Socialist', 'Black' say, 'You are not like us, you are
"enemy".' Joel Marcus in his Good Friday reflections on Jesus and the Holocaust tells this

story of Auschwitz:

> One survivor describes his arrival at Auschwitz as a teenager. He made it through
> selection - the fearsome process by which the arriving prisoners were sorted into two
> lines, a long line going to immediate death in the gas chambers, a short one going to
> slave labour and eventual death through starvation, disease, or execution. Like the
> other 'lucky ones', this young man immediately had his arm tattooed with a number.
> As he was given his number, an SS man came up to him. 'Do you know what this
> number's all about?' he asked. 'No, sir,' the youth replied. 'Okay, let me tell you now,'
> the SS man said. 'You are being dehumanised.'
> (Marcus 1997, pp.45-6)

The grim process continues. Here is Jesus, the Human One, being seen and treated as
less than human, a non-person. He is prepared to travel that road, allowing himself to be
humiliated and bound, to be with us and for us. In his identification with the victim, he
would enrol us in the battle against dehumanising those who are not 'one of us.'

Yet this picture of Jesus mocked before the soldiers is the gospel's supreme example of
double irony. In ironic mockery the soldiers cry, 'This is Jesus, the King.' 'Some king,' they
say. 'Some king indeed,' we say, for, before heaven and from heaven the voice has come
and will come saying, 'This is Jesus, the King.' Through Jesus the king, our view of kings,
kingship and kingdoms and our Christian view of power in the world will never be the same
again, however strong the temptation of the world's ways.

JESUS OR BARABBAS

We return to Barabbas and the scene with Pilate and the crowd. The disciples have
scattered, the High Priestly authorities are in full cry, the might of Imperial Rome is seen
and felt. Finally, with the appearance of the crowd all the forces in Mark's story of Jesus are
in place. 'Who is to die and who is to live?' asks Pilate. 'Who is to be set free?' (15:8) The
crowd is asked, 'On whom you will place your trust for the future, on Jesus, the Human One,
or Barabbas, terrorist and murderer (Barabbas has a bitterly ironic name, it means, 'son of
the father')? Whose way points forward? Is it the way of Jesus or Barabbas? To whom
belongs the future, the one who brings in his own person the new and living temple or the
one who would restore the old Temple by violent means?

The choice is stark. Are we to be like the crowd, fickle in our believing, prepared to be
with Jesus just so far and no further because we cling to the old ways of power, hanging on
to our worldly hopes, ready to follow any new power that guarantees self-interest? The
crowd's temptation is a perennial temptation.

The crowd seems at this moment all-powerful, with its frenzied shout for blood; 'Crucify
him, crucify him!' (15:13,14) Jesus has described the crowd as 'like sheep without a
shepherd.' (6:34) In truth their apparent power is hollow; Pilate is cynically manipulating

them, they are seduced by the appearance of power. We belong to a time which has seen much collective war fever and group hatred. In their frenzy, the crowd mimics the voice of the possessed; the people become for this moment, demonic.

They make the wrong choice, 'Give us Barabbas!' and Jesus is condemned. Jesus, the true son of the Father, goes on his way bound, humiliated, deserted, to be crucified. It looks like the end. But the whole movement of the gospel is of wrong becoming right, as death becomes life. The end is very near, yet in a strange and powerful way, signs of the way beyond the end multiply.

STUDY

BY YOURSELF

At his trial before Pilate, Jesus is condemned by state, or political, violence. He stands in solidarity with all victims of oppression, terror and violence. Think about such victims in our world, and pray for them. Think also about your role as a Christian, not only in prayer but in protest and positive political engagement.

PAUSE

JESUS, THE HUMAN ONE

> Alone thou goest forth, O Lord,
>   In sacrifice to die;
> Is this thy sorrow naught to us
>   Who pass unheeding by?...
>
> This is earth's darkest hour, but thou
>   Dost light and life restore;
> Then let all praise be given thee
>   Who livest evermore.
> (Peter Abelard, 1079-1142)

In the gospel story we are about to reach the foot of the cross. This is the time for watching and waiting for those who would learn the truth of the mystery, a time to pause and not pass, in the words of Peter Abelard's ancient hymn, 'unheeding by'. This pause is entitled, 'Jesus, the Human One'. However, this title is not here the key to understanding Jesus' role in fulfilling God's purposes, as it is in the gospel. It simply draws attention to three aspects of the human Jesus during these critical hours.

'Alone thou goest forth to die.' At the end, what a completely isolated figure Jesus is. Throughout the second half of the gospel, all the way along the journey to Jerusalem and the cross, Jesus becomes more cut-off and alone. There has long been a breach with family and neighbours. The crowd thins out until, before Pilate, it finally turns against him. In his conversations with the disciples the gulf between their understanding of his purpose and his own is gaping. Nowhere is that more obvious than when he tries to engage them with the reality of the cross (9:30-37, 10:32-45). As Jerusalem approaches, there is the graphic image of Jesus going on ahead while the disciples lag behind fearfully (10:32). We have just witnessed the collapse of the community of the disciples. The inner core, Peter, James and John, have succumbed to exhaustion at the start of the last day (14:32-42), Judas has betrayed him with the fatal kiss (14:45), at his arrest the disciples have fled (14:50) and finally, Peter has denied he ever knew Jesus (14:66-72).

Jesus stands alone. We can feel for this man and the agonies of his loneliness. Not the least of his sufferings must come from his sense of abandonment and betrayal. He experiences to the very depths all our feelings of loss and forsakenness. Indeed, we know that his feelings of being bereft are so strong that on the cross he cries out to the God in whom he has put all his trust. 'My God, my God why have you forsaken me?' (15:34)

Jesus stands alone. What he now accomplishes and what is brought to birth through him, comes from him alone, without human aid. Throughout the gospel there are pictures of Jesus going ahead of the disciples, going ahead of us. Now he goes alone ahead of us into the darkness and beyond. Nowhere is he more 'ahead of us' than at these moments of cross and resurrection. Nowhere is he more clearly 'Lord'.

JESUS IN THE HANDS OF OTHERS

There is a strange stillness at the centre of the cross. Alone, Jesus suffers and endures as all manner of things are done to him at the hands of 'sinful men.' W H Vanstone's book, *The Stature of Waiting*, invites reflection on the last days of Jesus' earthly life and a vital aspect of the human condition. A summary of his argument is as follows.

Throughout Mark's gospel, Jesus is portrayed as a thoroughly dynamic figure. The actions he initiates and the activity around him, particularly in the first half of the gospel, leave us breathless. Mark heightens our sense of Jesus' activity in two ways; by having us see situations through Jesus' eyes (for example, in 1:16, instead of saying, 'Simon and Andrew were catching fish with a net' he says, 'he saw Simon and Andrew... catching fish with a net') and by reporting to us Jesus' inner thoughts and feelings (as in 1:41, '[Jesus] was filled with pity'). From the moment of Jesus' receiving the kiss of Judas at his arrest, there is a change. Jesus remains at the centre of the picture, but instead of being the initiator of action, he is now shown as the sufferer at the hands of the actions of others. He is no longer the doer, he is the done to. He hardly speaks, and even when he does speak, his words are misunderstood or ignored. Vanstone puts it like this:

From the moment when Jesus is handed over in the Garden, Mark reports no single incident through Jesus' eyes and attributes nothing that happens to His initiative and activity. Whereas previously Mark has told us freely of what Jesus felt among the sceptical people of Nazareth and of what he thought when a woman touched the hem of His garment, now he tells us nothing whatever of what Jesus thought or felt, or of how He reacted, inwardly or outwardly, to what was done to Him. Preachers often tell us of the courage and patience of Jesus during his trial and crucifixion: and no doubt what they say is correct. But they cannot have learned what they say from Mark's gospel. For Mark writes no single word about Jesus' inward attitude or outward reactions. He does not even attribute to Jesus the relatively insignificant activities of 'going', or 'standing', or 'turning': always the expression is 'they took him', 'they led him,' 'they dressed him'.
(Vanstone 1982, p. 20)

The picture of the last hours of Jesus' life show him as the object of the actions of others, powerless to achieve anything himself. Of course, a prisoner has a limited sphere of action, yet there is something more. If we see Jesus as the one to 'follow' as Mark portrays him, and if we follow him because he shows us what being human really is, we need to see Jesus in the widest range of human situations. Our experience of being human is not only that of acting, doing, thinking, knowing, feeling - being active. It is also an experience of not knowing, being done to, being at the mercy of others and events, waiting, suffering. We are also passive receivers of good and ill, and many of our most significant moments are spent waiting.

It is this second vital aspect of being human which Vanstone highlights, helping us see it in Jesus as he goes to the cross, particularly in Mark's account of the final stages of his journey. Here we see Jesus live in what is an ever-present part of our humanity. In his suffering at the hands of sinful men, he shares this aspect of our lives; those times when we are inactive, powerless, can only wait. We are not only human when we are busy or achieving (and we do like to think today that 'being busy' is an accolade of virtue), Jesus dignifies 'the stature of our waiting'. Jesus alone, in the hands of sinners, is never more human than at this moment.

JESUS DEFENCELESS
The words of this verse from Graham Kendrick's song 'O Lord the Clouds are Gathering' give voice to a prayer which we continually make in face of the reality of our world.

Lord, over the nations now
where is the dove of peace?
Her wings are broken.
O Lord, while precious children starve,
the tools of war increase,
their bread is stolen.

Have mercy, Lord, have mercy, Lord,
forgive us, Lord, forgive us, Lord.
Restore us, Lord; revive your church again.
Let justice flow, let justice flow,
like rivers, like rivers,
and righteousness like a never-failing stream.
(Graham Kendrick, 'O Lord, the clouds are gathering')

We make this prayer because throughout the gospel we are shown a picture of a militant Jesus; Jesus the strong man (3:27), doing battle with the powers of darkness in whatever form they take. We have seen him not only reaching out to share with, heal and welcome real people in their pain, poverty and exclusion; we have also seen him do battle with injustice and domination. Today we would say he is heavily involved in justice issues. But how does he do battle? In the final, decisive battle centred round his trials and cross, as he stands alone in the hands of others, it is his will to be defenceless. 'And they made his grave with the wicked..... although he had done no violence...' (Isaiah 53:9, *NRSV*)

Walter Wink, in his study of authority then and now, *The Powers that Be* (a condensed edition of his much larger trilogy) writes, speaking of the twentieth century,

> Even if we inflate the probable total casualties from war for *all* centuries since agricultural civilisation began (c. 8000 BCE), *more people have already been killed in war in our century than in all the preceding ten thousand years combined.* Yet Christian ethicists still ponder the question of justifying certain wars!'
> (Wink 1998, p. 137)

What a horrific indictment of our times, made even worse by our current arsenal of weaponry with its awesome capacity to cause individual pain and mass destruction.

The writer to the Colossians says of Jesus, 'For in him all the fullness of God was pleased to dwell, and through him to reconcile to himself all things, whether on earth or heaven, making peace by the blood of his cross... he disarmed the principalities and powers and made public example of them, triumphing over them.' (Col 1:20, 2:15) At the cross we meet the justice of God and God's way of peace and reconciliation is made plain. Jesus defeats the forces of evil, not by force of arms, but by taking the force of evil to himself, by 'bearing all things.' (1 Cor 13:7) Yet 'he did no violence.' (Isaiah 53:9) Jesus is totally involved in the struggle against the powers for the establishing of justice; to that task he calls us. His struggle could not be more costly, but it is a way of committed non-violence. In a time like ours the way of non-violence shines from the cross, summoning us to attend and learn, as never before.

chapter 38

Crux: Jesus crucified, the justice of God

MARK 15: 21-47

Jesus is Crucified
(Matt 27:32-44; Lk 23:26-43; Jn 19:17-27)

On the way they met a man named Simon, who was coming into the city from the country, and the soldiers forced him to carry Jesus' cross. (Simon was from Cyrene and was the father of Alexander and Rufus.) They took Jesus to a place called Golgotha, which means 'The Place of the Skull'. There they gave him wine mixed with a drug called myrrh, but Jesus would not drink it. Then they crucified him and divided his clothes among themselves, throwing dice to see who would get which piece of clothing. It was nine o'clock in the morning when they crucified him. The notice of the accusation against him said, 'The King of the Jews' They also crucified two bandits with Jesus, one on his right and the other on his left.

People passing by shook their heads and hurled insults at Jesus: 'Aha! You were going to tear down the Temple and build it up again in three days! Now come down from the cross and save yourself!'

In the same way the chief priests and the teachers of the Law jeered at Jesus, saying to each other, 'He saved others, but he cannot save himself! Let us see the Messiah, the king of Israel, come down from the cross now, and we will believe in him!'

And the two who were crucified with Jesus insulted him also.

The Death of Jesus
(Matt 27:45-56; Lk 23:44-49; Jn 19:28-30)

At noon the whole country was covered with darkness, which lasted for three hours. At three o'clock Jesus cried out with a loud shout, '*Eloi, Eloi, lema sabachthani?*' which means, 'My God, my God, why did you abandon me?'

Some of the people there heard him and said, 'Listen, he is calling for Elijah!' One of them ran up with a sponge, soaked it in cheap wine, and put it on the end of a stick. Then he held it up to Jesus' lips and said, 'Wait! Let us see if Elijah is coming to bring him down from the cross!'

With a loud cry Jesus died.

The curtain hanging in the Temple was torn in two, from top to bottom. The army officer who was standing there in front of the cross saw how Jesus had died. 'This man was really the Son of God!' he said.

Some women were there, looking on from a distance. Among them were Mary Magdalene, Mary the mother of the younger James and of Joseph, and Salome. They had followed Jesus while he was in Galilee and had helped him. Many other women who had come to Jerusalem with him were there also.

The Burial of Jesus
(Matt 27:57-61; Lk 23:50-56; Jn 19:38-42)

It was towards evening when Joseph of Arimathea arrived. He was a respected member of the Council, who was waiting for the coming of the Kingdom of God. It was Preparation day (that is, the day before the Sabbath), so Joseph went boldly into the presence of Pilate and asked him for the body of Jesus. Pilate was surprised to hear that Jesus was already dead. He called the army officer and asked him if Jesus had been dead a long time. After hearing the officer's report, Pilate told Joseph he could have the body. Joseph bought a linen sheet, took the body down, wrapped it in the sheet, and placed it in a tomb which had been dug out of solid rock. Then he rolled a large stone across the entrance to the tomb. Mary Magdalene and Mary the mother of Joseph were watching and saw where the body of Jesus was placed.

George F MacLeod comments:

> I simply argue that the Cross be raised again at the centre of the market-place as
> well as on the steeple of the church. I am recovering the claim that Jesus was not
> crucified in a cathedral between two candlesticks, but on a cross between two
> thieves; on the town garbage-heap; at a crossroad so cosmopolitan that they had to
> write his title in Hebrew and in Latin and in Greek (or shall we say in English, in
> Bantu and in Afrikaans?); at the kind of place where cynics talk smut, and thieves
> curse, and soldiers gamble. Because that is where he died. And that is what he died
> about. And that is where church people should be and what being the church should
> be about.
> (George F MacLeod 1964, p.38)

'When I survey the wondrous cross,' writes Isaac Watts, and we often sing. Centuries of
Christian devotion have transformed the cross into something 'wondrous'. Yet we
appreciate the full wonder of the cross only if we understand something of its original
horror. Mark in his witness to the gospel brings us here to stand under the cross, the
ultimate political weapon in the Roman armoury and instrument of a death of hellish
torture and humiliation reserved for slaves and rebels. Here we stand.

> What a scene Mark paints, fraught with tragedy! In the foreground, beneath this
> Roman stake, all of Jesus' opponents have gathered to ridicule him. In the
> background, a few women disciples look on in horror. And what of us? Where do we
> stand on this pitiful finale, this consummate moment of desolation? Is there not a
> part of us lurking in each of the characters? A part that is, like the male disciples,
> altogether absent to this spectacle, having long ago abandoned Jesus at the first
> whiff of confrontation? A part that holds vigil with the women, incredulous and numb
> with horror? And also a part that, from the safety of the crowd, joins in the ridicule of
> this 'King' become 'Suffering Servant?' 'Who indeed can believe', as Isaiah asks
> (Isaiah 53) 'that it really has turned out this way?'
> (Myers 1988, pp.383-4)

That crucial question is anything but abstract. If this is indeed the end, then there is no
gospel, no good news. This is simply another episode in the saga of humanity's defeat
before the powers of evil. The agonising question of the Psalms, 'How long, how long, O
Lord?' receives no answer. In our need and longing we cry to a deaf and dumb God. This is
the crucial question about the meaning of our lives now. So, in spite of the awfulness of the
scene, we must attend closely.

Three crucial Old Testament references

To help us attend and understand, keep the number three firmly in mind. There are the three Old Testament passages rumbling away in the background which are critical for our understanding of the cross. There is Isaiah 53, the fourth and last of his 'Servant Songs', which pictures uniquely the Lord's servant suffering unjustly and vicariously on behalf of others. Through the servant's sufferings many are vindicated.

> Here hangs a man discarded,
> a scarecrow hanging high,
> a nonsense pointing nowhere
> to all who hurry by.
> (Wren, 1983)

Brian Wren's words could be a paraphrase of the words of Isaiah 53, and an all-too accurate description of the man on the cross. Isaiah's picture explicitly states that we turn our heads away in horror and yet, at the same time, alongside the servant's suffering, indeed hidden within it, are promises of a victory and a triumph (Isaiah 53:3,12).

Isaiah 53 speaks not only of the sufferings of God's servant but of his shame. Centuries of Christian devotion have concentrated our attention on the suffering of Jesus at Calvary. For his contemporaries and himself no less important was the shame of the cross. Auden in his poem in memory of Bonhoeffer calls this, 'Suffering in a public place, a death reserved for slaves'.

Crucifixion was the ultimate humiliation. There was a horror in the ancient world of being touched and handled against one's will. To be taken, bound, and hung naked in public to die in agony a death specifically reserved for those at the foot of the human pecking order was to be shamed beyond belief. Here is another depth to Jesus' self-giving, that for us he is prepared to 'disregard the shame' (Hebrews 12:2). In the letter to the Hebrews we are given that text which links Jesus' cross with our mission. 'Jesus also suffered outside the city gate... Let us therefore go out to him, outside the camp, and bear the abuse he endured.' (Hebrews 13:12-13, NRSV)

The second Old Testament passage is Psalm 22. Its first line forms Jesus' cry from the cross, considered by Mark of such importance that he renders it in Jesus' own words, 'Eloi, eloi, lema sabachthani', 'My God, my God, why have you forsaken me?' (15:34) Three times the psalm is either quoted from or alluded to (Ps 22:1,7,18, RSV). Psalm 22 is a cry to God for justice, for the plaintiff's vindication in face of his enemies. Is the cry heard? The psalm begins in pain and desolation and ends in quiet assurance that, before God, the psalmist's cry has been heard. God is neither deaf, nor dumb, nor powerless.

The third crucial passage is Daniel 7 with its vision of the coming of the Son of Man, the Human One.

I saw in the night visions, and behold, with the clouds of heaven there came one like a son of man, and he came to the Ancient of Days and was presented before him. And to him was given dominion and glory and kingdom, that all peoples, nations, and languages should serve him; his dominion is an everlasting dominion, which shall not pass away, and his kingdom one that shall not be destroyed.
(Daniel 7:13-14, *RSV*)

We've seen how often Jesus uses that title to describe himself throughout the gospel. In the gospel, Jesus specifically relates the coming of the Son of Man (Dan 13:7) to himself at the time when he first announces his cross (8:38-9:1); in the major sermon of the gospel's second half, before the cross, (13:26); and in his words to Caiaphas at his first trial (14:62). Joel Marcus comments:

> The scene of which Daniel 7:13 is a part, describes four beasts that arise out of the sea and represent the four world empires that have oppressed Israel (Dan 7:1-8 cf v18). Opposed to them is the God of Israel, who is pictured as a numinous 'one that was ancient of days' surrounded by millions of angels (7:9-12). A human-like figure, 'the one like a son of man' is presented before this venerable figure and given a share in his dominion (7:13-14); later in the chapter the same dominion is granted to 'the saints of the Most High' (7:18) and 'the people of the saints of the Most High' (7:27). Correspondingly, dominion is taken away from the final beast (7:26), an act that is interpreted as a judgement upon it. The theme of judgement, indeed, pervades the latter half of the chapter: 'the court sat in judgement, and the books were opened' (7:10); 'judgement was given to (or for) the saints of the Most High' (7:26); 'the court shall sit in judgement' (7:26). The 'one like a son of man' is not himself described as a judge, but judgement is given to or for 'the saints of the Most High', who were associated with him. (7:22)
> (Marcus 1997, p. 165)

The apocalyptic signs around Jesus' death - 'the whole country was covered in darkness... for three hours' (15:33); 'the curtain hanging in the Temple was torn in two, from top to bottom' (15:38); intimate the cross as the moment of judgement and recall the significance of the court of heaven in the Daniel passage. The contemporary powers of evil represented by Rome and the forces of reaction gathered round the Jerusalem Temple will be overthrown. Mark however makes two significant additions to the Daniel tradition. The Son of Man figure in Daniel is above and beyond suffering, Mark's Jesus has gone to great lengths to make plain that 'the Son of Man must suffer' before he enters his kingdom (8:31; 9:12, 31; 10:33,45; 14:21, 41). Further, the sufferings of the Son of Man are intimately linked with the cross-bearing and sufferings of the following disciple community. After each of the three predictions of his cross and resurrection, Jesus teaches of the cost of the way of discipleship for those who follow (8:31-38; 9:31-37; 10:32-45).

This is of great importance for us on the road of discipleship now. It is in and through our sufferings that we receive intimations of glory. 'Mark's community finds grounds for hope not only in the promise of its vindication in the near future but also in a mysterious empowerment that it experiences now in the very midst of tribulation.' (Marcus 1997, p.171)

THE THREE WATCHING HOURS

With the three Old Testament passages in the background, Mark divides the events of the crucifixion into three 'Watches'. These are three periods of time, the first two clearly of three hours duration. 'It was nine o'clock in the morning when they crucified him.' (15:25)

We pick up the narrative again at 15:21: 'On the way they met a man named Simon, who was coming into the city from the country, and the soldiers forced him to carry Jesus' cross.' The story is thick with allusions and contrasts. Mark's gospel begins with a voice crying in the wilderness and reaches a climax around the story of Jesus' final journey into the wilderness of death. Jesus, we also remember, has very recently entered Jerusalem with crowds around him feting his arrival, his way strewn with a carpet of clothes and palm branches; here he leaves the city quite alone, with no follower or friend even to carry his cross. The second half of the gospel has been full of Jesus' urgent demand to his disciples that they become 'cross-bearing' people. It has fallen on deaf ears. Jesus is now so bereft of friends that the soldiers press a stranger into service as a cross-bearer. His name is Simon of Cyrene. There is such irony in that name - 'Simon' - the same name as the one who was first called to follow, whose own confession allowed Jesus to unveil the way of the cross. Come the crunch, Simon the disciple is absent. Another Simon, another man from the countryside, another outsider, has this reluctant place of honour.

The sad procession makes its way up the *via dolorosa*. The original purpose of this pitiful spectacle, and the sad and depraved rationale for public punishment, is to make an example. 'Don't do as he did or you'll end up like him!' Rome went to great lengths to ensure that its subject people were in no doubt where real power lay, even to the squalid ritual of the display of prisoners on their way to execution. Yet even in this cruel spectacle Jesus' enemies bear unconscious witness, 'Tear down the temple and build it in three days!' they jeer (15:29). This man's words and way are so significant and so dangerous that only elimination will silence him. Or will it?

JESUS LIFTED HIGH

The company makes its way to the foot of the cross. Jesus is hoisted high. Before he is nailed up he is stripped once again. This is the first allusion to Psalm 22. 'They divide my garments among them and for my raiment they cast lots.' (Ps 22:18, *RSV*)

On a small tablet of wood above each prisoner's head is written a brief description of the crime for which they have been condemned. What has Pilate had written, irony on irony, above Jesus? 'The King of the Jews' (15:26). Round the foot of the cross gathers a strange and motley crowd, collaborators, cynics, soldiers, members of the priestly family, no doubt also the ghoulish and the curious. Disciples are noticeably absent. Crucified with Jesus are two bandits, one on his right hand and one on his left. Right and left hands, where have we recently heard these words? From James and John who ask to sit in places of honour on either side of Jesus when he comes in glory (10:37).

Mark, particularly in Chapter 13, makes it clear that Jesus does not endorse the methods of the bandits' freedom struggle. Jesus explicitly warns his disciples to have nothing to do with guerrilla warfare or armed insurrection. Yet Jesus' whole ministry can also be seen as making common cause with the bandits in the struggle to free his people. We have a choice. On the one hand we can read this scene of Jesus' hanging between the bandits as one of grotesque parody, a sign of profound lawlessness, of the one without sin becoming sin for our sake. Alternatively, we can also read this as an act of solidarity whereby, while Jesus disassociates himself from the bandits' bloody means, he does not disavow the justice of their cause. He dies alongside them and they die alongside him. In a strange way, they are the ones, not the disciples, who share the fearful baptism he has predicted (10:38-39).

The bandits suffer with him, the bystanders cruelly mock (15:29-31). Here is the second reference to Psalm 22,

> All who see me mock at me,
> they make mouths at me, they wag their heads;
> 'He committed his cause to the Lord;
> let him deliver him,
> let him rescue him, for he delights in him!'
> (Ps 22:7,8, *RSV*)

What is the nature of the bystanders' mockery? They raise again the critical issue of the Temple. What is the true Temple? What is this sanctuary which will be destroyed and rebuilt in three days? We know that it is not the massive pile on Mount Zion; it is this frail body of flesh here before us. The mockery of the crowd serves to focus our gaze on where it should truly be, on Jesus himself.

The chief priests and the Scribes say, 'He saved others, he cannot save himself. Let the Christ, the King of Israel, come down from the cross that we may see and believe.' (15:31, *RSV*) They give him his full title and, in their malice, they tell the truth. 'He saved others', yes, indeed; 'he will not save himself', yes, indeed also. Out of the mouths of his enemies we hear of Jesus' true vocation. This is his calling; the saving of others, by the giving of himself. It is in and through that giving that we learn that he is the Christ. It is by refusing to save himself that he becomes the Saviour. He is indeed, in words which have journeyed with me for many years, 'the Incarnate Word in the bleeding helplessness of utter service' (Smith 1956, p.100).

DARKNESS AT NOON

So the drama moves to the second watch: the sixth hour, or noon, to darkness at noon. The sun disappears, as in Exodus 10:22 when for three days the mighty Egyptian Sun-god Ra was blotted out by Yahweh, God of Israel. Here is the moment of Judgement, of the critical clash of the powers. There comes from Jesus that most terrible of cries, *'Eloi, eloi, lama sabachthani'*; 'My God, my God, why have you forsaken me?' These are the first words of Psalm 22 (the third reference). We have already seen that these words are the cry of a righteous man for justice and deliverance. The cry ascends to heaven. Will it simply echo unheard and unanswered in the vast darkness of space? Will the heavens remain silent? Will the darkness prevail? For the moment, there is nothing. The crowd get it wrong again. They think they hear Jesus calling Elijah, mishearing *'Eloi'*. Jesus has already said, 'Elijah has come and they did with him as they pleased.' (9:13) He expects no help from that quarter. Jesus is and has always been clear that there will be no last minute rescue. It is no use waiting to see if Elijah will cut him down. The waiting is short. Jesus gives a loud cry, a great gasp, and dies (15:37). That's it, finished. On the cross now there is but the bleeding shell of a man; this broken, beaten, bound temple hangs now deserted, empty, lifeless.

Except, wait a minute! At the very moment of Jesus' death, in the other temple, the great Temple on the hill, the curtain which separated the Holy of Holies, God's place on earth, from the rest of the world, that veil is rent in two from top to bottom. Here is the final reversal; it is not the new order that is dead, it is the old order that is utterly finished. 'You can't put new cloth on an old garment, the tearing is simply irreparable.' (2:21) The old Temple cannot contain the word and spirit of God. Word and spirit dwell in the new humanity created by Christ's sacrifice. They are out in the world and Christ's people are called, after Bonhoeffer, to a new 'holy worldliness'.

THE STRONG MAN BOUND

At the very moment of the strong man's triumph, he has not prevailed. Victory has been snatched from the jaws of defeat. The strong man's house is ransacked. Here is the third and final key moment of the gospel, standing alongside and completing the moments of the baptism and transfiguration. Look at these parallels.

> At the baptism, the heavens are rent open and the dove descends. (1:10)
> At the transfiguration, Jesus' garments turn white and the cloud descends. (9:3,7)
> At the cross, the veil of the Temple is rent open and the darkness spreads. (15:33)
>
> At the baptism, the voice says, 'You are my son, the beloved'. (1:11)
> At the transfiguration, the voice says, "This is my son, the beloved". (9:7)
> At the cross, the soldier says, 'Truly this man was the son of God'. (15:39)

At the baptism, John the Baptist appears as Elijah. (1:4-6)

At the transfiguration, Jesus appears with Elijah. (9:4)

At the cross, the crowd asks, 'Is he calling Elijah?' (15:35)

The close parallels between each of the three passages are clear. Each points to a key moment where Jesus is revealed, at the start, the pivot and the end of the gospel. At each, Jesus is shown as son of God. Yet we recall that the title which Jesus himself most fully owns is 'Son of Man', 'Human One'. Jesus has made very plain that the Son of Man is a servant whose vocation is to suffer and to die and in his suffering and dying he will bring victory over the powers.

Here is the resolution of Jesus' prediction of the coming of the Son of Man with reference to Daniel. In the Daniel passage it is precisely at the point where the beast, symbolising the powers of evil, seems to triumph that a counter vision appears and the Human One (or, Son of Man) emerges in power and glory. Mark is saying that Jesus' death on earth completes the battle of the heavenly powers. So the Human One who has come on earth to serve and give his life as a ransom for many (10:45) is revealed as the same Human One to whom is given glory, power and dominion. The judgement has indeed come. The Human One is vindicated and enthroned, not for his sake alone, but as the supreme witness to the way God works to establish justice here on earth, through the Human One and the way of his cross, which is the way of those who will follow.

The watch began six hours ago when the procession reached the place of the skull and the Human One's cross was raised. It was intensified by darkness at noon, the foreshadowing of judgement. It is now ended. If we have truly watched and waited ourselves, then we have seen not defeat but victory, not death but life, not the end but a new beginning. The new beginning speaks of the future of the new Temple, razed and raised in three days. We will learn how through the victory of the cross the new Temple expands from Jesus' own body into the life of the new community as it continues life on the way, the way to which we are all called.

THREE WITNESSES

There remains the third watch of the day of the cross, before evening brings the Passover itself. And, at the end, there are three witnesses. There's the witness of the Roman soldier, representative of the power that kills. 'Truly this man was a Son of God.' (15:39) Without irony; it is given to one of Jesus' opponents to see and declare 'Who He is'. Second, there is the part played by Joseph of Arimathea, the representative of the other power, the Sanhedrin. He takes Jesus' body for burial (15:42-46). Is the taking down and burying of Jesus an act of love, of witness, of commitment at the last or is this simply a way of getting the dead Jesus finally and hastily buried before the Passover, shutting the door on an unsavoury episode the sooner and the better forgotten? It's a door that won't stay shut.

The last witnesses are the women. Three of them (three again!) are named; Mary

Magdalene, Mary the mother of James and Joseph, and Salome. They remain. They have stayed with Jesus throughout the journey and are, in their own way, faithful to the end when there is no sign of the three named disciples, Peter, James and John. They are tellingly described as those who in Galilee have followed and served him (15:41). There is no higher and more worthy description. To have followed and served is what it's all about. The witness of the women represents the continuing lifeline of discipleship when the male of the species is conspicuously and significantly absent. In a moment we will see that they are the ones who will be the living witnesses of the way from death to life. That is the wonder of the gift given to and received from those who follow and serve. They witness to the way from death to life.

We wait with the women, for the three days, in the sure knowledge that 'the world order is being overturned, from the highest political power to the deepest cultural pattern and it begins within the new community.' (Myers 1988 p. 397) This is the new community to which we belong, now.

STUDY

BY YOURSELF

'At the foot of the cross is the place where discipleship ends and/or begins.'
• Reflect on this statement.

FOR GROUP WORK

'Jesus wasn't crucified in a cathedral between two candlesticks, but on a cross between two thieves.' (George MacLeod)
• How does the cross of Jesus influence/shape/ change our view of God?
• How does the cross of Jesus influence/shape/ change our view of ourselves and what our lives are for?
• Discuss together what steps your church takes, or should develop, to show that you are a people committed to the way of the cross.

chapter 39

Gone to Galilee: Beginning Again

MARK 16:1-8

The Resurrection

(Matt 28:1-8; Lk 24:1-12; Jn 20:1-10)

After the Sabbath was over, Mary Magdalene, Mary the mother of James, and Salome brought spices to go and anoint the body of Jesus. Very early on Sunday morning, at sunrise, they went to the tomb. On the way they said to one another, 'Who will roll away the stone for us from the entrance to the tomb?' (It was a very large stone.) Then they looked up and saw that the stone had already been rolled back. So they entered the tomb, where they saw a young man sitting on the right, wearing a white robe - and they were alarmed.

'Don't be alarmed,' he said. 'I know you are looking for Jesus of Nazareth, who was crucified. He is not here - he has been raised! Look, here is the place where they put him. Now go and give this message to his disciples, including Peter: 'He is going to Galilee ahead of you; there you will see him, just as he told you.'

So they went out and ran from the tomb, distressed and terrified. They said nothing to anyone, because they were afraid.

A TEXTUAL QUESTION

We have come to the end of the text of Mark's gospel. There is a question about the text. Most scholars agree that the original gospel text ends at verse 8. Some ancient manuscripts have either one or other of the alternative endings provided at the end of the Good News Bible and other versions (see Appendix). However, the weight of opinion is very strong that neither of these alternatives is authentic Mark, because they are far from universally attested and, more importantly, because they clash with the sense and spirit of the rest of the gospel. These alternative endings represent a not very subtle borrowing from the resurrection stories of the other gospels. These stories have meaning and authenticity within their own narrative framework, but intruded into Mark they distract and distort the sense of his own particular witness.

Looking at these alternatives, the shorter ending, instead of leaving us with the witness of the women, the young man and the empty tomb, gives an appearance of Jesus himself and the restoration of the place of Peter and the male disciples. It's nice and neat and comfortable, but very doubtful. The longer ending is even more suspect. Myers is scathing:

> The longer endings represent the work of those who cannot see 16:8 as an invitation to which to respond, but only as a scandal which must be resolved. Instead of disturbing questions that reflect the human struggle and ambiguity of practice, we have pat answers... We might, for the sake of argument, even refer to these longer endings as 'imperial rewritings' of Mark, which symbolise our unending attempts to domesticate the gospel. Life in the imperial sphere depends on triumphal narrative; the eleventh-hour Hollywood rescues, the arrival of the cavalry, the "happily ever after". Such endings allow us to avoid confronting ourselves, our mistakes and our frailty. Why else would the story of the Vietnam war need a heavily cosmetic face-lift before appearing in high school history texts?
> (Myers 1988, p. 402)

The longer ending sounds three particularly jarring notes. In the first place it confuses the dominant theme of following Jesus with the practice of baptism and the theology of correct belief. 'Follow the right cultic practices, believe the right things and you'll be all right. Tough luck on the rest!' (cf.16:15-16) Such a view is quite at odds with a gospel which has as one of its key texts, 'Lord, I believe, help my unbelief.' (9:24) It clashes with the constant theme of a continuing struggle for discipleship. Jesus calls disciples to struggle and suffer to establish the justice of God in the world, by way of the cross, not to be snake charmers (16:18). The view of discipleship here sits ill with Mark's portrayal of Jesus for ever travelling out to break down the man-made barriers which exclude and condemn. It ill behoves any church seeking to follow Mark's Jesus to settle behind a secure stockade protected by doctrinal razor wire.

Secondly, the longer ending gives the disciples new power as miracle workers, while Mark's gospel is particularly sparing and ambiguous over the question of miracles. Even more dissonant is the implication in these verses that to the church is given power and success while the whole thrust of the second half of the gospel, culminating in the cross itself, is about an inversion of all that we and the world see as power and success. These idols are unmasked and dethroned in the gospel's most critical moments, as we stand before the dying Lord.

Thirdly, it elevates Jesus conveniently to heaven. Of course such an elevation has its place within the whole witness of the New Testament. However, Mark, on several occasions and crucially in 16:7, clearly locates the future of the risen Christ in Galilee. 'Tell the disciples, and Peter, he is going to Galilee, ahead of you. There you will see him, just as he told you.' It is to despised, disregarded, poor, troublesome, marginalised, provincial Galilee, scene of past and future struggles of the believing community, that Jesus goes ahead and will be found.

The alternative endings will not do. What's left? There are two possibilities. One is that the original ending of the gospel was lost, or frayed and became detached or some uncouth fellow tore it off to light a fire. One of the elders in the congregation I serve firmly believes that in a cave in upper Egypt an authentic original will turn up some day with the 'proper' ending. All things are possible. We will embrace the final possibility, which is simply to make our cloak with the cloth we've got and assume that verses 1-8 contain all that was written, so verse 8 is the Marcan conclusion. The gospel *seems* to end with a group of frightened women saying nothing to anyone (16:8). Yet wait! Someone must have said something to someone. You, the reader, know! Such a reading may not turn out to be so disastrous at all.

EVIDENCE OF RESURRECTION

What do the first eight verses of Chapter 16 tell us? There are the women who have been there from the beginning, following and serving throughout Jesus' ministry. They were there until the bitter end at the foot of the cross, albeit at a distance. They were present at the sealing of the tomb. In and through them, the story of discipleship continues, the thread remains unbroken. They are the ones who return to the tomb, very early on Sunday morning. They come, thinking to perform a last act of love for their dead Lord and practically wondering how the heavy stone might be moved. The stone has been moved already; the grave is empty. Of the dead Christ, there is no trace. This mute witness is full of powerful eloquence. We talk of folk being 'dead and gone', yet the opposite is here the case. Jesus is alive and gone, gone ahead of them, still ahead. To the end Mark remains a gospel full of surprises.

The young man

There is someone there, not an angel or two angels, just a young man in a white robe. At a crucial point in Jesus' last day, a young man appeared who had, at that point, no robe at all (14:51). He had been forced to leave it behind in his helter-skelter flight from the soldiers who were trying to lay hands on him. Now he waits in a robe of white, the colour of the martyr, the supreme witness. White was also the colour of Jesus' robe at the transfiguration. The young man's witness is, 'You are looking for Jesus of Nazareth, (despised old Nazareth), he is risen, he is not here, he has been raised. He is alive and gone. Here is where he lay. See for yourselves he is not here.' (16:6) 'There's a message, a message for you to take to his disciples who are not here either, still posted missing since they've turned and run because their faith has failed. Tell his disciples... and Peter.' What a world of meaning there is in these words! Tell the disciples whose community has disintegrated as their faith has dissolved... and Peter, first disciple, first confessor, enthusiast, misunderstander, deserter. 'Tell them, tell him, it's not all over, he's not dead and gone, he *is* going to Galilee, ahead of them. There they will find him, just as he told them.' (16:7)

It is a new beginning. Where has he gone and where will they meet him? It will happen back in Galilee, back at the beginning, back where it all started.

The call renewed

There they will 'see' him. How important sight has been as a theme throughout the gospel. The word used for 'see' here is used only in the gospel when Jesus foretells the coming of the Human One. 'You will see the Son of Man coming in clouds with great power and glory'(13:26, 14:62). Through the cross the Human One has come into his own, has been revealed. It is Jesus now revealed in his full meaning and glory, Jesus who can be clearly 'seen', who goes before the disciples into Galilee where the whole mission will begin again. Here is the third great call to discipleship. The first was by the lakeside with the fishermen, the second around the events of Caesarea Philippi and the Transfiguration, the third is here, before the empty tomb. 'He goes before you, there you will see him.' (16:7)

The witness of the women

Yet the women are far from exultant, they are distressed, terrified and silent. The disciples were in a similar state when Jesus calmed the storm (4:35-41) and when they stood before him on the mount of the Transfiguration (9:2-8). Throughout the Bible, initial human reaction to an epiphany of God is shown as fright, wonder and confusion. Both these incidents were unveilings of the presence of God in Jesus. Both also raised the question for the disciples - will we continue to follow? That is also the question here.

The gospel ends with this final clash between the announcement of the Jesus who goes before into Galilee, which fills us with hope, and the portrayal of the women's consternation and fear. To the end there is an unresolved ambiguity. Yet the result of this final tension is fascinating. Instead of an unambiguous happy ending with which we can put his book down and say, 'Goody, goody, Jesus has won, it's all come out right in the end,' Mark typically leaves us with a question, a question which will send us back to the gospel to read more carefully between the lines. More significantly, he leaves us with a question requiring an answer in our lives now.

THE QUESTION FOR US

What will the end result be for us? 'This is the Good News about Jesus Christ.' (1:1) Now we have heard the whole story. Will we end in consternation or silence or will we read the living signs of Jesus and move on to where he goes before us in our contemporary Galilee? Will we rise from a cowed defeat in the face of the state of our church, nation and world (which insidiously saps the strength to love and the will to resist in our souls) and get out into Galilee to meet and be revived by the crucified and risen one, going ahead of us in the struggles and complexities of our world today? Through the events of the cross and resurrection, the secret is out. There is no more need of silence. It is now made plain who Jesus is. Will people be able to 'read' who Jesus is in the testimony of our lives?

'The power of Mark's gospel lies ultimately not in what it tells the disciples/readers, but in what it asks of them.' (Myers 1988, p. 403) The question is Jesus' own question, at the heart of the quest, 'Who am I? Who do you say that I am?'

The invitation is, 'Follow me - just follow, in the midst of your life now.'

TRUE RESURRECTION

The promise in the challenge is that as we respond to Jesus' invitation and seek to take his way, with all that such a way involves in the reality of our lives, then we too will learn on the way - for there's no other place to learn - 'Who he is.'

That open, living question and invitation, constantly renewed, lies before us every day. This is the invitation to the transforming journey. Jesus says,

Will you come and follow me,
if I but call your name?
Will you go where you don't know
and never be the same?
(Extract from Bell and Maule 1987, p. 116)

STUDY

Reflection

- Reflect on your journey through the gospel of Mark. In what ways has it taught you more about Jesus or changed your view of him?
- Ask yourself now the question from the introduction: 'What about Jesus excites, scares, perplexes, challenges, reassures me?' (See 'Suggestions on how to use this book', in the Introduction.)

A Prayer from the Iona Community:

> O Christ, the Master Carpenter, who at the last, through wood and nails, purchased our whole salvation, wield well your tools in the workshop of your world, so that we who come rough-hewn to your bench may here be fashioned to a truer beauty of your hand. We ask it for your own name's sake. *Amen.*
> (The Iona Community Worship Book 1998, p.30)

FOR GROUP WORK

- Share your personal reflections about your view of Jesus now. (You may want to prepare for this in advance by writing a piece of poetry or prose, or making a drawing or collage to share with the group - and for the group to share with others in your faith community).
- 'He has gone before you into Galilee. There you will see him.' Share with one another evidences of the presence of Jesus, hints of resurrection you have known.
- Celebrate 'resurrection now' with a meal together. You deserve it!

chapter 40

EpilOgue

The journey through Mark is over. Your faith journey and mine begins again every day. For much of my life, the nation of Scotland and the city of Glasgow, both in times of transition, have been my 'Galilee' and I would share one picture and one poem from each as a final reflection. Glasgow comes first.

The Iona Community for many years had a mainland centre beside the river Clyde in the heart of Glasgow. The bottom floor of this Community House was a public restaurant, much frequented by the bus drivers, conductors and passengers from the stand opposite, by those on the edges of homelessness, and by those who lived and worked in the city centre. To reflect the breaking of barriers the whole floor was open plan. The kitchen was open, at one end you could see your soup simmering and your mince cooking, and at the other end, the chapel was also open, lunchtime prayers took place in the context of the buzz of the restaurant all around. And on one wall was a huge mural of the life of the city of Glasgow, with the life of the tenement houses open to view, with children playing in the streets and the cranes and the workers of the shipyards all around. In the centre, at an ordinary kitchen table with a family gathered round it, was the figure of Jesus, breaking bread, at the heart of the common life of the city. It's a picture to carry with us. For it's:

> Not just once with special people,
> not just hidden deep in time,
> but wherever Christ is followed,
> earthly fare becomes sublime.
> (Extract from Bell and Maule 1989, p.109)

In the middle of the ordinary, at the heart of the life of the world, Jesus makes community and calls us into communion. There we are bid find faith together. And we will, if we take the words of Jesus according to Mark to heart and 'see', 'listen', 'reflect', 'share' and 'act'. There we will see him, discovering and being surprised by the glory in the grey, as Kathy Galloway's poem 'Christ of Scotland' says so movingly.

Christ of Scotland

He walks among the yellow and the grey.
Grey of stone and slate and steely rivers
running through grey towns where steel ran yesterday,
and grey mists lifting where the coming day
delivers grey-edged intimations of
a grey mortality,
and a shadier morality.
Here, poverty and pain are dirty-fingered currency
in the market-place of souls,
and stunted possibility hobbles on the bleeding stumps
of legs hacked off from under it.
Here in the grey forgotten wasteland
that is not fate or accident or fecklessness
but just the grey, inevitable result
of choices made,
and burdens shifted,
and cost externalised out of the magic circle of prosperity,
here, he walks.

But in his heart, he carries yellow.
Yellow for the daffodils that surge across the banks
of railway lines.
Yellow for the crocuses that parade in Charlotte Square.
Yellow for the primroses that gleam in crevices of island rock.
Yellow for the irises that wave from glittering ditches.
Yellow for the broom that flashes fire across a thousand summer hills.
Yellow for the barren land cloaked in winter snow,
Awaiting yellow springtime's sun
to kiss it into bloom.
He carries yellow in his heart.
Held high like the lion raised upon the terraces.
Yellow for courage.
Yellow for beauty.
Yellow for resistance.
Yellow for love.
Yellow to obliterate the grey.
He walks, yellow, in the grey.
(Galloway 1993)

Appendix

ALTERNATIVE ENDINGS TO MARK 16: 9-20

Shorter ending

The women went to Peter and his friends and gave them a brief account of all they had been told. After this, Jesus himself set out through his disciples from the east to the west the sacred and ever-living message of eternal salvation.

Longer ending

After Jesus rose from death early on Sunday, he appeared first to Mary Magdalene, from whom he had driven out seven demons. She went and told his companions. They were mourning and crying; and when they heard her say that Jesus was alive and that she had seen him, they did not believe her.

After this, Jesus appeared in a different manner to two of them while they were on their way to the country. They returned and told the others, but they would not believe it.

Last of all, Jesus appeared to the eleven disciples as they were eating. He scolded them, because they did not have faith and because they were too stubborn to believe those who had seen him alive. He said to them, 'Go throughout the whole world and preach the gospel to the whole human race. Whoever believes and is baptised will be saved; whoever does not believe will be condemned. Believers will be given the power to perform miracles: they will drive out demons in my name; they will speak in strange tongues; if they pick up snakes or drink any poison, they will not be harmed; they will place their hands on sick people, who will get well.'

After the Lord Jesus had talked with them, he was taken up to heaven and sat at the right hand of God. The disciples went and preached everywhere, and the Lord worked with them and proved that their preaching was true by the miracles that were performed.

REFERENCES

Abelard, Peter: Hymn 242 in *Church Hymnary, third edition*, Oxford: Oxford University Press (1973). Translation by Francis Bland Tucker.

Auden, W H (1963): 'Friday's Child, in memory of Dietrich Bonhoeffer', in *Collected Poems*; (1966) 'City WIthout Walls' in *City without Walls*, New York: Random House

Bell, John and Maule, Graham (1987, 1989): 'Will you come and follow me' from *Heaven Shall Not Wait* (1987) & 'The hand of heaven', from *Love From Below* (1989); Glasgow: Wild Goose Publications

Belo F (1981) *A Materialist Reading of the Gospel of Mark*, New York: Orbis (also quoted in Myers 1988)

Berry, Jan (see Christian Aid)

Bonhoeffer, Dietrich (1953 first English translation): *Letters and Papers from Prison*, London: SCM Press

Brooke, S A: 'It fell upon a summer day', *Church Hymnary 3*, Oxford: Oxford University Press *(1973)*. Translation by Francis Bland Tucker.

Burleigh, J H S (1960): *A Church History of Scotland*, Oxford: Oxford University Press

Christian Aid (1992): *Bread of Tomorrow, Praying with the World's Poor*, London: SPCK/Christian Aid

Davies, John and Vincent, John (1986): *Mark at Work* , London: The Bible Reading Fellowship

Donovan, V (1989, 1991): *The Church in the Midst of Creation*, first published 1989, Maryknoll, NY: Orbis Books; British publication 1991, London: SCM Press

Eliot, T S (1959): 'East Coker' in *Four Quartets*, London: Faber

Frostensen, Anders (1974, 1989): 'The love of God is broad like beach and meadow', transl. Fred Kaan. *Chalice Hymnal*, London: Stainer and Bell.

Galloway, Kathy (1993) 'Christ of Scotland', in *Love Burning Deep*, London: SPCK

Good News Bible, Second Edition 1994, Bath: The Bible Societies/ Harper Collins

Hengel, Martin (1978): *Crucifixion*, Philadelphia: Fortress Press

Iona Community Worship Group (1991): *The Iona Community Worship Book*, Glasgow: Wild Goose Publications

Kendrick, Graham 1987): Verse 2 of 'O Lord, the clouds are gathering', Croydon: Make Way Music

Lorimer, W L (1983): *The New Testament in Scots*, Edinburgh: Southside

McIlvanney, William (1991): *Strange Loyalties*, London: Hodder & Stoughton

MacLeod, George F (1964): *Only One Way Left*, Glasgow: Iona Community

Marcus, Joel (1992): *The Way of the Lord*, Louisville, Kentucky: Westminster/John Knox Press
   - (1997): *Jesus and the Holocaust. Reflections on Suffering and Hope*, New York: Doubleday

Miller, Arthur (1953): *The Crucible: A Play in Four Acts*, New York: Viking Penguin Inc

Myers, Ched (1988): *Binding the Strong Man: A Political Reading of Mark's Story of Jesus*, Maryknoll, NY: Orbis

Nagle, Joe (1991): 'Meditations for Holy Week', *Sojourners* April, Washington DC: Sojourners Community

Newbigin, Lesslie (1983):*The Other Side of 84*, London: British Council of Churches

Rowland, C (1985): *Christian Origins*, London: SPCK

Schweitzer, A (1910): *The Quest for the Historical Jesus* (trans W Montgomery), London: A & C Black - (1952): *Albert Schweitzer: An Anthology*, A & C Black, London.

Shairp, John Campbell, ' 'Twixt gleams of joy and clouds of doubt', *Church Hymnary 3rd edition 675*, Oxford: Oxford University Press (1973).

Silf, Margaret (1999), *Taste and See: Adventuring into Prayer*, London: Darton, Longman and Todd

Smith, Donald C (1987): *Passive Obedience and Prophetic Criticism: Social Criticism in the Scottish Church 1830-1945*, Lang Publishing

Smith, R G (1956): *The New Man*, London: SCM Press

Soelle, Dorothy (1977): *Revolutionary Patience*, Maryknoll, NY: Orbis
Taylor, John (1972), *The Go-Between God*, London: SCM Press

Telford,William (1980): *The Barren Temple and the Withered Tree,* Sheffield: JSOT Press

Thomas, R S (1993): 'The Moon in Lleyn', in *Collected Poems* London: JM Dent/Orion Publishing Group

Vanstone, W H (1982): *The Stature of Waiting,* London: DLT

Via, Dan O (1985): *The Ethics of Mark's Gospel - In the Middle of Time,* Philadelphia: Fortress Press

Wallis, Jim (1981): *The Call to Conversion,* Tring: Lion Publishing

Waetjen, H (1989): *A Reordering of Power,* Minneapolis: Fortress Press

Watts, Isaac: 'When I survey the wondrous cross', *Church Hymnary 3rd edition* 254, Oxford: Oxford University Press (1973)

Weber, Hans-Reudi (1989): *Power: Focus for a Biblical Theology,* Geneva: World Council of Churches Publications

Williams, Rowan (1983): *The Truce of God,* London: Fount Paperbacks - (2002) *Writing in the Dust, Reflections on 11 September,* London: Harper Collins

Wink, Walter (1998): *The Powers that Be,* New York: Doubleday

Wren, Brian (1983): Verse from 'Here hangs a man discarded' in *Faith Looking Forward,* Oxford: Oxford University Press

Abbreviations:

AV	Authorised Version
GNB	Good News Bible
NEB	New English Bible
NRSV	New Revised Standard Version
REB	Revised English Bible (revision of the NEB)
RSV	Revised Standard Version

ACKNOWLEDGEMENTS

Except where otherwise attributed, scriptures and additional materials quoted from the Good News Bible published by the Bible Societies/HarperCollins Publishers Ltd., UK, © American Bible Society, 1966, 1971, 1976, 1992, 1994. Used by permission.

Ched Myers, *Binding the Strong Man: A Political Reading of Mark's Story of Jesus*. Copyright © 1988 by Ched Myers. Published by Orbis Books, Maryknoll, New York; excerpts used by permission.

Iona Worship material © 1991 WGRG, Iona Community, G2 3DH. Excerpts used by permission.

'Christ of Scotland', Copyright © Kathy Galloway, is reprinted by kind permission of the author.

'O Lord the Clouds Are Gathering', by Graham Kendrick, Copyright © 1987 Make Way Music, PO Box 263, Croydon, CR9 5AP. Excerpt used by permission.

'The Moon in Lleyn' from *Collected Poems* by R S Thomas; Copyright © 1993 J M Dent/Orion Publishing. Reprinted by permission.

9 781904 325031